To my mom,
who never got to see me draw.

And to Moggy,
I love you with all of my heart.

D1319145

Each morning when I open my eyes,
I say to myself,
"I, not events, have the power
to make me happy or unhappy today.
I can choose which it shall be.
Yesterday is dead;
tomorrow hasn't arrived yet.
I have just one day,
TODAY
and I'm going to be
happy in it."

- Attributed to Groucho Marx

the road to god knows...

von allan

a von allan studio book

Ottawa

Library and Archives Canada Cataloguing in Publication

Allan, Von, 1974-
    The road to god knows... / written and illustrated by
Von Allan.

ISBN 0-9781237-0-0

    I. Title.

PN6733.A46R63 2007   741.5'971
C2006-903474-5

Published by Von Allan Studio, P.O. Box 20520, 390 Rideau Street,
Ottawa, Ontario, Canada K1N 1A3. Email: von@vonallan.com
Web: www.vonallan.com Phone: 613-236-9957

Excerpt from *Mr. Canoehead* taken from *Canadian Comics Cavalcade*
Volume 1 Number 1. ™ and © 1986, 2006 The Frantics. Web:
www.the frantics.com

Please note that the song fragments used for each chapter are in the
"traditional" (i.e.: public) domain. However, if any reader discovers
an instance where this is not the case, please contact Von Allan
Studio and let us know.

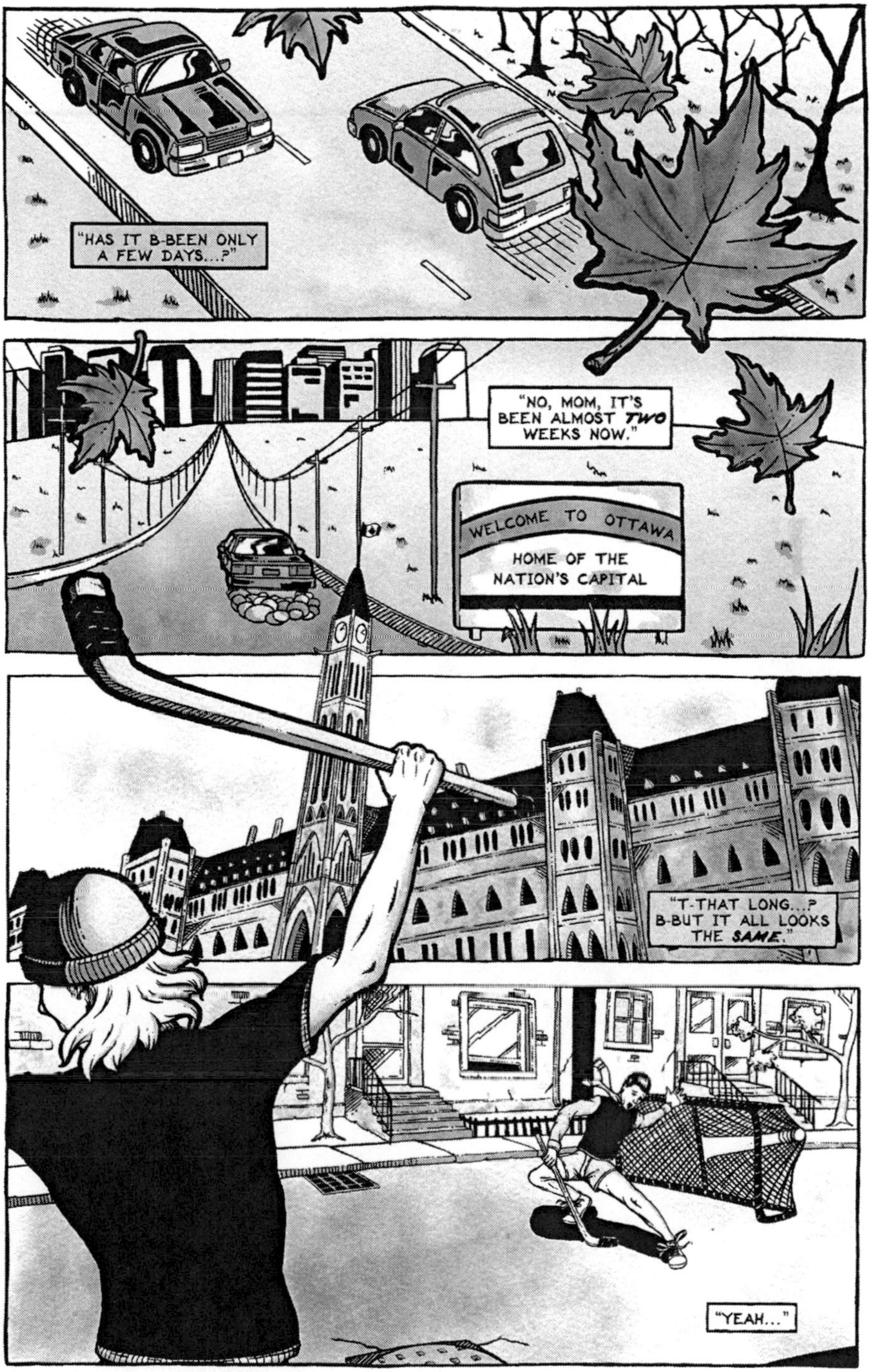
"HAS IT B-BEEN ONLY A FEW DAYS...?"
"NO, MOM, IT'S BEEN ALMOST *TWO* WEEKS NOW."
WELCOME TO OTTAWA
HOME OF THE NATION'S CAPITAL
"T-THAT LONG...? B-BUT IT ALL LOOKS THE *SAME*."
"YEAH..."

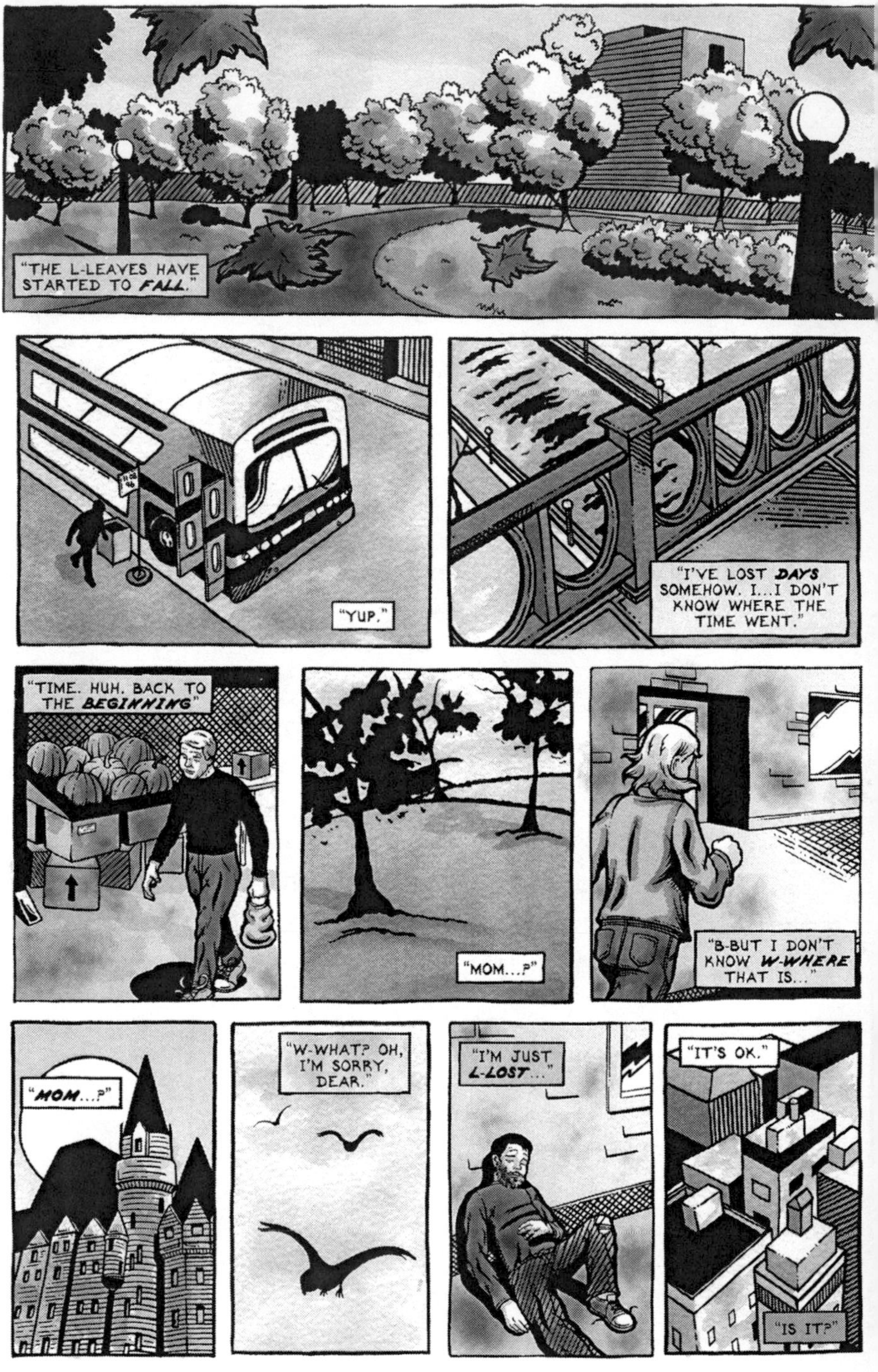
"THE L-LEAVES HAVE STARTED TO FALL."
"YUP."
"I'VE LOST DAYS SOMEHOW. I...I DON'T KNOW WHERE THE TIME WENT."
"TIME. HUH. BACK TO THE BEGINNING"
"MOM...?"
"B-BUT I DON'T KNOW W-WHERE THAT IS..."
"MOM...?"
"W-WHAT? OH, I'M SORRY, DEAR."
"I'M JUST L-LOST..."
"IT'S OK."
"IS IT?"

"WHAT?"
"IS IT OK?"
"I…I'M NOT SURE I…"
"HOW DO WE KNOW?"
"WHAT?"

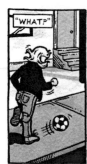

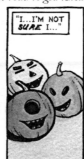

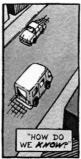

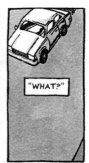

The road to god knows...

"HOW DO WE KNOW IF WE'RE OK, MARIE? HOW DO WE EVER KNOW?

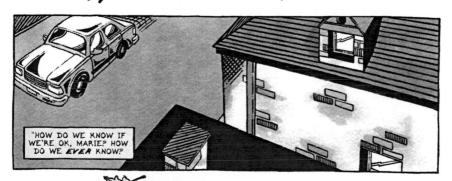

by Von Allan

edited by Sam Boswell

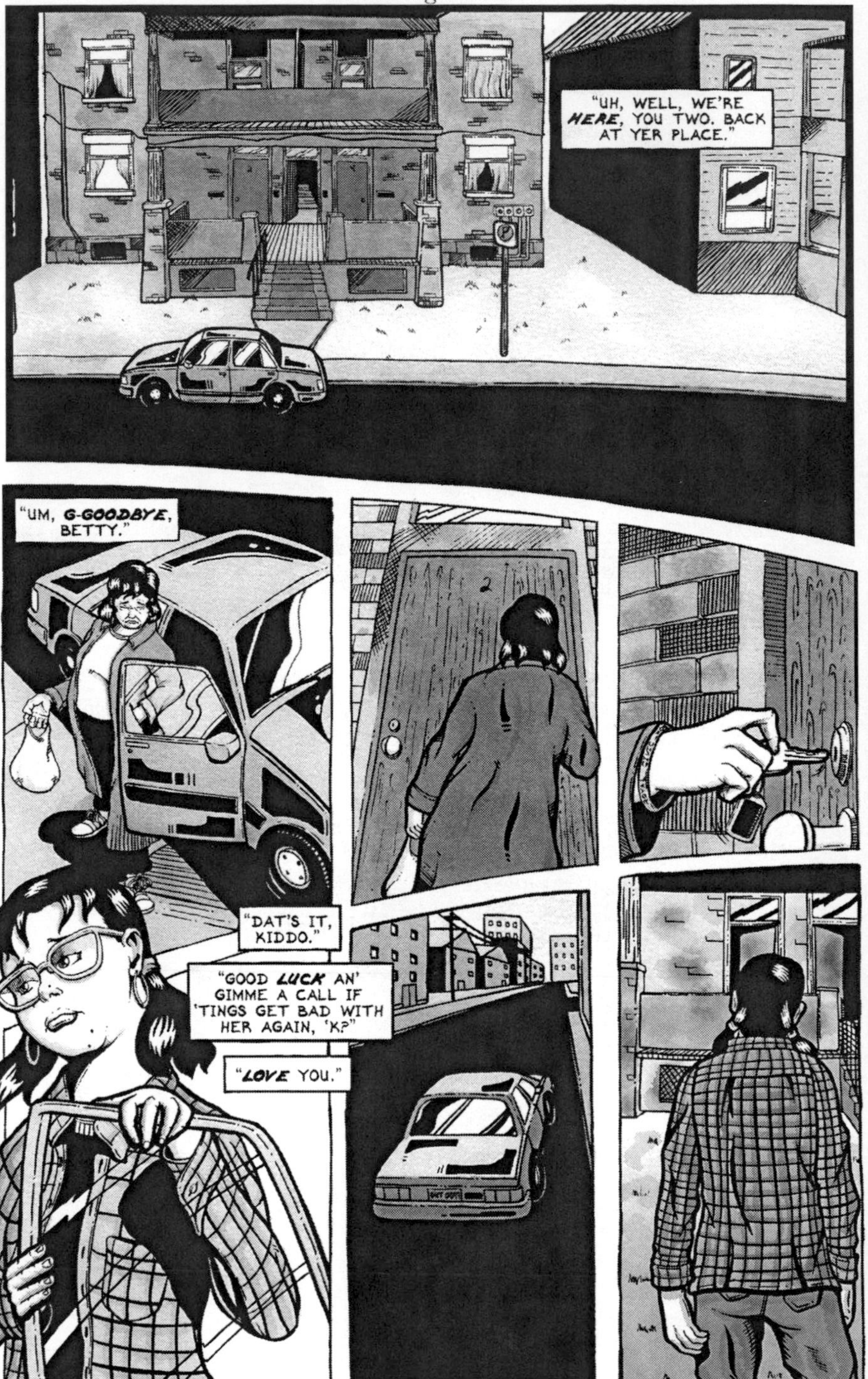
"UH, WELL, WE'RE HERE, YOU TWO. BACK AT YER PLACE."
"UM, G-GOODBYE, BETTY."
"DAT'S IT, KIDDO."
"GOOD LUCK AN' GIMME A CALL IF 'TINGS GET BAD WITH HER AGAIN, 'K?"
"LOVE YOU."

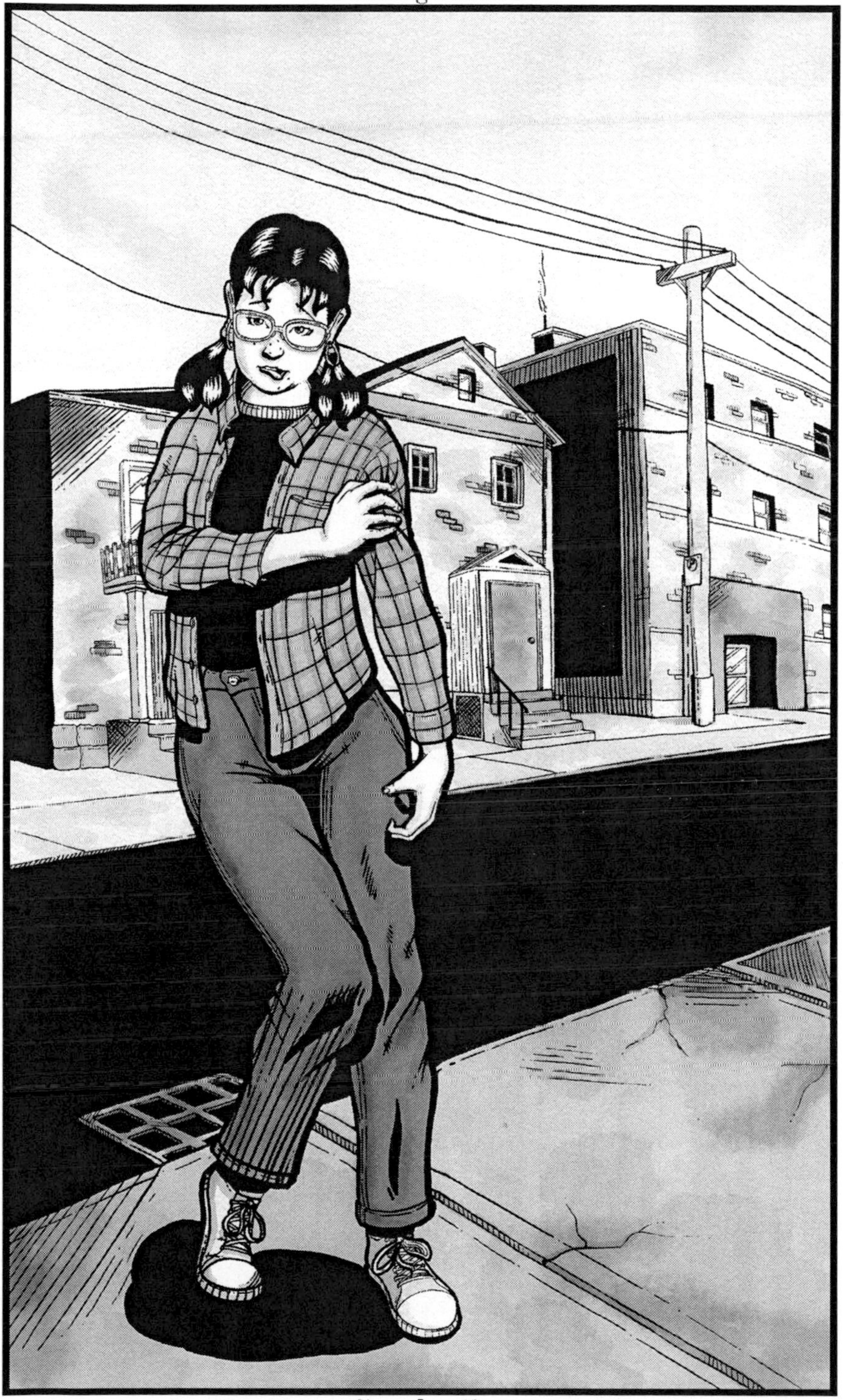

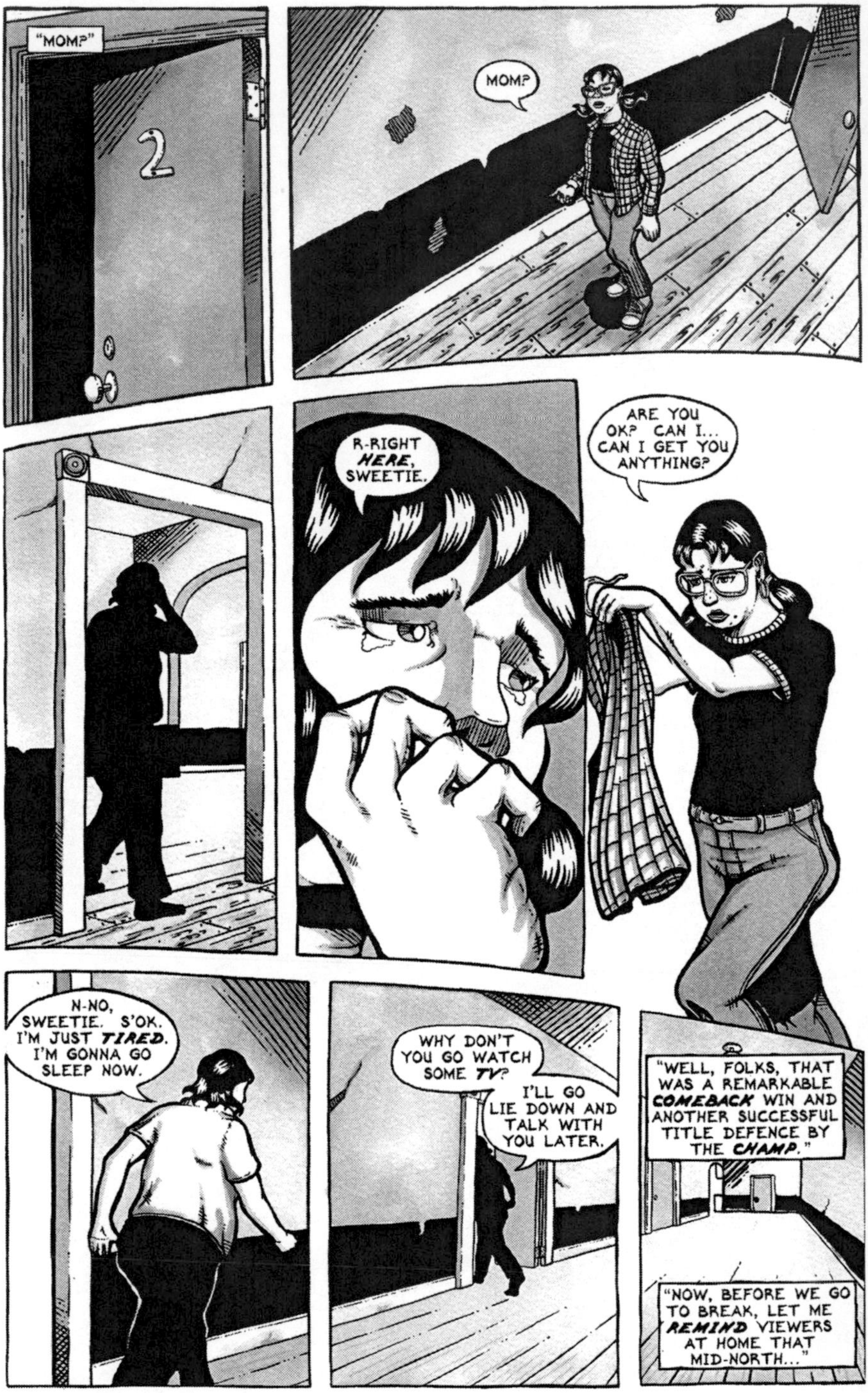
"MOM?"
MOM?
R-RIGHT HERE, SWEETIE.
ARE YOU OK? CAN I... CAN I GET YOU ANYTHING?
N-NO, SWEETIE. S'OK. I'M JUST TIRED. I'M GONNA GO SLEEP NOW.
WHY DON'T YOU GO WATCH SOME TV?
I'LL GO LIE DOWN AND TALK WITH YOU LATER.
"WELL, FOLKS, THAT WAS A REMARKABLE COMEBACK WIN AND ANOTHER SUCCESSFUL TITLE DEFENCE BY THE CHAMP."
"NOW, BEFORE WE GO TO BREAK, LET ME REMIND VIEWERS AT HOME THAT MID-NORTH..."

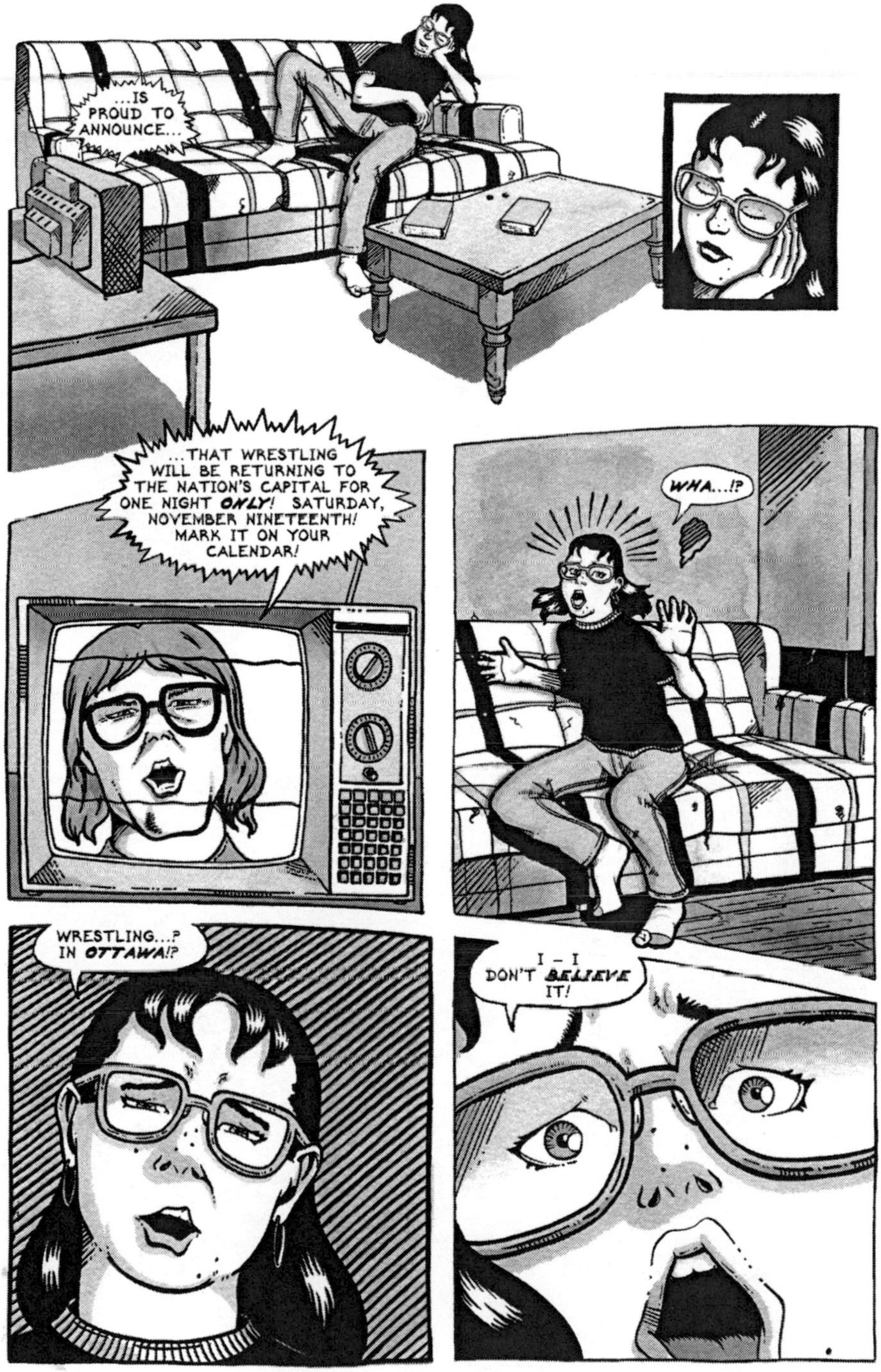
...IS PROUD TO ANNOUNCE...
...THAT WRESTLING WILL BE RETURNING TO THE NATION'S CAPITAL FOR ONE NIGHT ONLY! SATURDAY, NOVEMBER NINETEENTH! MARK IT ON YOUR CALENDAR!
WHA...!?
WRESTLING...? IN OTTAWA!?
I - I DON'T BELIEVE IT!

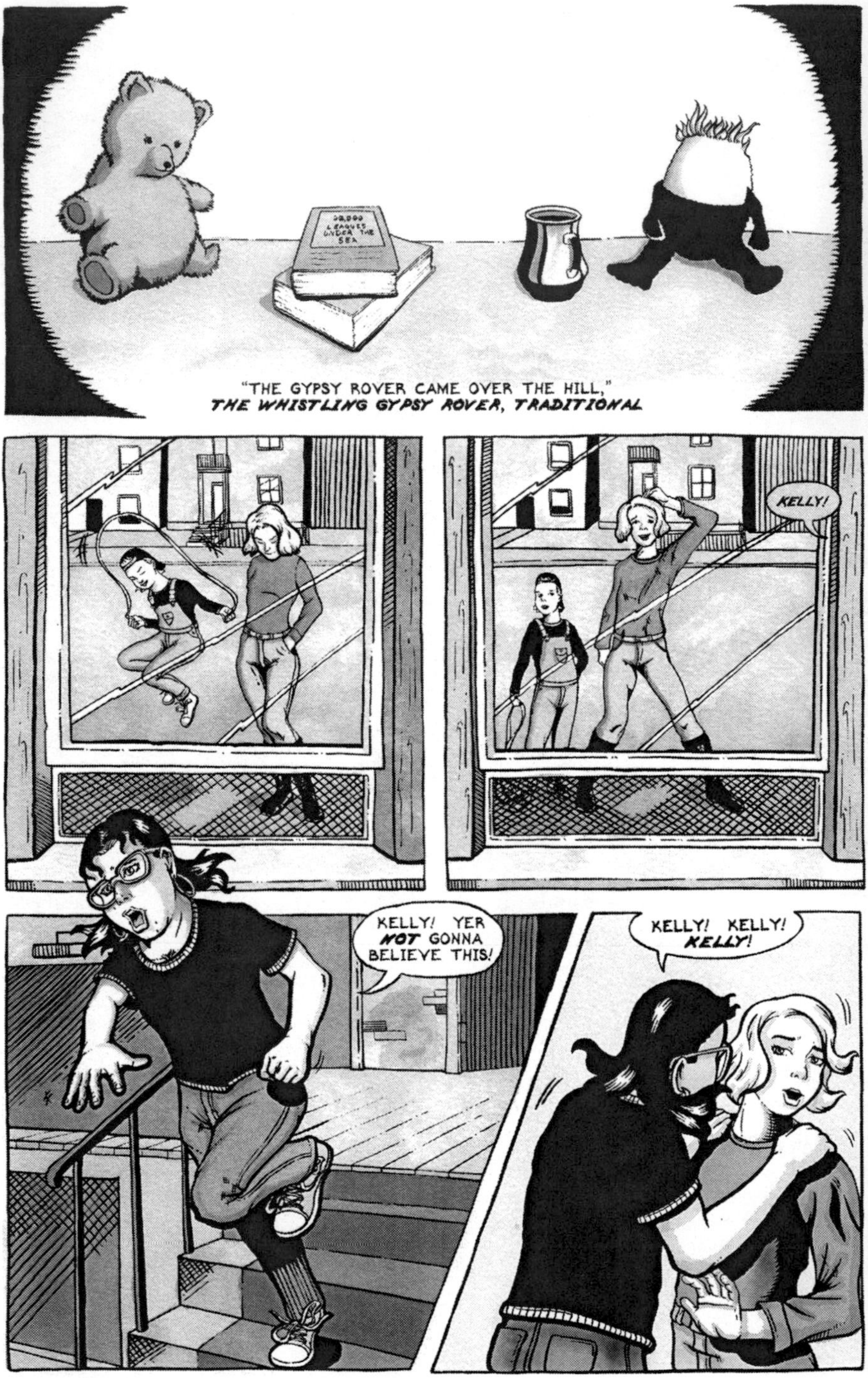
20,000 LEAGUES UNDER THE SEA
"THE GYPSY ROVER CAME OVER THE HILL,"
THE WHISTLING GYPSY ROVER, TRADITIONAL
KELLY!
KELLY! YER NOT GONNA BELIEVE THIS!
KELLY! KELLY! KELLY!

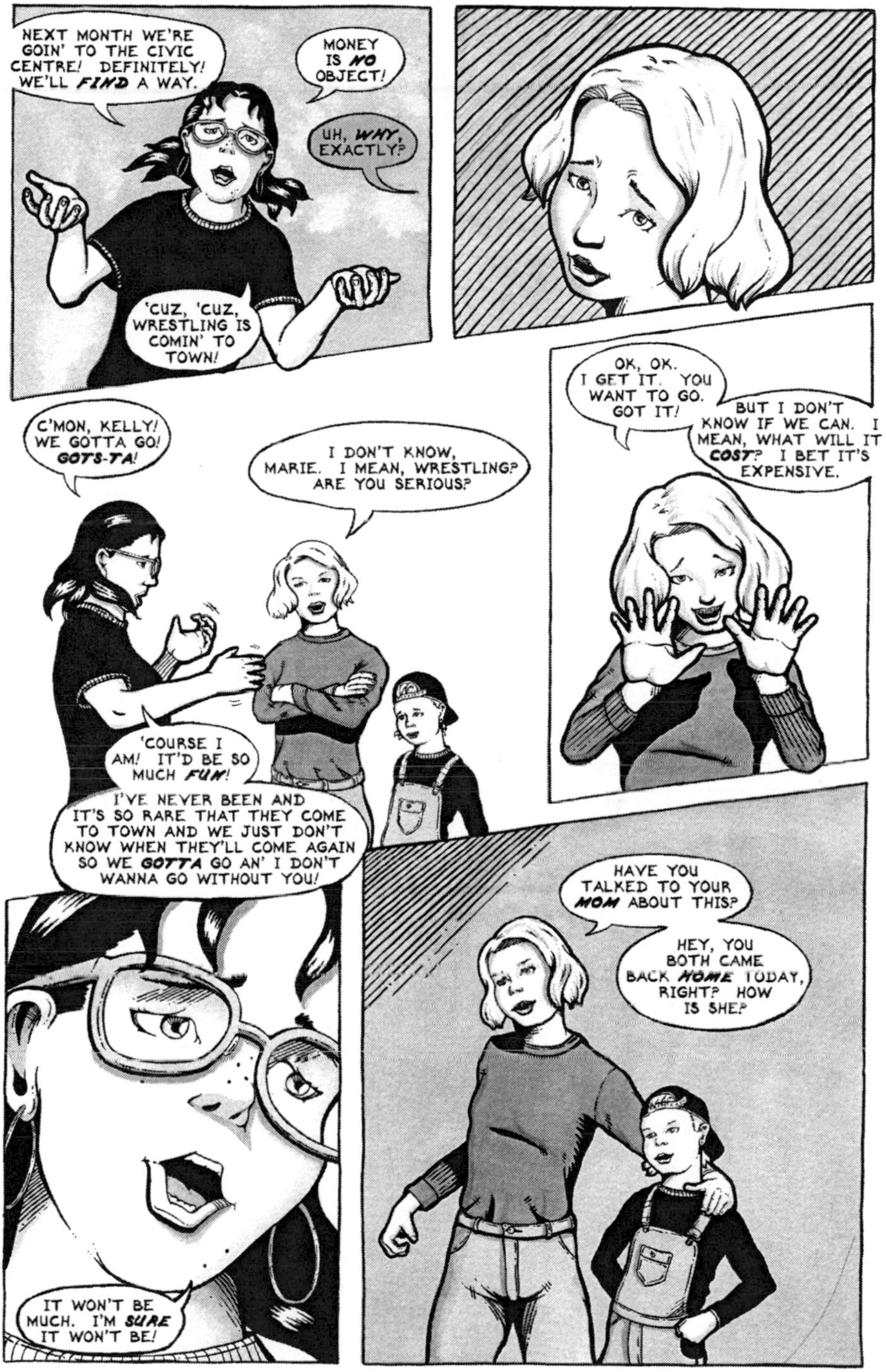
NEXT MONTH WE'RE GOIN' TO THE CIVIC CENTRE! DEFINITELY! WE'LL FIND A WAY.
MONEY IS NO OBJECT!
UH, WHY, EXACTLY?
'CUZ, 'CUZ, WRESTLING IS COMIN' TO TOWN!
C'MON, KELLY! WE GOTTA GO! GOTS-TA!
I DON'T KNOW, MARIE. I MEAN, WRESTLING? ARE YOU SERIOUS?
'COURSE I AM! IT'D BE SO MUCH FUN!
I'VE NEVER BEEN AND IT'S SO RARE THAT THEY COME TO TOWN AND WE JUST DON'T KNOW WHEN THEY'LL COME AGAIN SO WE GOTTA GO AN' I DON'T WANNA GO WITHOUT YOU!
OK, OK. I GET IT. YOU WANT TO GO. GOT IT!
BUT I DON'T KNOW IF WE CAN. I MEAN, WHAT WILL IT COST? I BET IT'S EXPENSIVE.
IT WON'T BE MUCH. I'M SURE IT WON'T BE!
HAVE YOU TALKED TO YOUR MOM ABOUT THIS?
HEY, YOU BOTH CAME BACK HOME TODAY, RIGHT? HOW IS SHE?

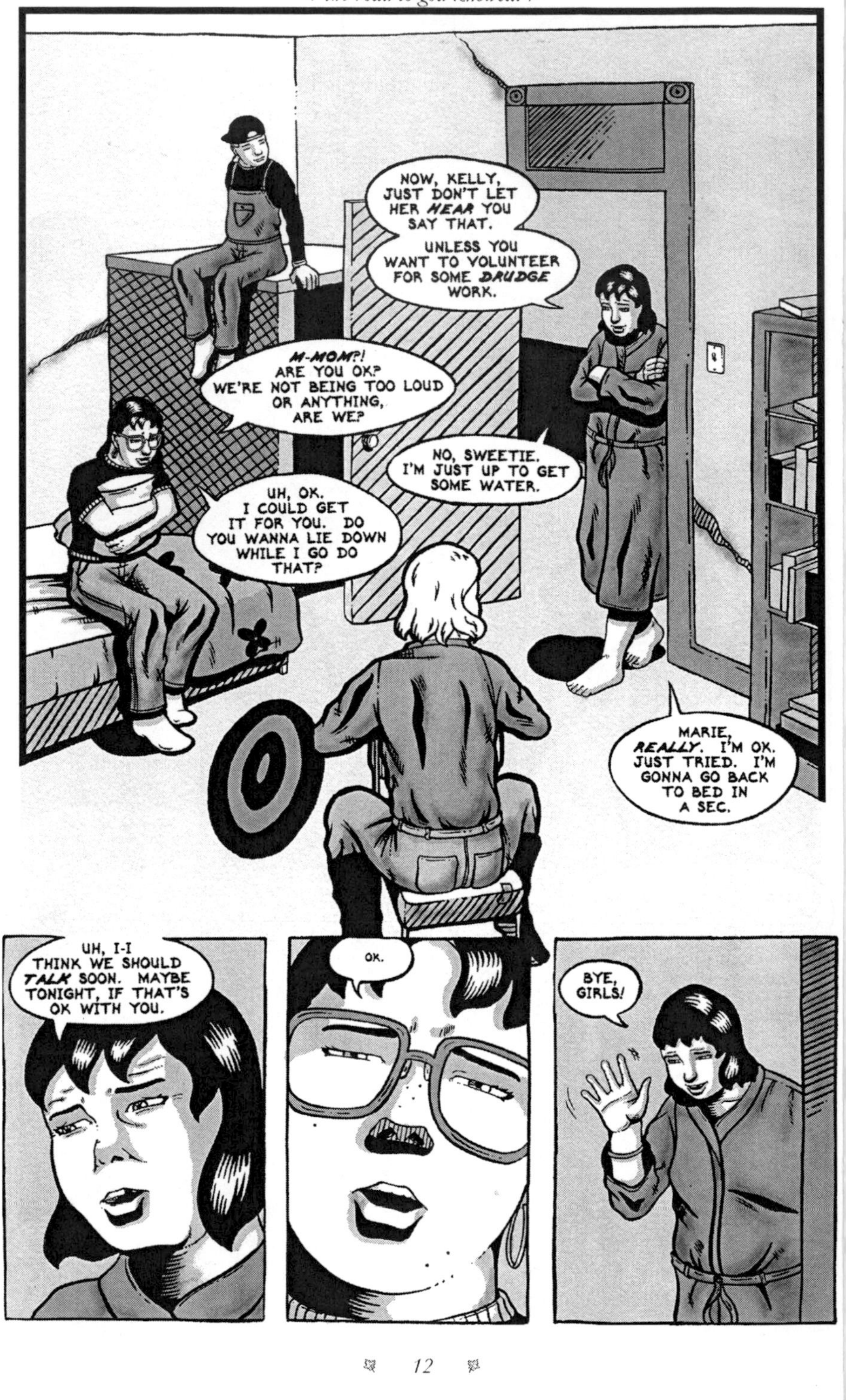
NOW, KELLY, JUST DON'T LET HER *HEAR* YOU SAY THAT.
UNLESS YOU WANT TO VOLUNTEER FOR SOME *DRUDGE* WORK.
M-MOM?! ARE YOU OK? WE'RE NOT BEING TOO LOUD OR ANYTHING, ARE WE?
NO, SWEETIE. I'M JUST UP TO GET SOME WATER.
UH, OK. I COULD GET IT FOR YOU. DO YOU WANNA LIE DOWN WHILE I GO DO THAT?
MARIE, *REALLY*. I'M OK. JUST TRIED. I'M GONNA GO BACK TO BED IN A SEC.
UH, I-I THINK WE SHOULD *TALK* SOON. MAYBE TONIGHT, IF THAT'S OK WITH YOU.
OK.
BYE, GIRLS!

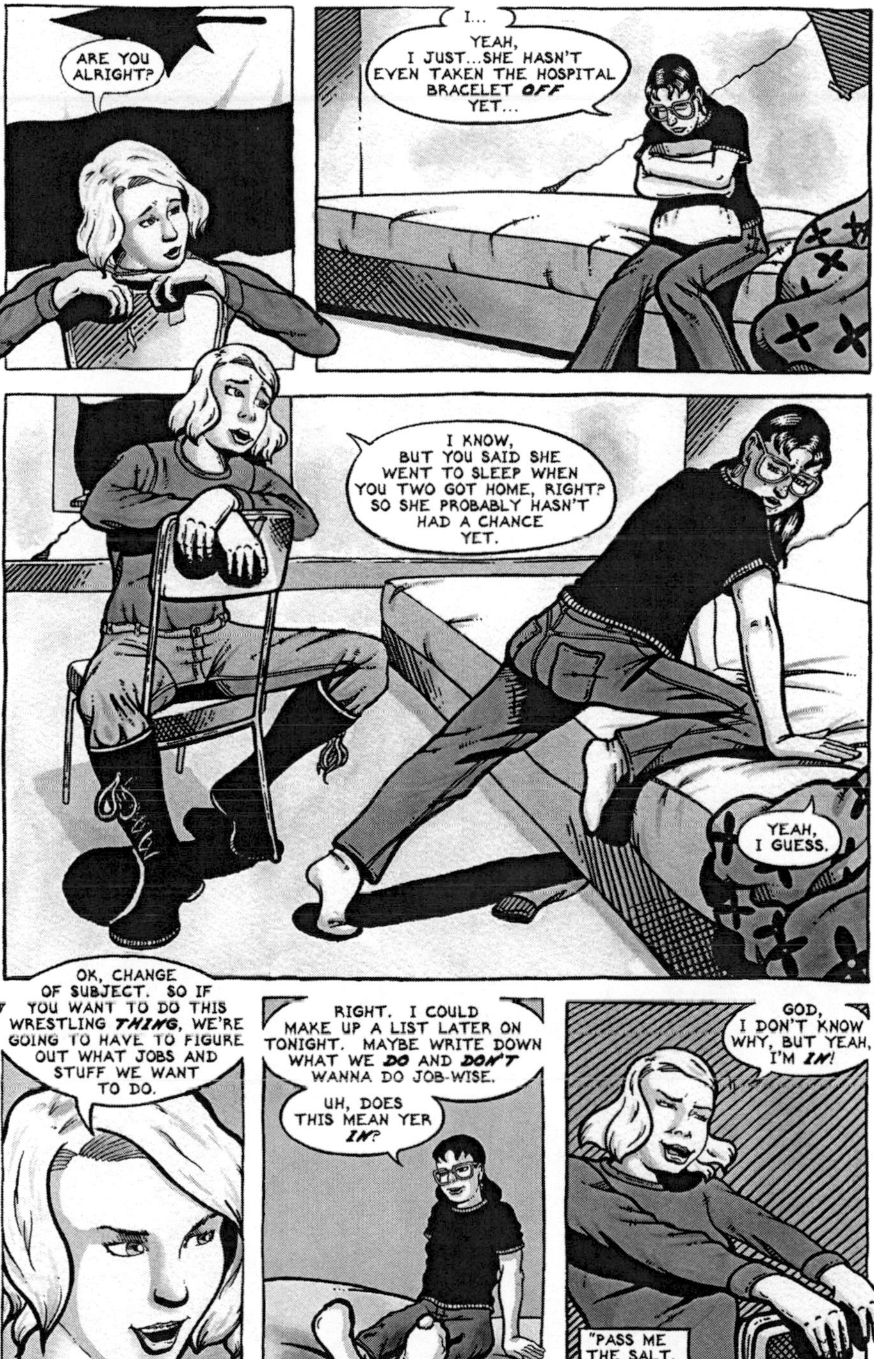
ARE YOU ALRIGHT?
I...
YEAH, I JUST...SHE HASN'T EVEN TAKEN THE HOSPITAL BRACELET OFF YET...
I KNOW, BUT YOU SAID SHE WENT TO SLEEP WHEN YOU TWO GOT HOME, RIGHT? SO SHE PROBABLY HASN'T HAD A CHANCE YET.
YEAH, I GUESS.
OK, CHANGE OF SUBJECT. SO IF YOU WANT TO DO THIS WRESTLING THING, WE'RE GOING TO HAVE TO FIGURE OUT WHAT JOBS AND STUFF WE WANT TO DO.
RIGHT. I COULD MAKE UP A LIST LATER ON TONIGHT. MAYBE WRITE DOWN WHAT WE DO AND DON'T WANNA DO JOB-WISE.
UH, DOES THIS MEAN YER IN?
GOD, I DON'T KNOW WHY, BUT YEAH, I'M IN!
"PASS ME THE SALT, SWEETIE?"

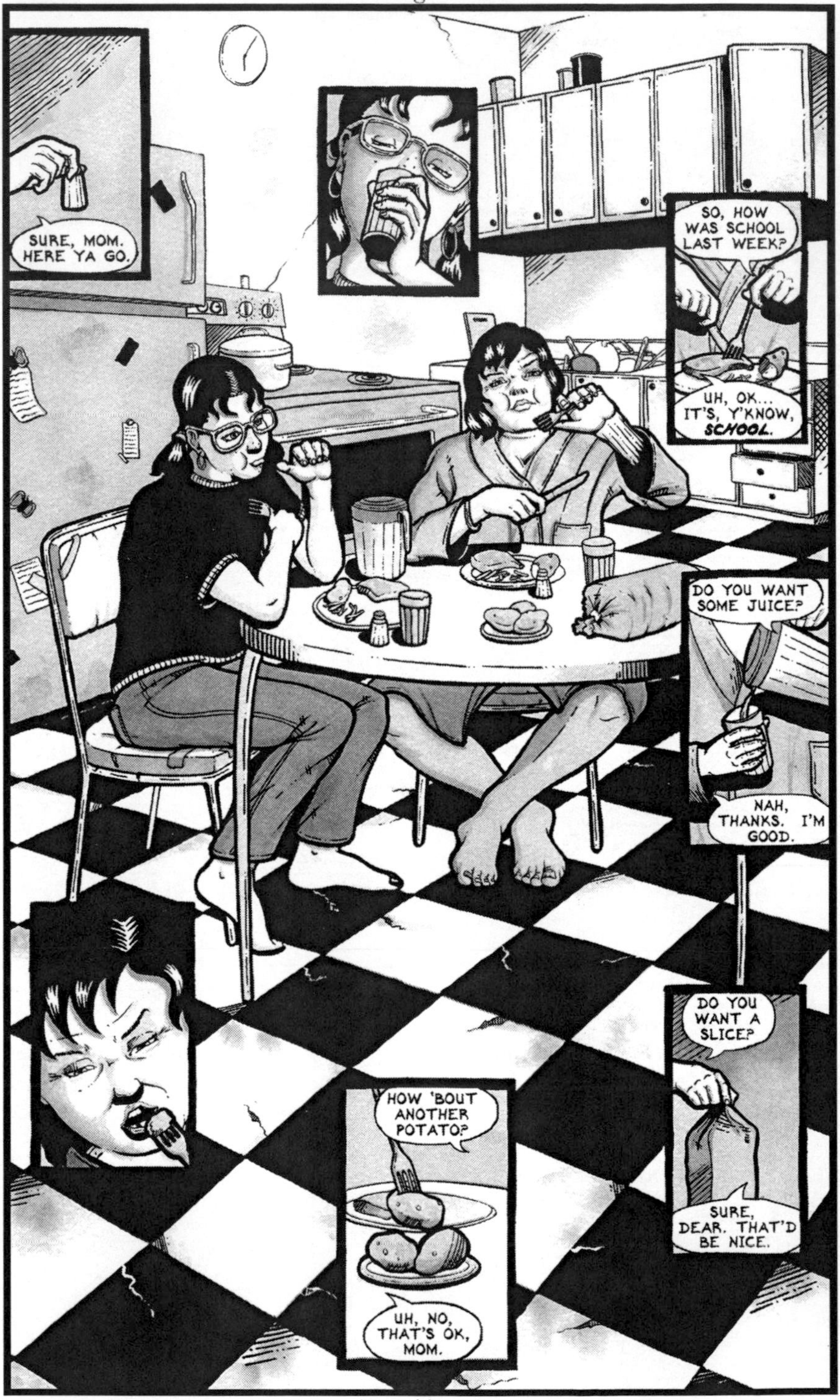
SURE, MOM. HERE YA GO.
SO, HOW WAS SCHOOL LAST WEEK?
UH, OK... IT'S, Y'KNOW, SCHOOL.
DO YOU WANT SOME JUICE?
NAH, THANKS. I'M GOOD.
DO YOU WANT A SLICE?
SURE, DEAR. THAT'D BE NICE.
HOW 'BOUT ANOTHER POTATO?
UH, NO, THAT'S OK, MOM.

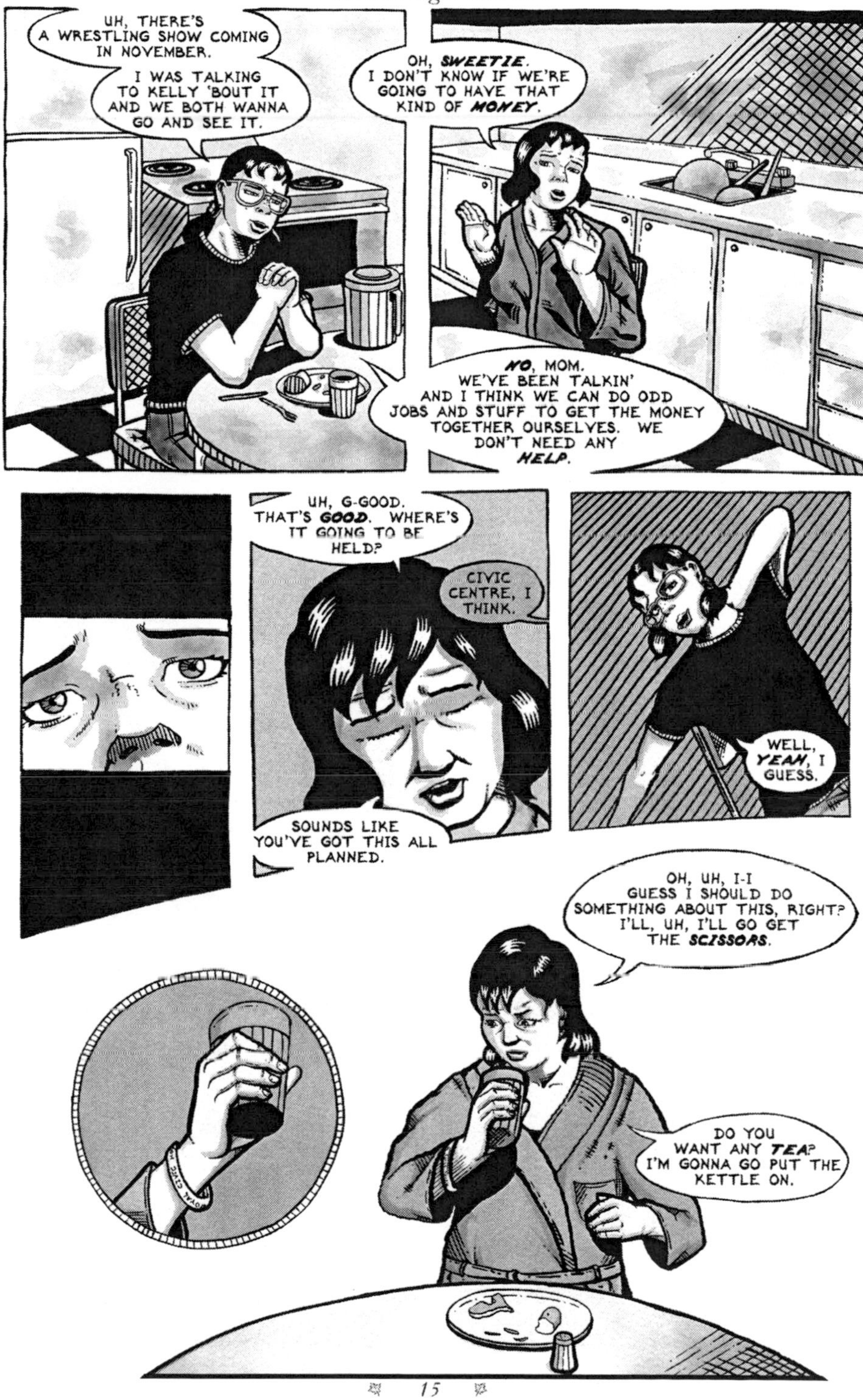
UH, THERE'S A WRESTLING SHOW COMING IN NOVEMBER.
I WAS TALKING TO KELLY 'BOUT IT AND WE BOTH WANNA GO AND SEE IT.
OH, SWEETIE. I DON'T KNOW IF WE'RE GOING TO HAVE THAT KIND OF MONEY.
NO, MOM. WE'VE BEEN TALKIN' AND I THINK WE CAN DO ODD JOBS AND STUFF TO GET THE MONEY TOGETHER OURSELVES. WE DON'T NEED ANY HELP.
UH, G-GOOD. THAT'S GOOD. WHERE'S IT GOING TO BE HELD?
CIVIC CENTRE, I THINK.
SOUNDS LIKE YOU'VE GOT THIS ALL PLANNED.
WELL, YEAH, I GUESS.
OH, UH, I-I GUESS I SHOULD DO SOMETHING ABOUT THIS, RIGHT? I'LL, UH, I'LL GO GET THE SCISSORS.
DO YOU WANT ANY TEA? I'M GONNA GO PUT THE KETTLE ON.

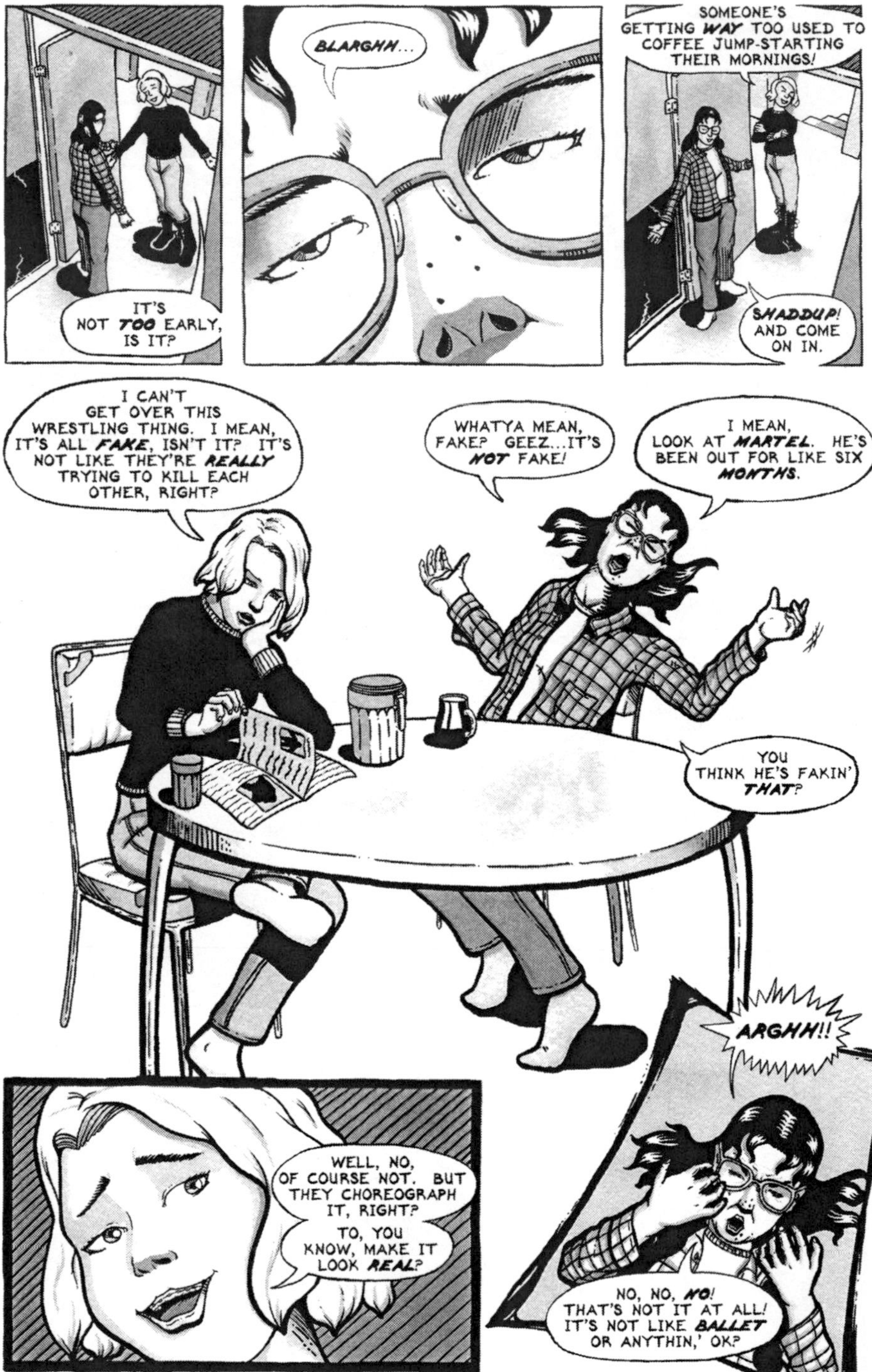
IT'S NOT TOO EARLY, IS IT?
BLARGHH...
SOMEONE'S GETTING WAY TOO USED TO COFFEE JUMP-STARTING THEIR MORNINGS!
SHADDUP! AND COME ON IN.
I CAN'T GET OVER THIS WRESTLING THING. I MEAN, IT'S ALL FAKE, ISN'T IT? IT'S NOT LIKE THEY'RE REALLY TRYING TO KILL EACH OTHER, RIGHT?
WHATYA MEAN, FAKE? GEEZ...IT'S NOT FAKE!
I MEAN, LOOK AT MARTEL. HE'S BEEN OUT FOR LIKE SIX MONTHS.
YOU THINK HE'S FAKIN' THAT?
WELL, NO, OF COURSE NOT. BUT THEY CHOREOGRAPH IT, RIGHT?
TO, YOU KNOW, MAKE IT LOOK REAL?
ARGHH!!
NO, NO, NO! THAT'S NOT IT AT ALL! IT'S NOT LIKE BALLET OR ANYTHIN,' OK?

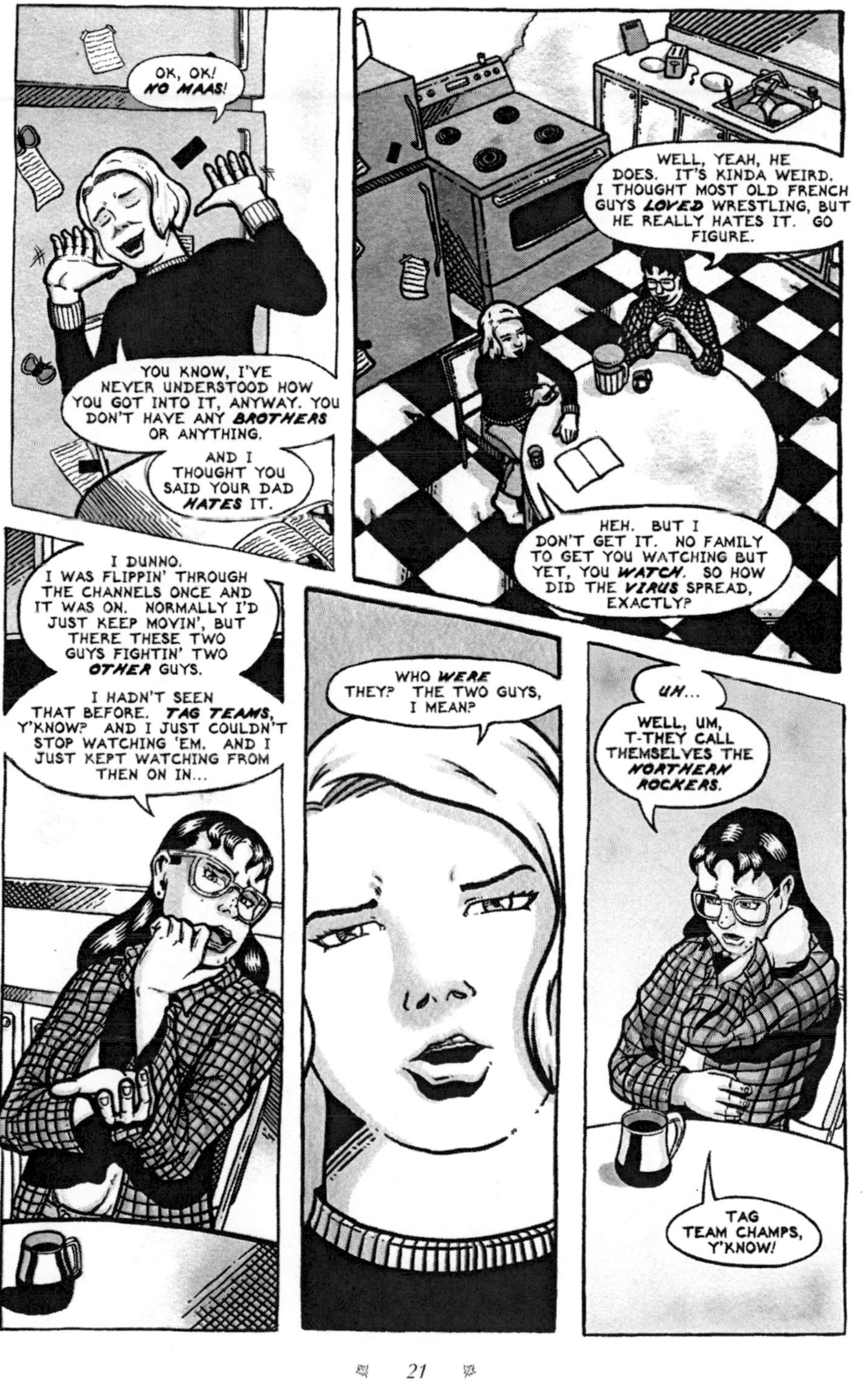
OK, OK! NO MAAS!
YOU KNOW, I'VE NEVER UNDERSTOOD HOW YOU GOT INTO IT, ANYWAY. YOU DON'T HAVE ANY BROTHERS OR ANYTHING.
AND I THOUGHT YOU SAID YOUR DAD HATES IT.
WELL, YEAH, HE DOES. IT'S KINDA WEIRD. I THOUGHT MOST OLD FRENCH GUYS LOVED WRESTLING, BUT HE REALLY HATES IT. GO FIGURE.
HEH. BUT I DON'T GET IT. NO FAMILY TO GET YOU WATCHING BUT YET, YOU WATCH. SO HOW DID THE VIRUS SPREAD, EXACTLY?
I DUNNO. I WAS FLIPPIN' THROUGH THE CHANNELS ONCE AND IT WAS ON. NORMALLY I'D JUST KEEP MOVIN', BUT THERE THESE TWO GUYS FIGHTIN' TWO OTHER GUYS.
I HADN'T SEEN THAT BEFORE. TAG TEAMS, Y'KNOW? AND I JUST COULDN'T STOP WATCHING 'EM. AND I JUST KEPT WATCHING FROM THEN ON IN...
WHO WERE THEY? THE TWO GUYS, I MEAN?
UH...
WELL, UM, T-THEY CALL THEMSELVES THE NORTHERN ROCKERS.
TAG TEAM CHAMPS, Y'KNOW!

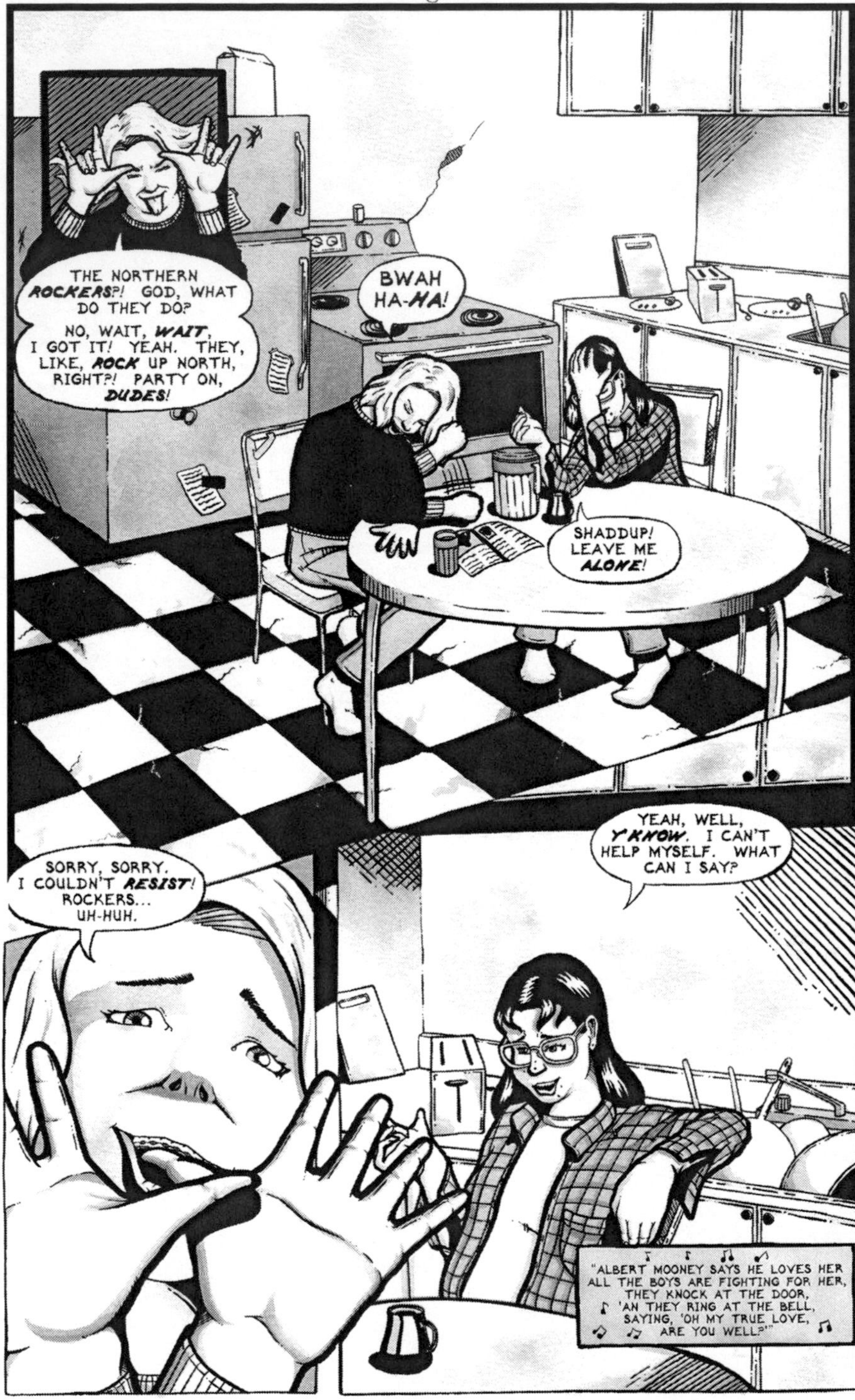
THE NORTHERN ROCKERS?! GOD, WHAT DO THEY DO?
NO, WAIT, WAIT, I GOT IT! YEAH. THEY, LIKE, ROCK UP NORTH, RIGHT?! PARTY ON, DUDES!
BWAH HA-HA!
SHADDUP! LEAVE ME ALONE!
SORRY, SORRY. I COULDN'T RESIST! ROCKERS... UH-HUH.
YEAH, WELL, Y'KNOW. I CAN'T HELP MYSELF. WHAT CAN I SAY?
"ALBERT MOONEY SAYS HE LOVES HER ALL THE BOYS ARE FIGHTING FOR HER, THEY KNOCK AT THE DOOR, 'AN THEY RING AT THE BELL, SAYING, 'OH MY TRUE LOVE, ARE YOU WELL?'"

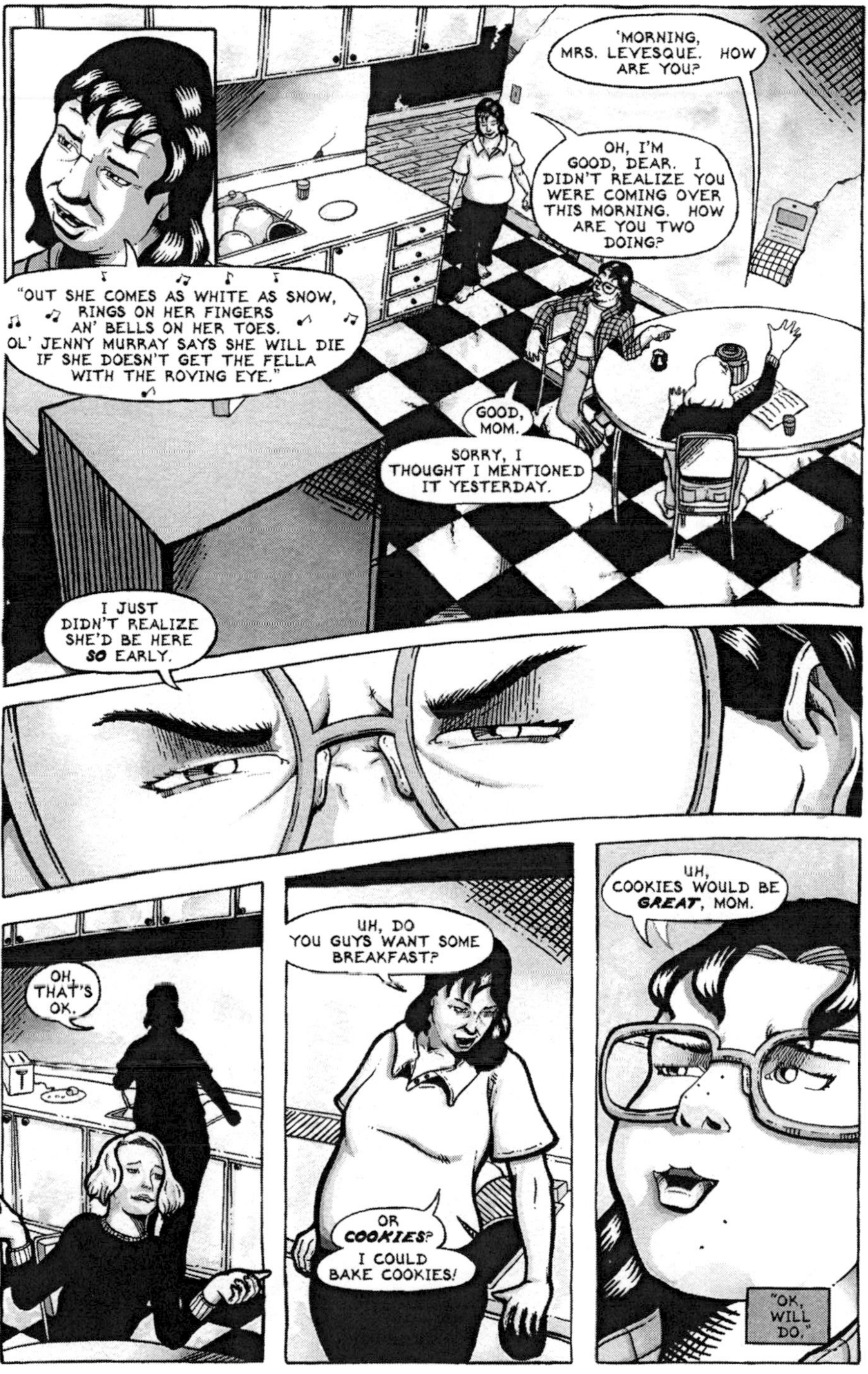
'MORNING, MRS. LEVESQUE. HOW ARE YOU?
OH, I'M GOOD, DEAR. I DIDN'T REALIZE YOU WERE COMING OVER THIS MORNING. HOW ARE YOU TWO DOING?
"OUT SHE COMES AS WHITE AS SNOW, RINGS ON HER FINGERS AN' BELLS ON HER TOES. OL' JENNY MURRAY SAYS SHE WILL DIE IF SHE DOESN'T GET THE FELLA WITH THE ROVING EYE."
GOOD, MOM.
SORRY, I THOUGHT I MENTIONED IT YESTERDAY.
I JUST DIDN'T REALIZE SHE'D BE HERE SO EARLY.
OH, THAT'S OK.
UH, DO YOU GUYS WANT SOME BREAKFAST?
OR COOKIES? I COULD BAKE COOKIES!
UH, COOKIES WOULD BE GREAT, MOM.
"OK, WILL DO."

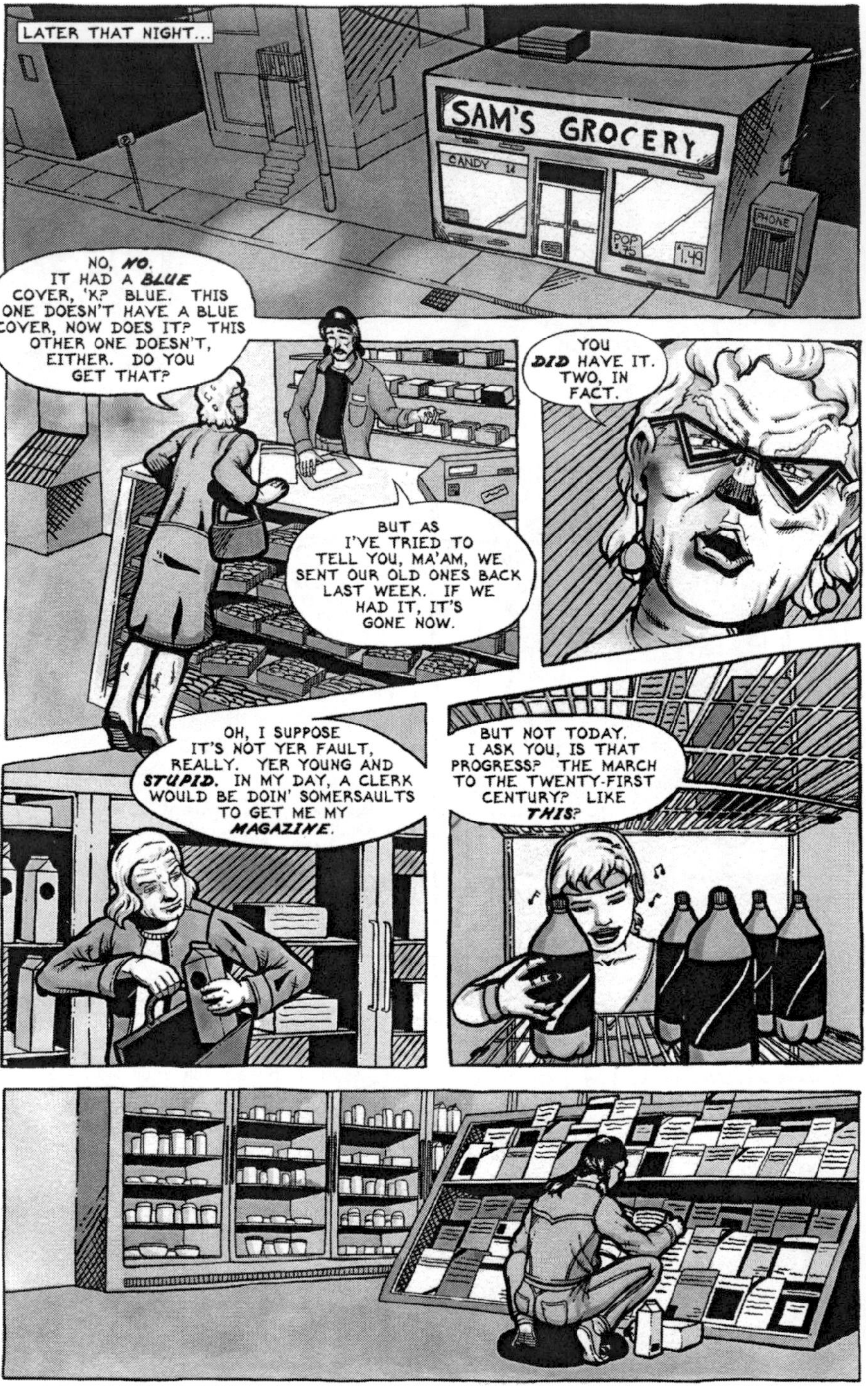
LATER THAT NIGHT...
SAM'S GROCERY
CANDY
PHONE
POP
1.49
NO, NO. IT HAD A BLUE COVER, 'K? BLUE. THIS ONE DOESN'T HAVE A BLUE COVER, NOW DOES IT? THIS OTHER ONE DOESN'T, EITHER. DO YOU GET THAT?
BUT AS I'VE TRIED TO TELL YOU, MA'AM, WE SENT OUR OLD ONES BACK LAST WEEK. IF WE HAD IT, IT'S GONE NOW.
YOU DID HAVE IT. TWO, IN FACT.
OH, I SUPPOSE IT'S NOT YER FAULT, REALLY. YER YOUNG AND STUPID. IN MY DAY, A CLERK WOULD BE DOIN' SOMERSAULTS TO GET ME MY MAGAZINE.
BUT NOT TODAY. I ASK YOU, IS THAT PROGRESS? THE MARCH TO THE TWENTY-FIRST CENTURY? LIKE THIS?

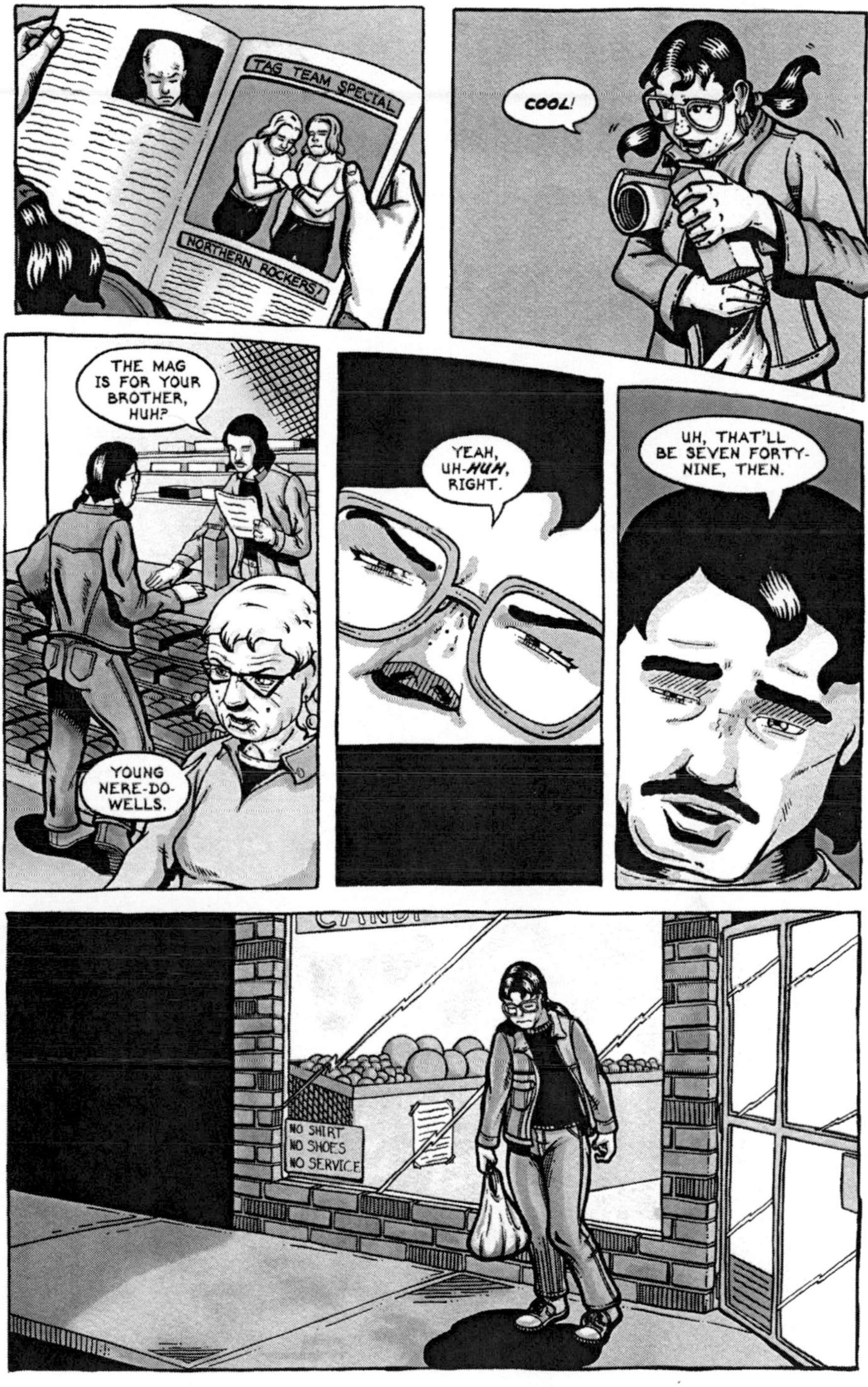
TAG TEAM SPECIAL
NORTHERN ROCKERS!
COOL!
THE MAG IS FOR YOUR BROTHER, HUH?
YOUNG NERE-DO-WELLS.
YEAH, UH-HUH, RIGHT.
UH, THAT'LL BE SEVEN FORTY-NINE, THEN.
NO SHIRT NO SHOES NO SERVICE

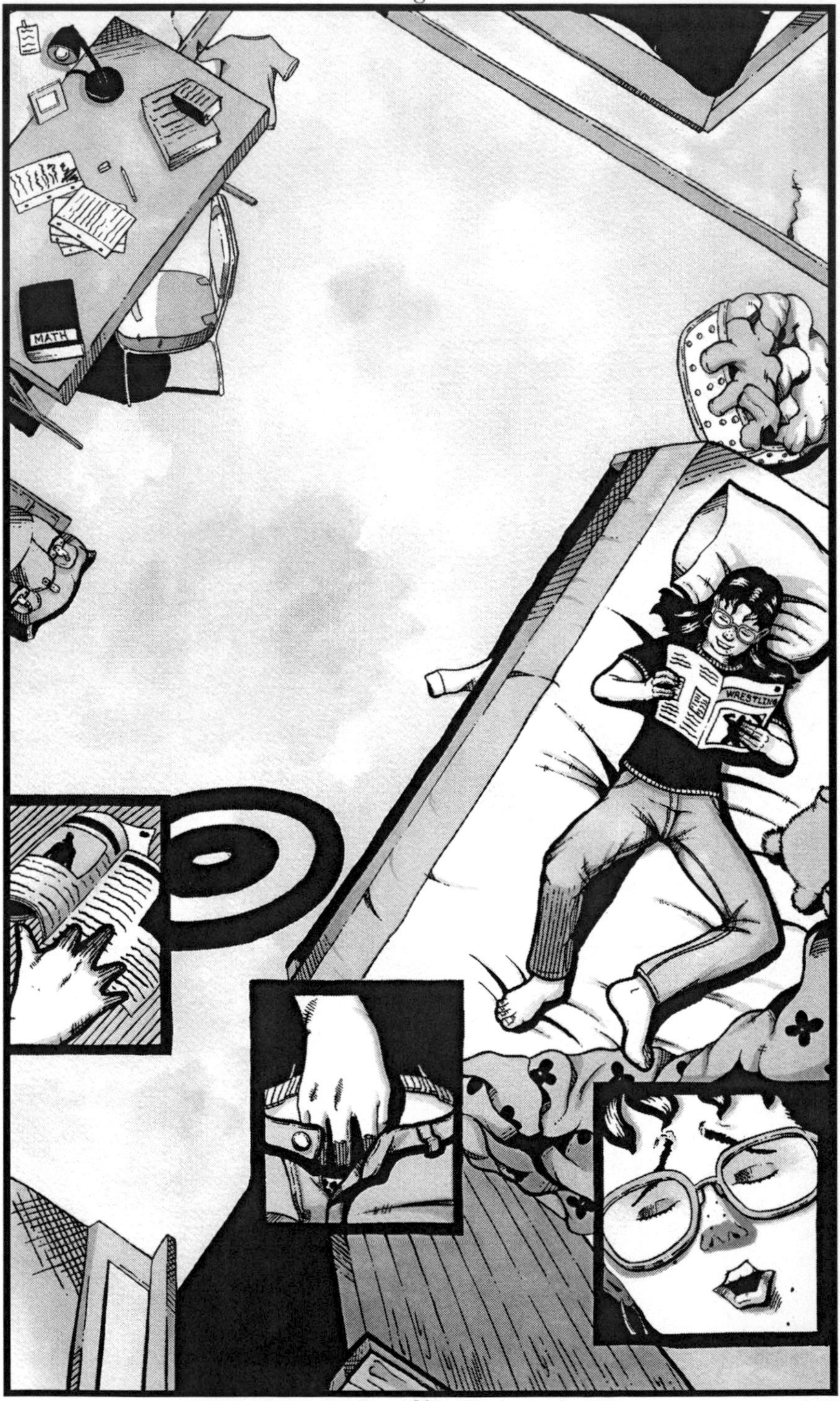
MATH
WRESTLING

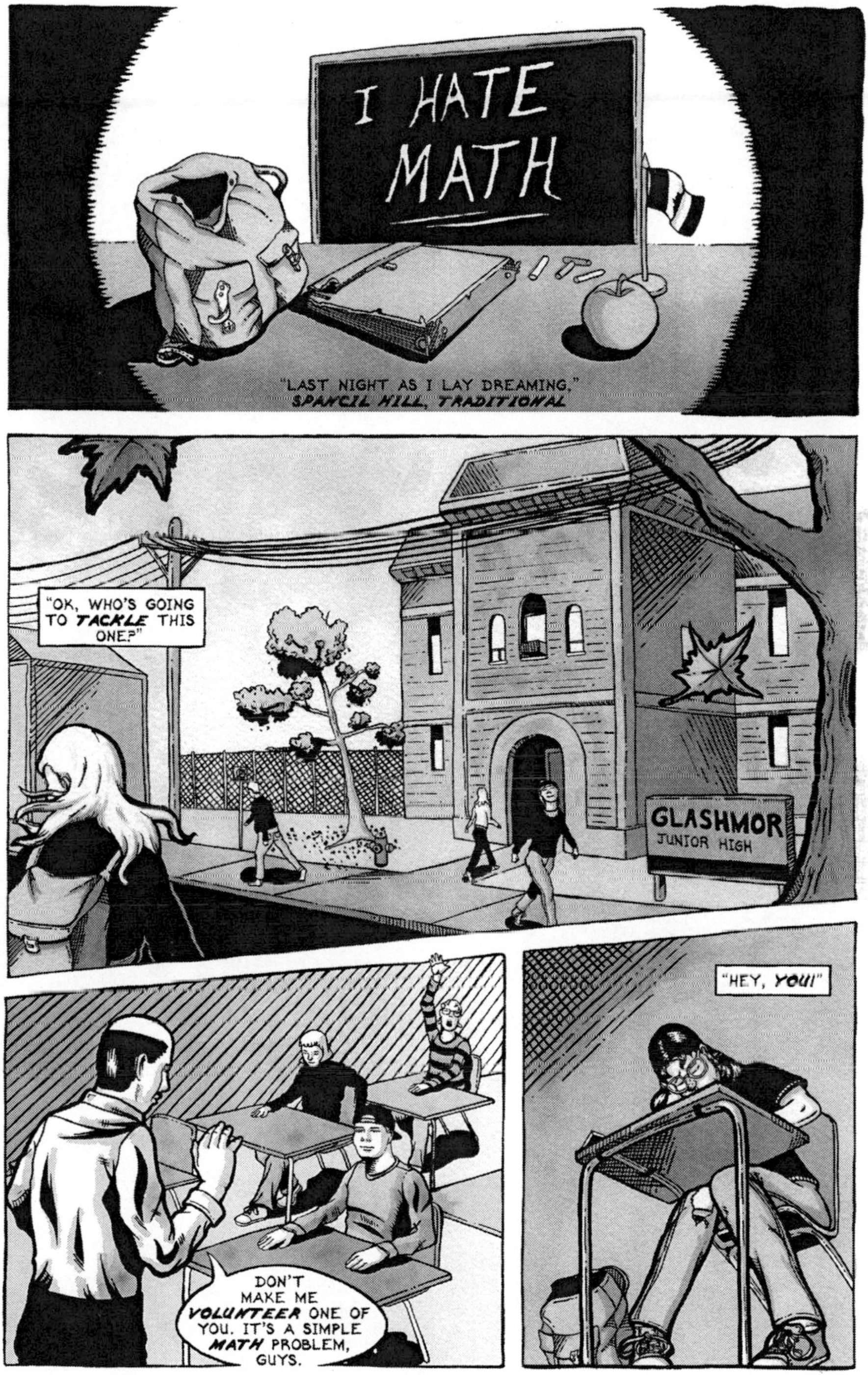
I HATE MATH
"LAST NIGHT AS I LAY DREAMING,"
SPANCIL HILL, TRADITIONAL
"OK, WHO'S GOING TO TACKLE THIS ONE?"
GLASHMOR JUNIOR HIGH
DON'T MAKE ME VOLUNTEER ONE OF YOU. IT'S A SIMPLE MATH PROBLEM, GUYS.
"HEY, YOU!"

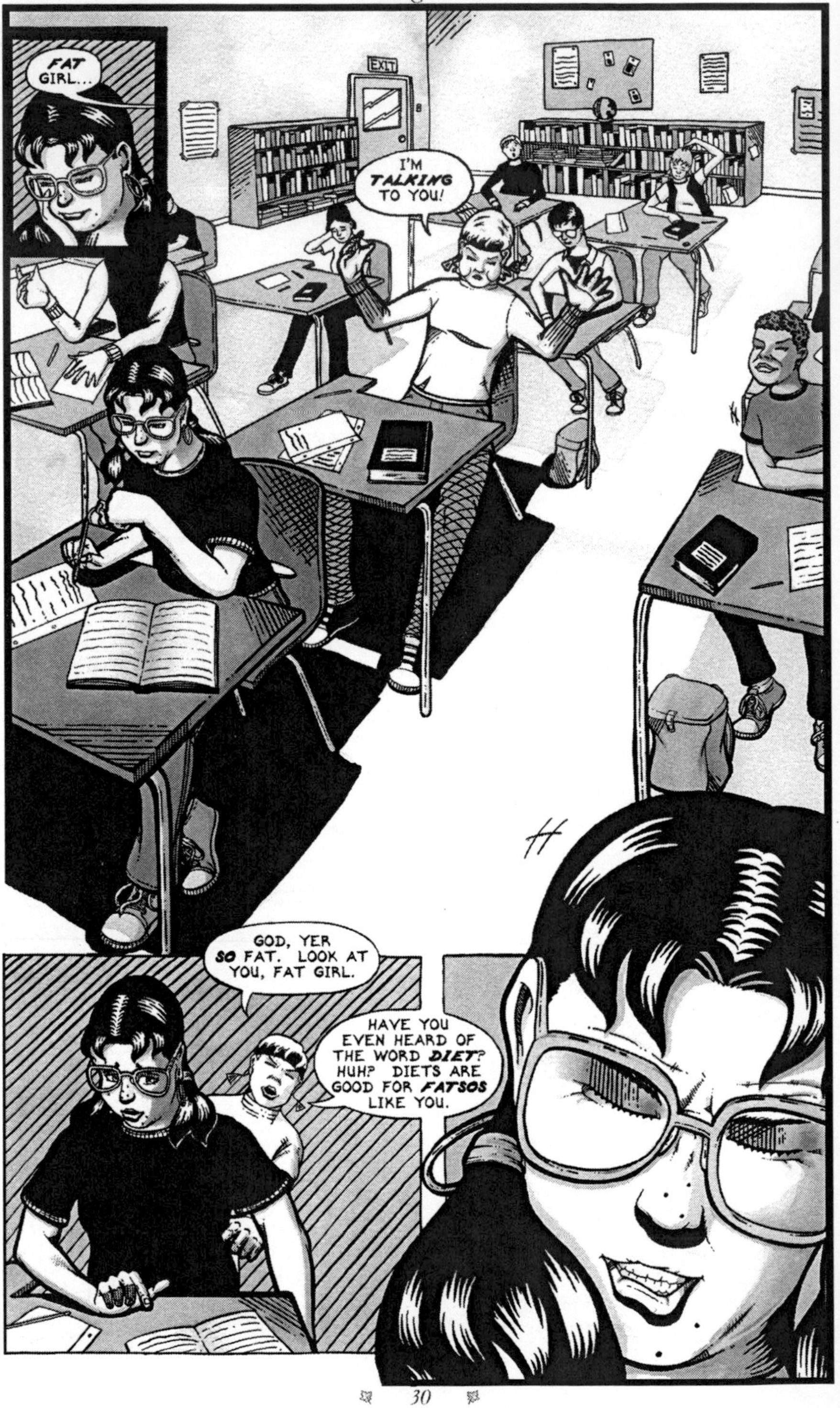
FAT GIRL...
I'M TALKING TO YOU!
GOD, YER SO FAT. LOOK AT YOU, FAT GIRL.
HAVE YOU EVEN HEARD OF THE WORD DIET? HUH? DIETS ARE GOOD FOR FATSOS LIKE YOU.

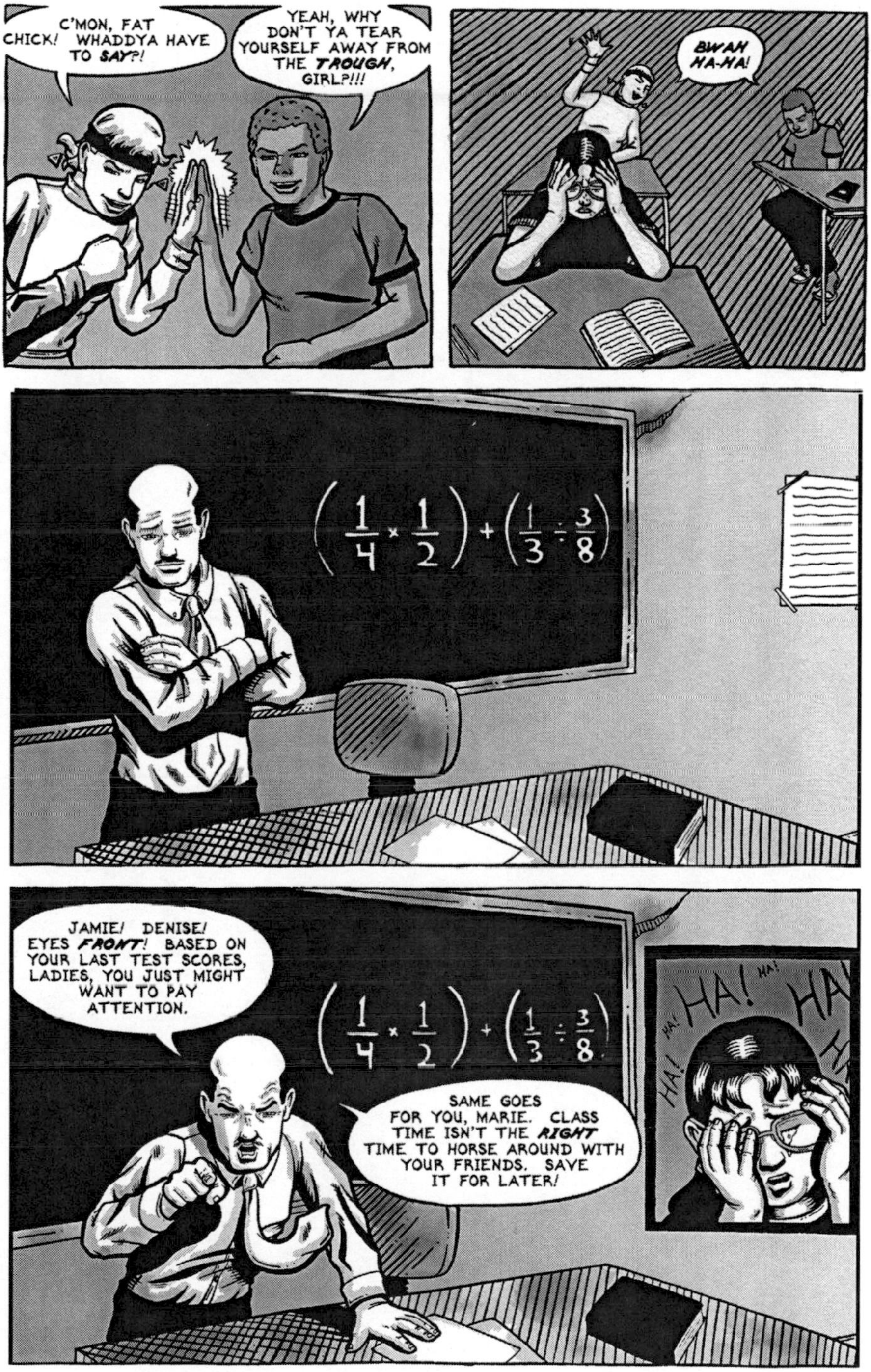
C'MON, FAT CHICK! WHADDYA HAVE TO *SAY*?!
YEAH, WHY DON'T YA TEAR YOURSELF AWAY FROM THE *TROUGH*, GIRL?!!!
BWAH HA-HA!
(1/4 × 1/2) + (1/3 ÷ 3/8)
JAMIE! DENISE! EYES *FRONT*! BASED ON YOUR LAST TEST SCORES, LADIES, YOU JUST MIGHT WANT TO PAY ATTENTION.
SAME GOES FOR YOU, MARIE. CLASS TIME ISN'T THE *RIGHT* TIME TO HORSE AROUND WITH YOUR FRIENDS. SAVE IT FOR LATER!
HA! HA! HA! HA!

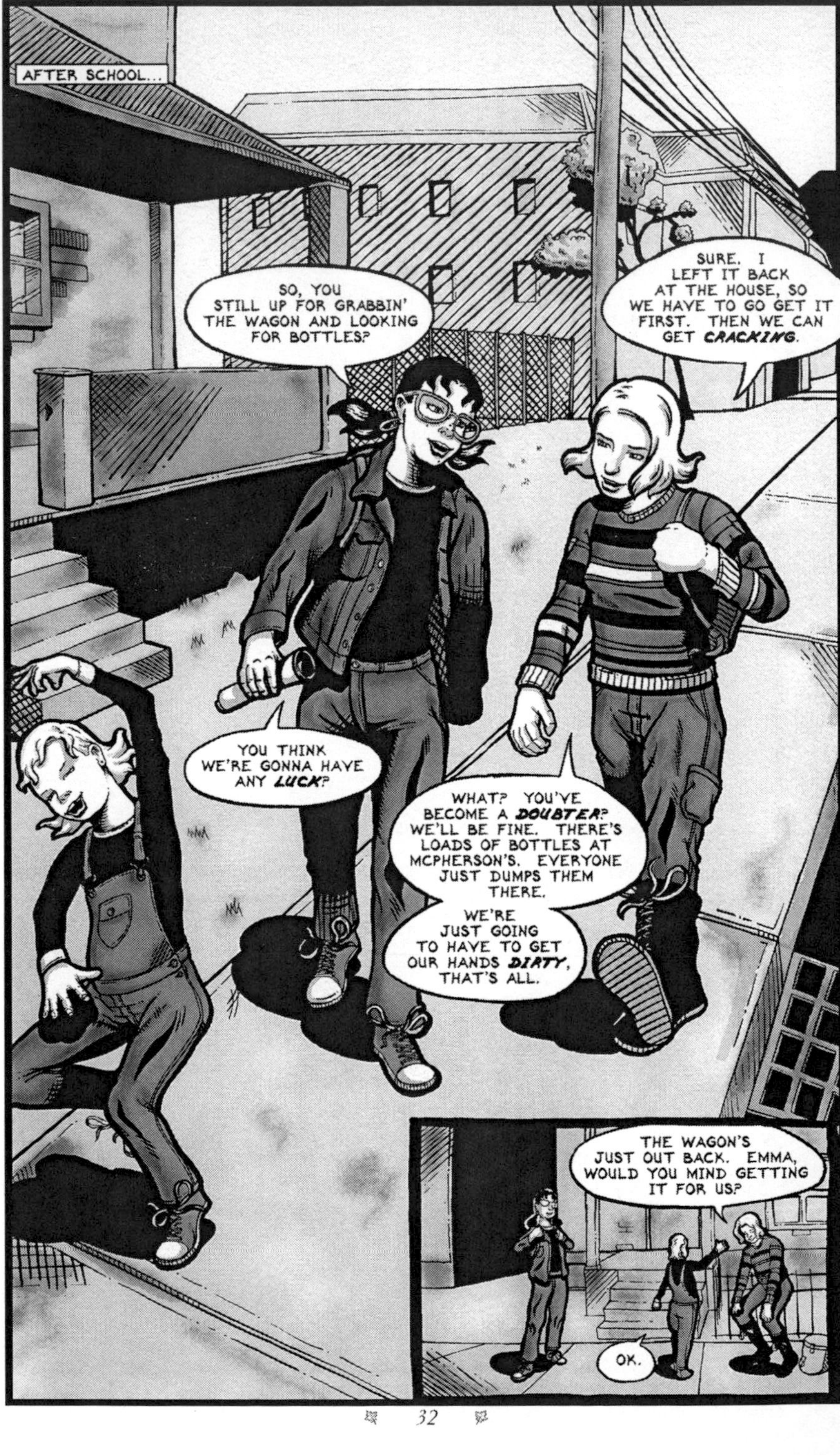
AFTER SCHOOL...
SO, YOU STILL UP FOR GRABBIN' THE WAGON AND LOOKING FOR BOTTLES?
SURE. I LEFT IT BACK AT THE HOUSE, SO WE HAVE TO GO GET IT FIRST. THEN WE CAN GET CRACKING.
YOU THINK WE'RE GONNA HAVE ANY LUCK?
WHAT? YOU'VE BECOME A DOUBTER? WE'LL BE FINE. THERE'S LOADS OF BOTTLES AT MCPHERSON'S. EVERYONE JUST DUMPS THEM THERE.
WE'RE JUST GOING TO HAVE TO GET OUR HANDS DIRTY, THAT'S ALL.
THE WAGON'S JUST OUT BACK. EMMA, WOULD YOU MIND GETTING IT FOR US?
OK.

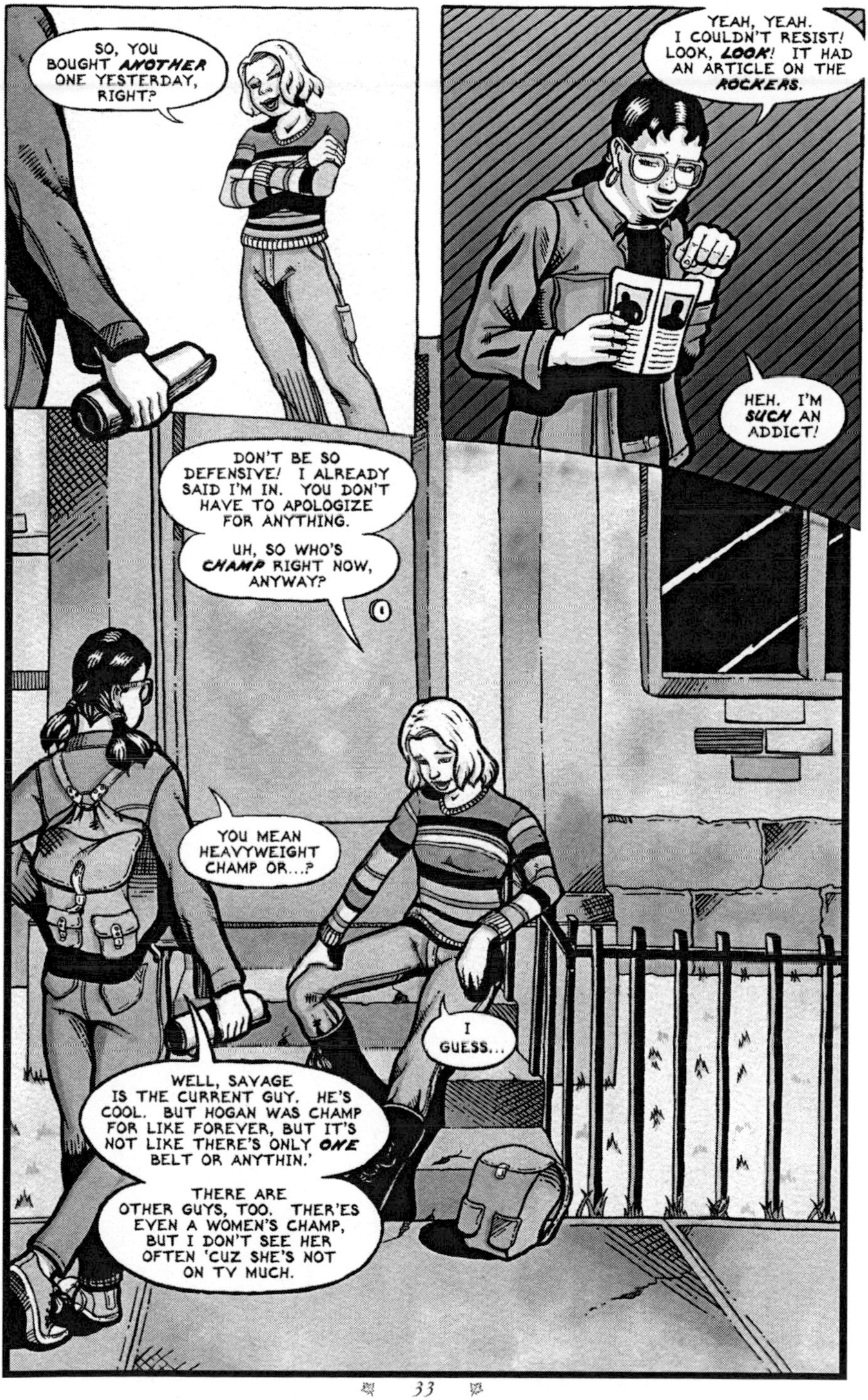
SO, YOU BOUGHT ANOTHER ONE YESTERDAY, RIGHT?
YEAH, YEAH. I COULDN'T RESIST! LOOK, LOOK! IT HAD AN ARTICLE ON THE ROCKERS.
HEH. I'M SUCH AN ADDICT!
DON'T BE SO DEFENSIVE! I ALREADY SAID I'M IN. YOU DON'T HAVE TO APOLOGIZE FOR ANYTHING.
UH, SO WHO'S CHAMP RIGHT NOW, ANYWAY?
YOU MEAN HEAVYWEIGHT CHAMP OR...?
I GUESS...
WELL, SAVAGE IS THE CURRENT GUY. HE'S COOL. BUT HOGAN WAS CHAMP FOR LIKE FOREVER, BUT IT'S NOT LIKE THERE'S ONLY ONE BELT OR ANYTHIN.'
THERE ARE OTHER GUYS, TOO. THER'ES EVEN A WOMEN'S CHAMP, BUT I DON'T SEE HER OFTEN 'CUZ SHE'S NOT ON TV MUCH.

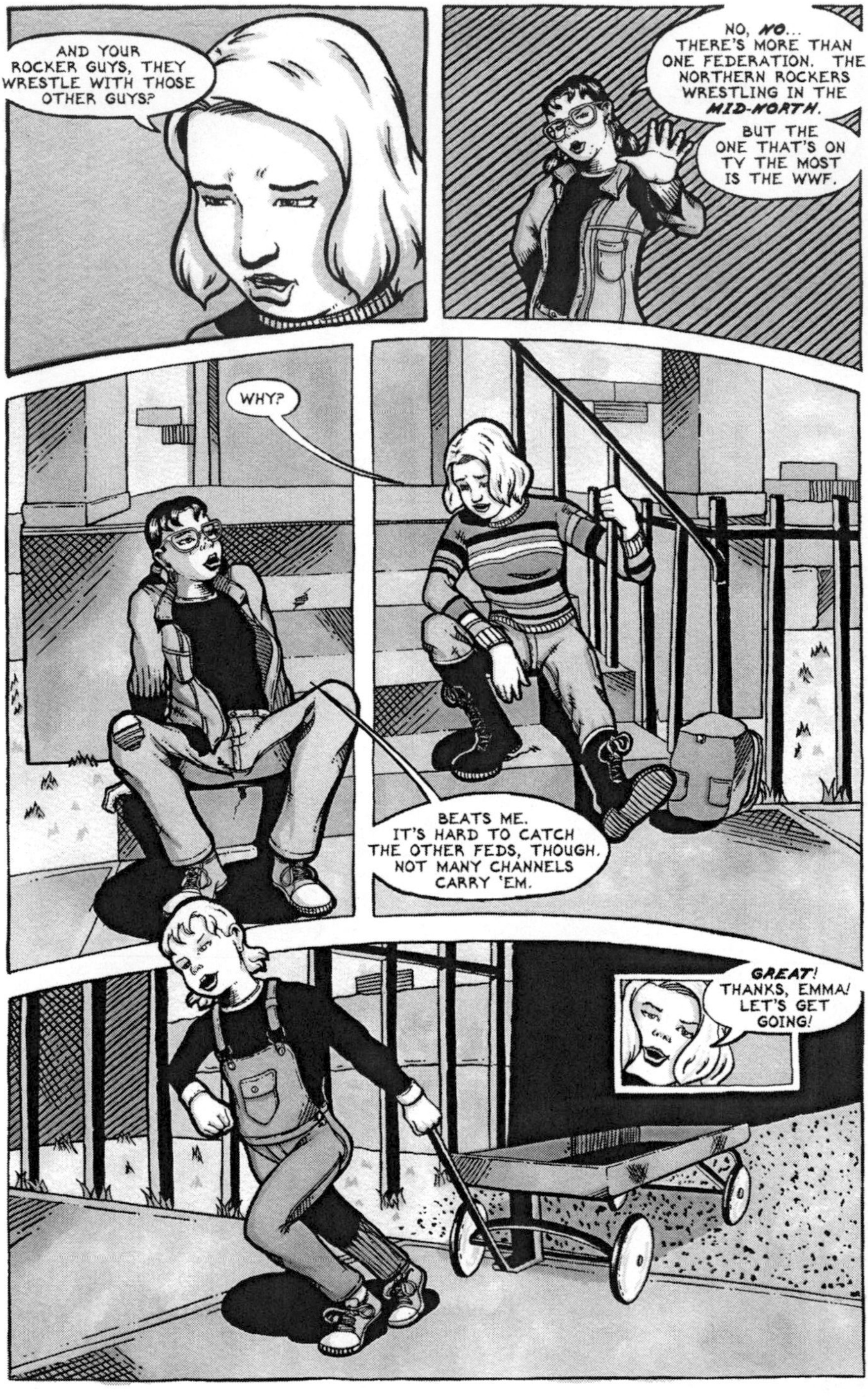
AND YOUR ROCKER GUYS, THEY WRESTLE WITH THOSE OTHER GUYS?
NO, NO... THERE'S MORE THAN ONE FEDERATION. THE NORTHERN ROCKERS WRESTLING IN THE MID-NORTH.
BUT THE ONE THAT'S ON TV THE MOST IS THE WWF.
WHY?
BEATS ME. IT'S HARD TO CATCH THE OTHER FEDS, THOUGH. NOT MANY CHANNELS CARRY 'EM.
GREAT! THANKS, EMMA! LET'S GET GOING!

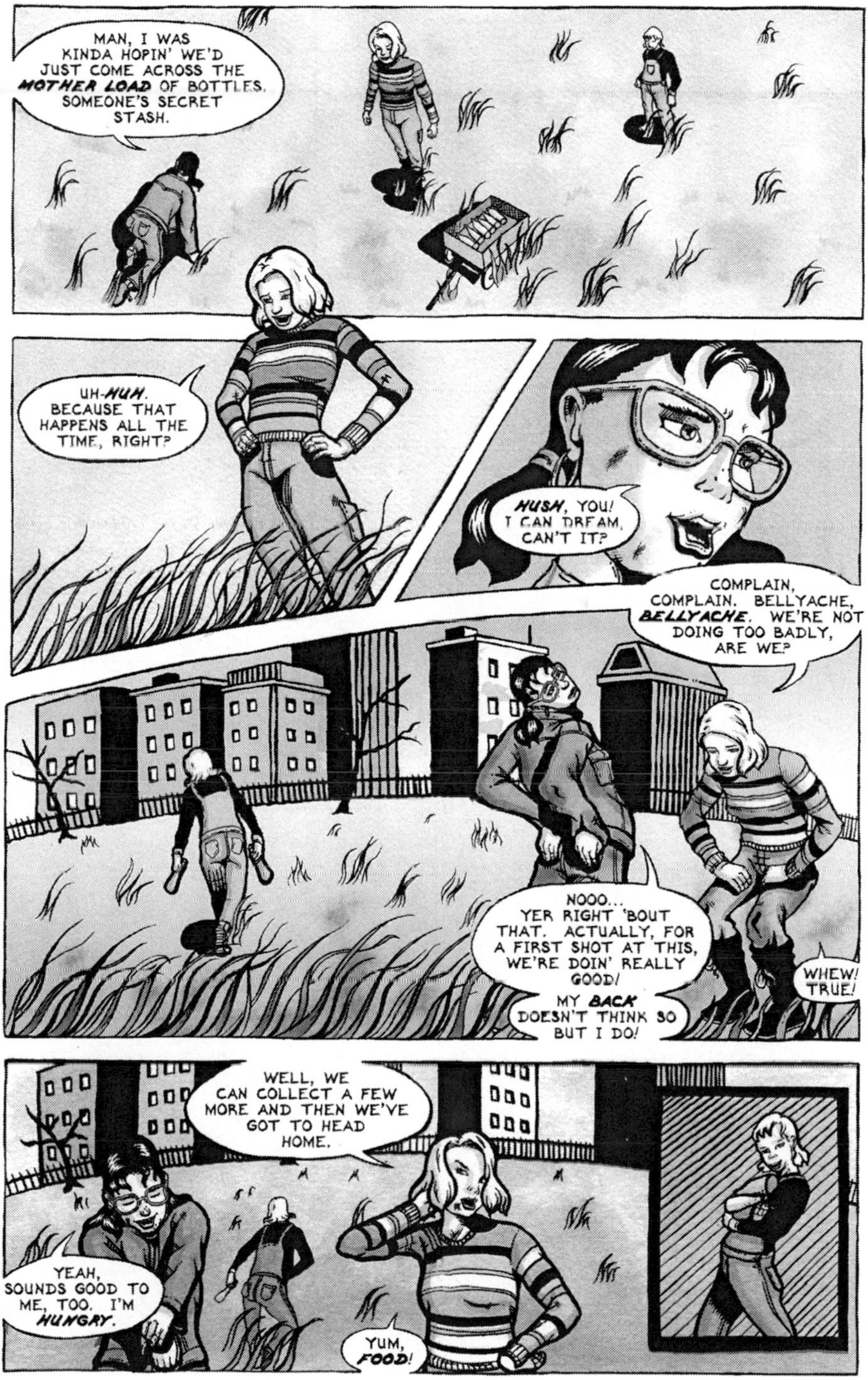
MAN, I WAS KINDA HOPIN' WE'D JUST COME ACROSS THE MOTHER LOAD OF BOTTLES. SOMEONE'S SECRET STASH.
UH-HUH. BECAUSE THAT HAPPENS ALL THE TIME, RIGHT?
HUSH, YOU! I CAN DREAM, CAN'T I?
COMPLAIN, COMPLAIN. BELLYACHE, BELLYACHE. WE'RE NOT DOING TOO BADLY, ARE WE?
NOOO... YER RIGHT 'BOUT THAT. ACTUALLY, FOR A FIRST SHOT AT THIS, WE'RE DOIN' REALLY GOOD!
MY BACK DOESN'T THINK SO BUT I DO!
WHEW! TRUE!
WELL, WE CAN COLLECT A FEW MORE AND THEN WE'VE GOT TO HEAD HOME.
YEAH, SOUNDS GOOD TO ME, TOO. I'M HUNGRY.
YUM, FOOD!

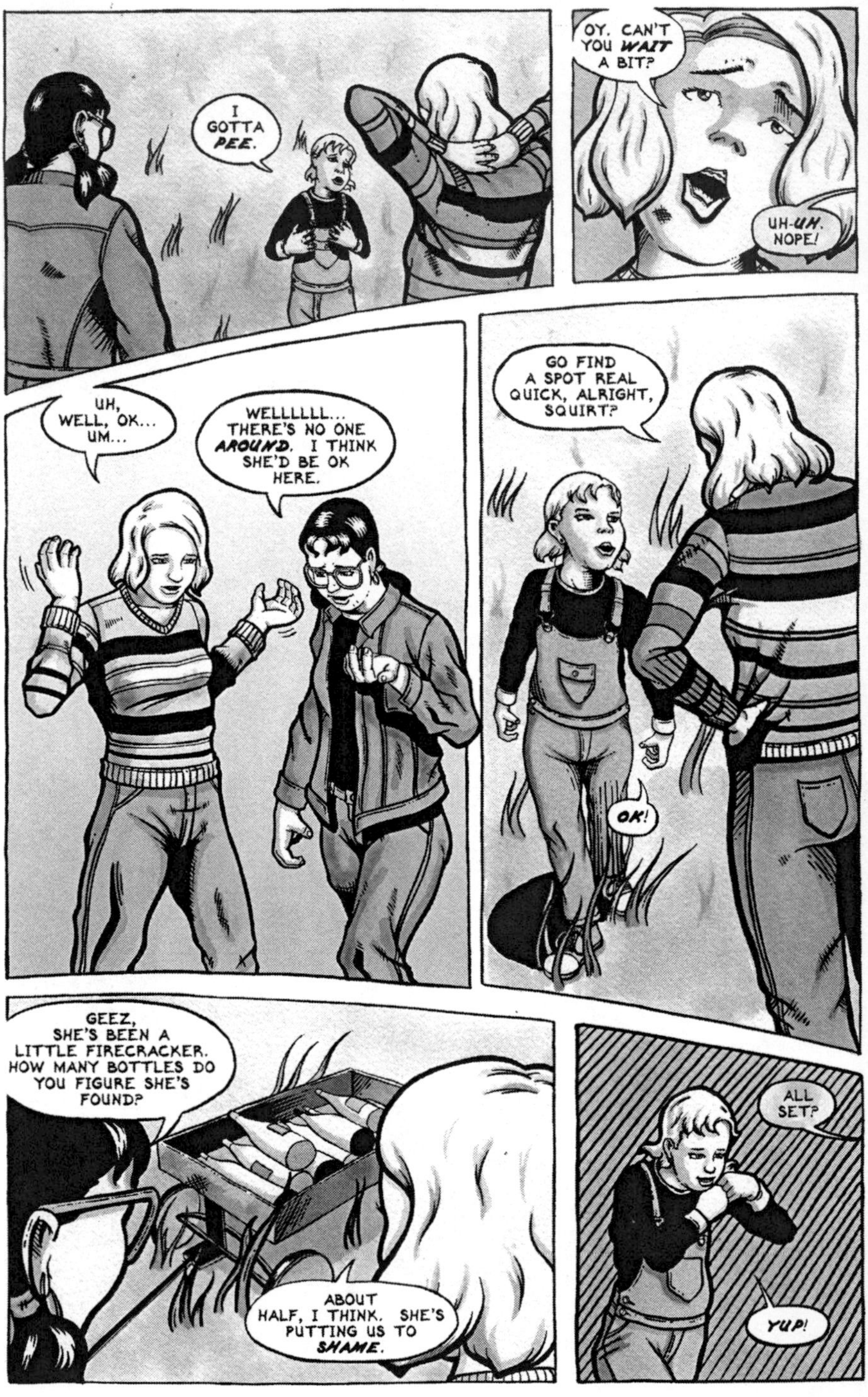
I GOTTA PEE.
OY. CAN'T YOU WAIT A BIT?
UH-UH. NOPE!
UH, WELL, OK... UM...
WELLLLLL... THERE'S NO ONE AROUND. I THINK SHE'D BE OK HERE.
GO FIND A SPOT REAL QUICK, ALRIGHT, SQUIRT?
OK!
GEEZ, SHE'S BEEN A LITTLE FIRECRACKER. HOW MANY BOTTLES DO YOU FIGURE SHE'S FOUND?
ABOUT HALF, I THINK. SHE'S PUTTING US TO SHAME.
ALL SET?
YUP!

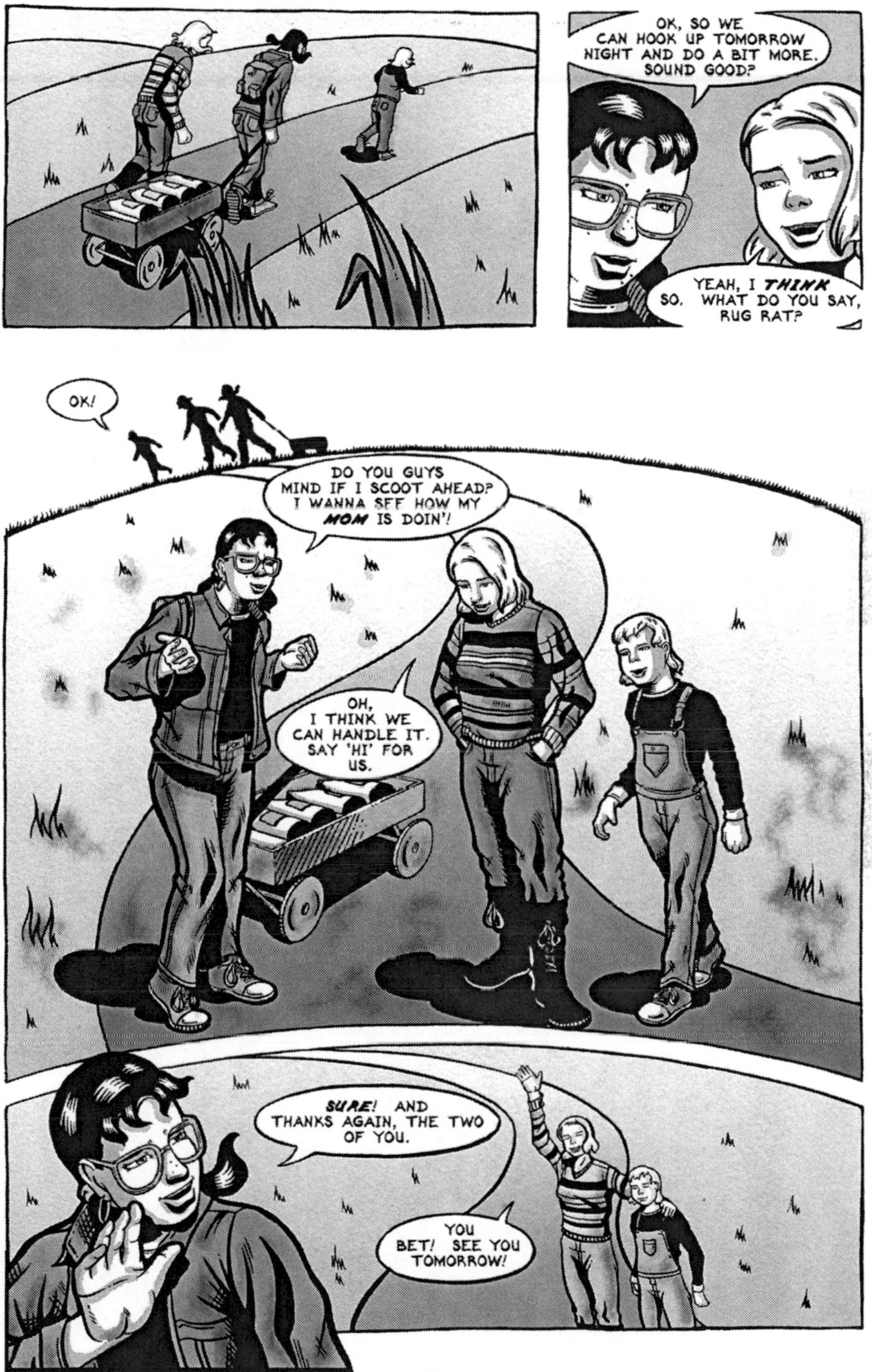
OK, SO WE CAN HOOK UP TOMORROW NIGHT AND DO A BIT MORE. SOUND GOOD?
YEAH, I THINK SO. WHAT DO YOU SAY, RUG RAT?
OK!
DO YOU GUYS MIND IF I SCOOT AHEAD? I WANNA SEE HOW MY MOM IS DOIN'!
OH, I THINK WE CAN HANDLE IT. SAY 'HI' FOR US.
SURE! AND THANKS AGAIN, THE TWO OF YOU.
YOU BET! SEE YOU TOMORROW!

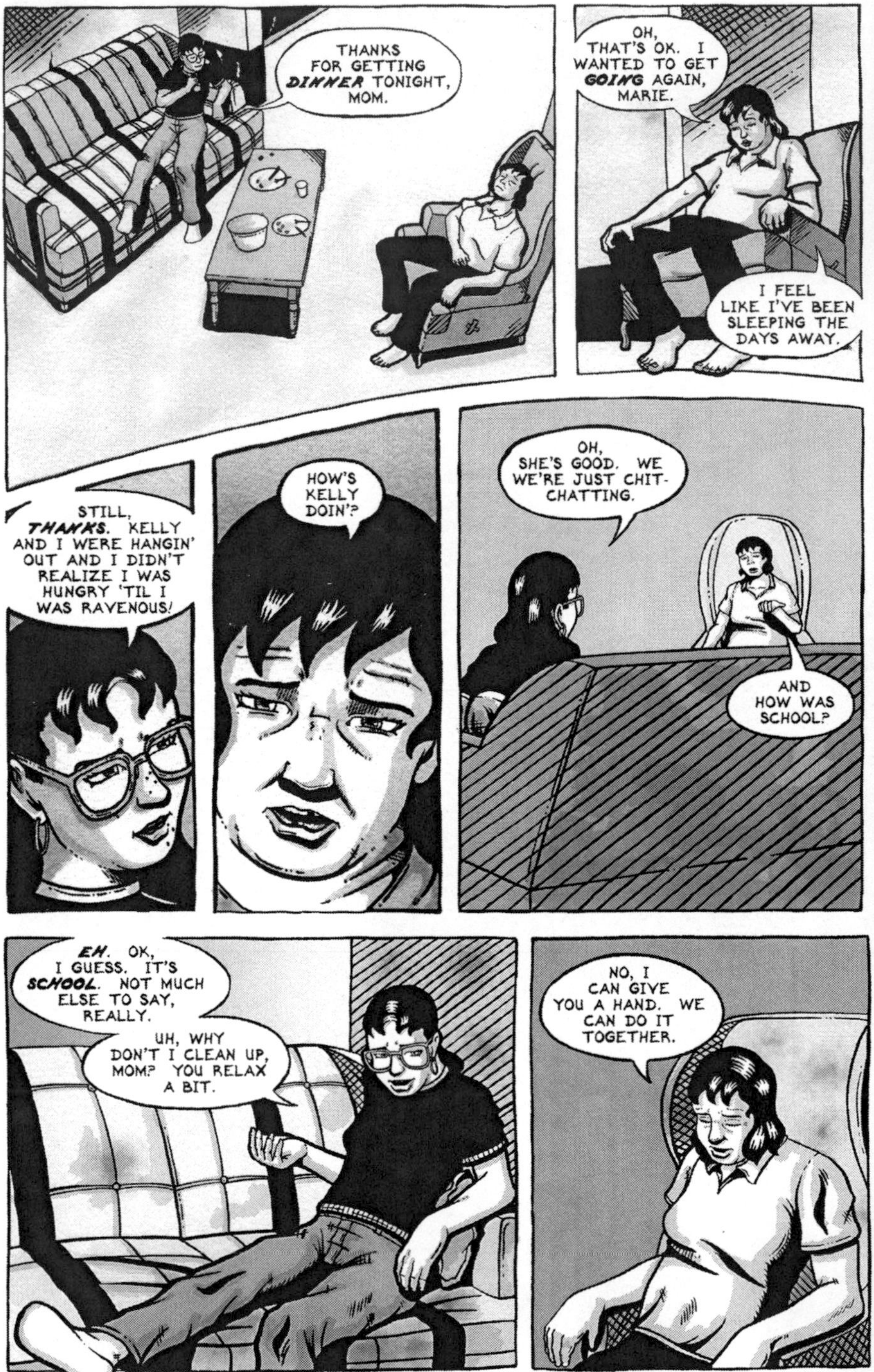
THANKS FOR GETTING DINNER TONIGHT, MOM.
OH, THAT'S OK. I WANTED TO GET GOING AGAIN, MARIE.
I FEEL LIKE I'VE BEEN SLEEPING THE DAYS AWAY.
STILL, THANKS. KELLY AND I WERE HANGIN' OUT AND I DIDN'T REALIZE I WAS HUNGRY 'TIL I WAS RAVENOUS!
HOW'S KELLY DOIN'?
OH, SHE'S GOOD. WE WE'RE JUST CHIT-CHATTING.
AND HOW WAS SCHOOL?
EH. OK, I GUESS. IT'S SCHOOL. NOT MUCH ELSE TO SAY, REALLY.
UH, WHY DON'T I CLEAN UP, MOM? YOU RELAX A BIT.
NO, I CAN GIVE YOU A HAND. WE CAN DO IT TOGETHER.

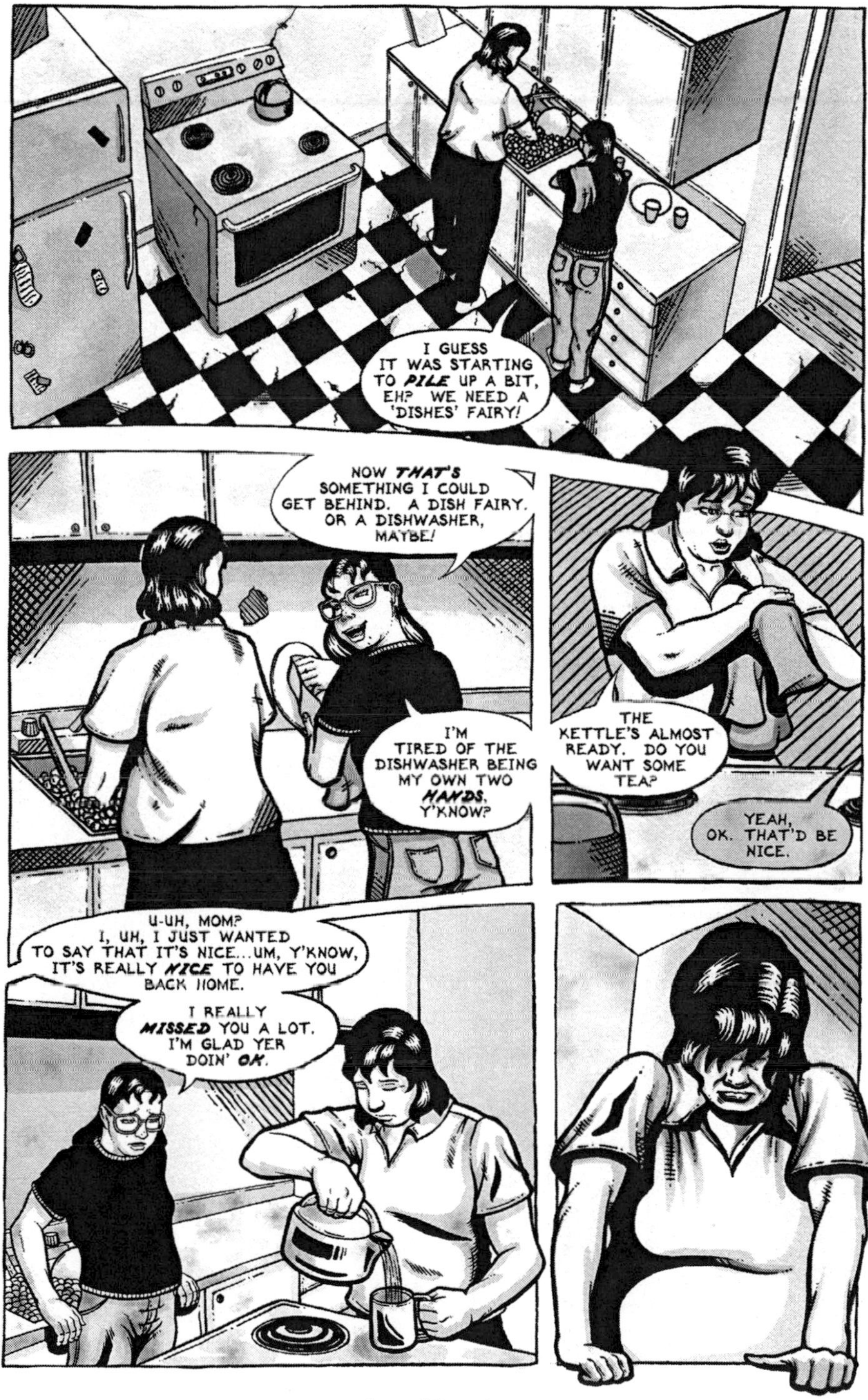
I GUESS IT WAS STARTING TO PILE UP A BIT, EH? WE NEED A 'DISHES' FAIRY!
NOW THAT'S SOMETHING I COULD GET BEHIND. A DISH FAIRY. OR A DISHWASHER, MAYBE!
I'M TIRED OF THE DISHWASHER BEING MY OWN TWO HANDS, Y'KNOW?
THE KETTLE'S ALMOST READY. DO YOU WANT SOME TEA?
YEAH, OK. THAT'D BE NICE.
U-UH, MOM? I, UH, I JUST WANTED TO SAY THAT IT'S NICE...UM, Y'KNOW, IT'S REALLY NICE TO HAVE YOU BACK HOME.
I REALLY MISSED YOU A LOT. I'M GLAD YER DOIN' OK.

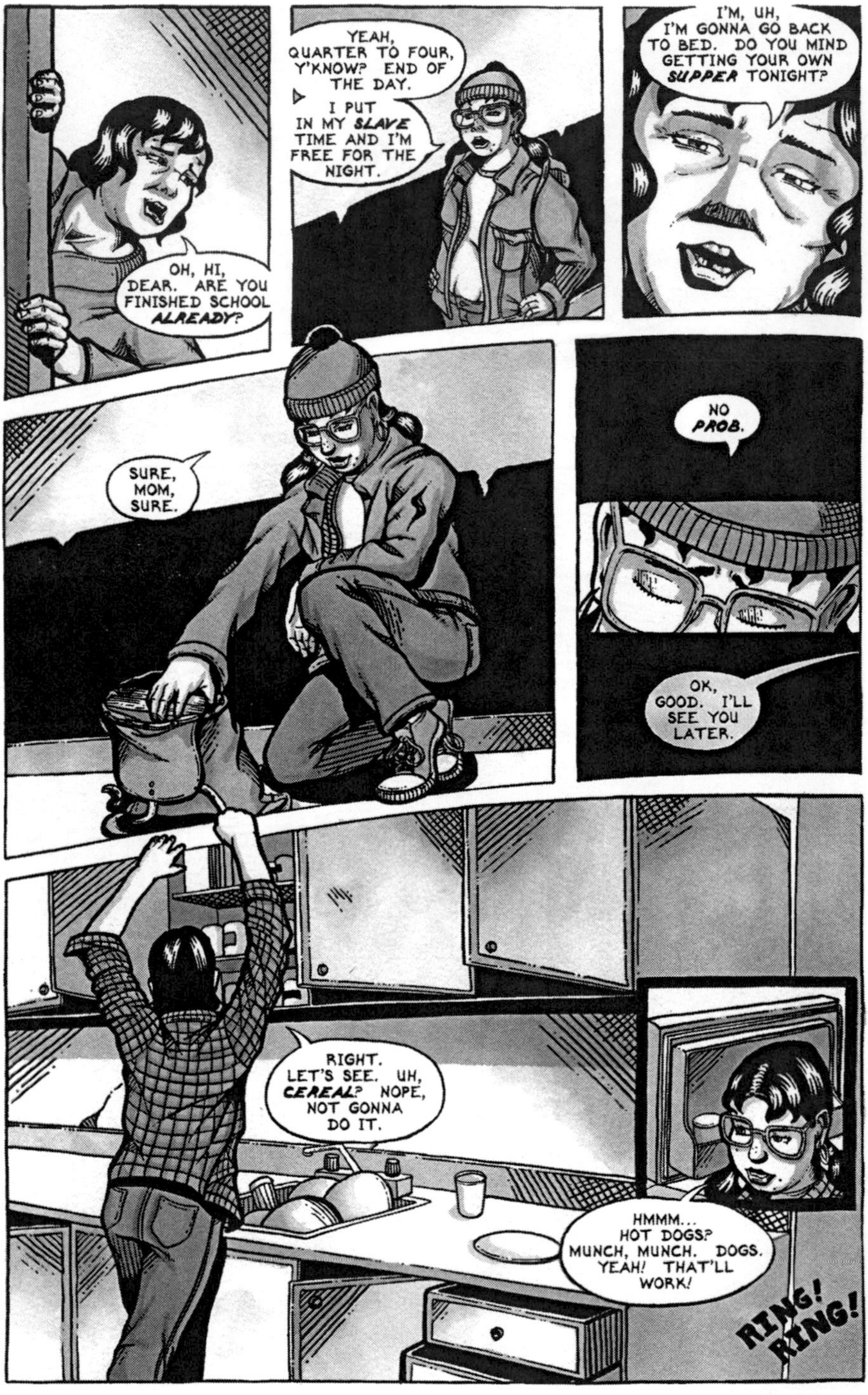
OH, HI, DEAR. ARE YOU FINISHED SCHOOL ALREADY?
YEAH, QUARTER TO FOUR, Y'KNOW? END OF THE DAY.
I PUT IN MY SLAVE TIME AND I'M FREE FOR THE NIGHT.
I'M, UH, I'M GONNA GO BACK TO BED. DO YOU MIND GETTING YOUR OWN SUPPER TONIGHT?
SURE, MOM, SURE.
NO PROB.
OK, GOOD. I'LL SEE YOU LATER.
RIGHT. LET'S SEE. UH, CEREAL? NOPE, NOT GONNA DO IT.
HMMM... HOT DOGS? MUNCH, MUNCH. DOGS. YEAH! THAT'LL WORK!
RING! RING!

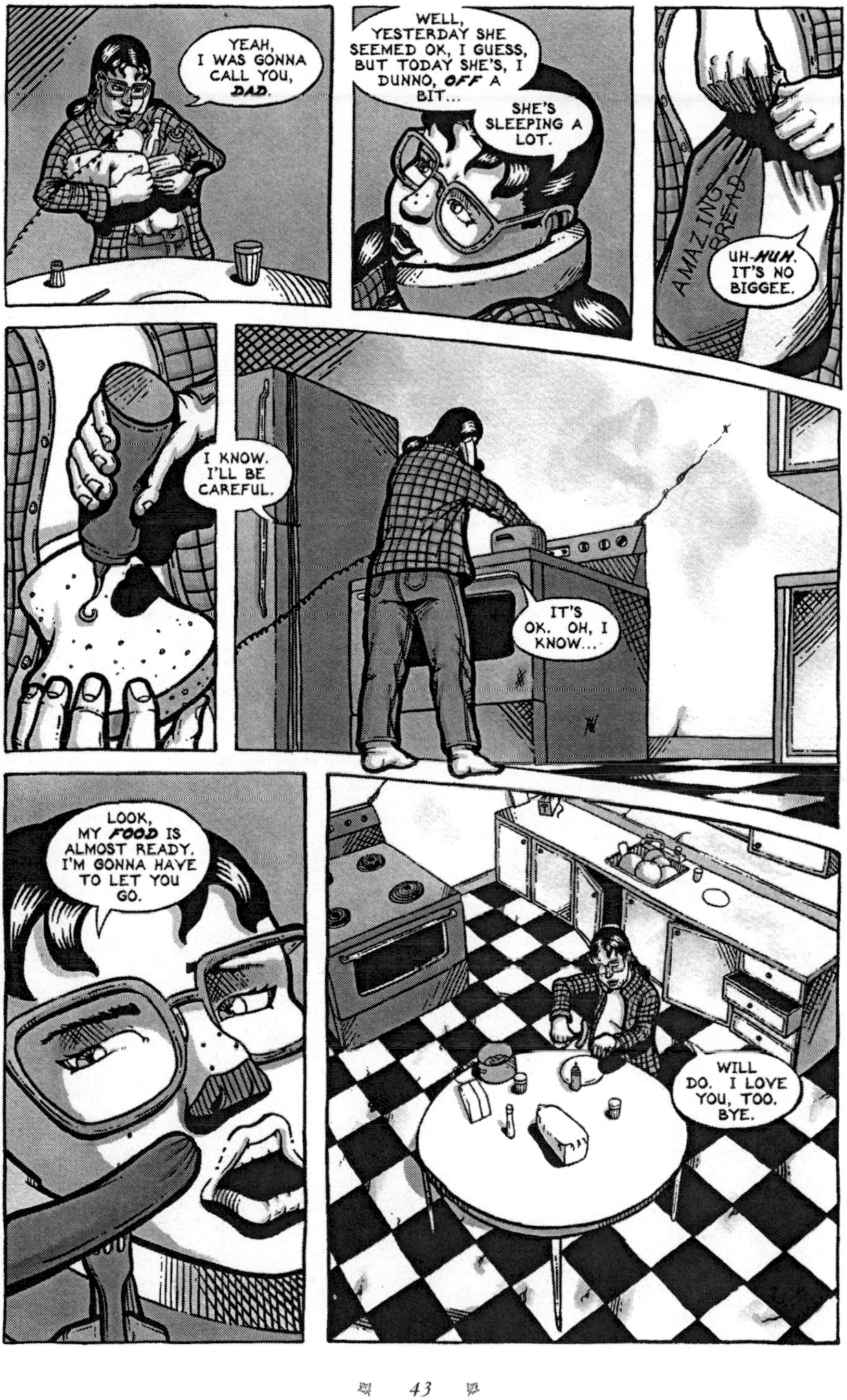
YEAH, I WAS GONNA CALL YOU, DAD.
WELL, YESTERDAY SHE SEEMED OK, I GUESS, BUT TODAY SHE'S, I DUNNO, OFF A BIT...
SHE'S SLEEPING A LOT.
AMAZING BREAD
UH-HUH. IT'S NO BIGGEE.
I KNOW. I'LL BE CAREFUL.
IT'S OK. OH, I KNOW...
LOOK, MY FOOD IS ALMOST READY. I'M GONNA HAVE TO LET YOU GO.
WILL DO. I LOVE YOU, TOO. BYE.

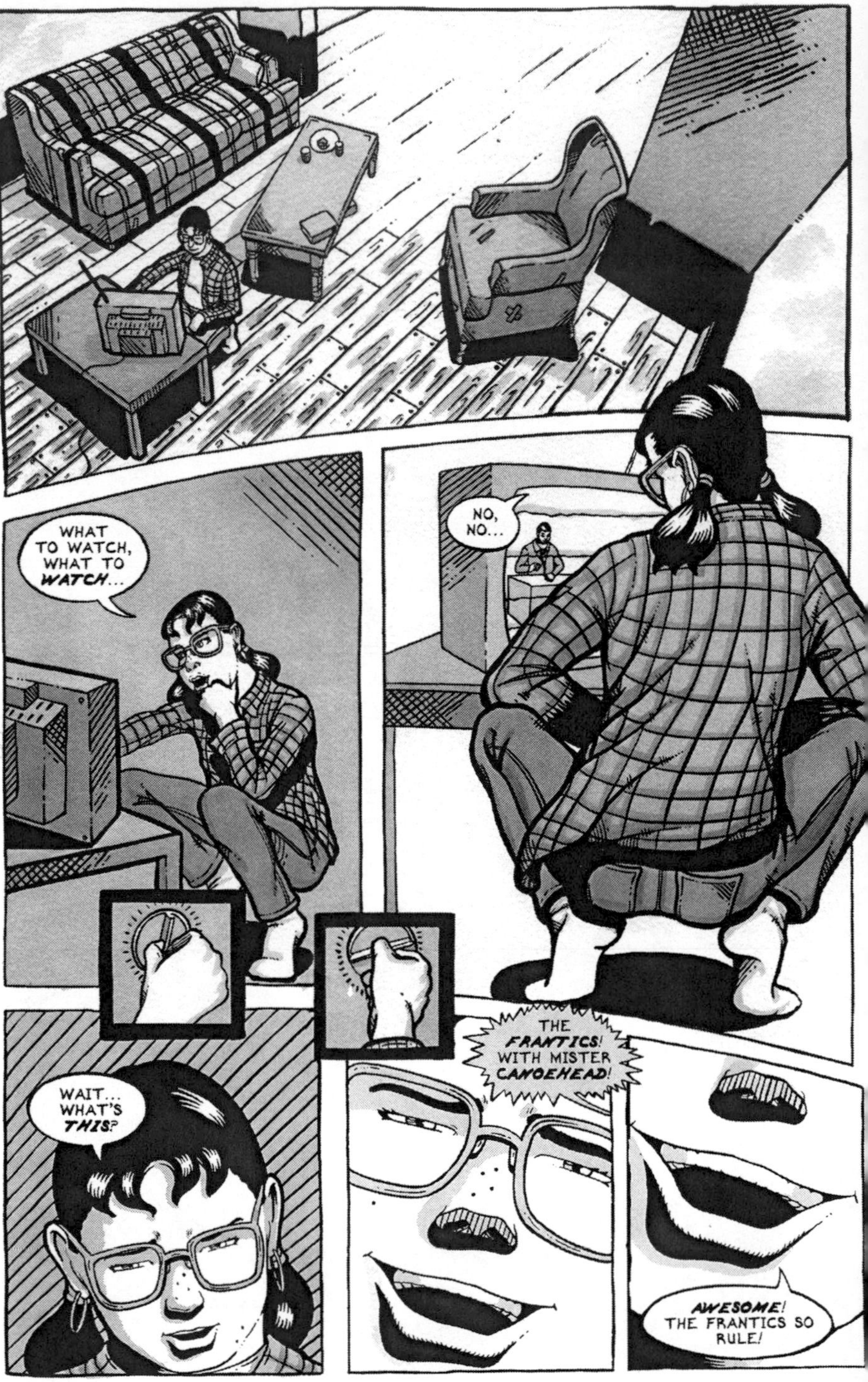
WHAT TO WATCH, WHAT TO WATCH...
NO, NO...
WAIT... WHAT'S THIS?
THE FRANTICS! WITH MISTER CANOEHEAD!
AWESOME! THE FRANTICS SO RULE!

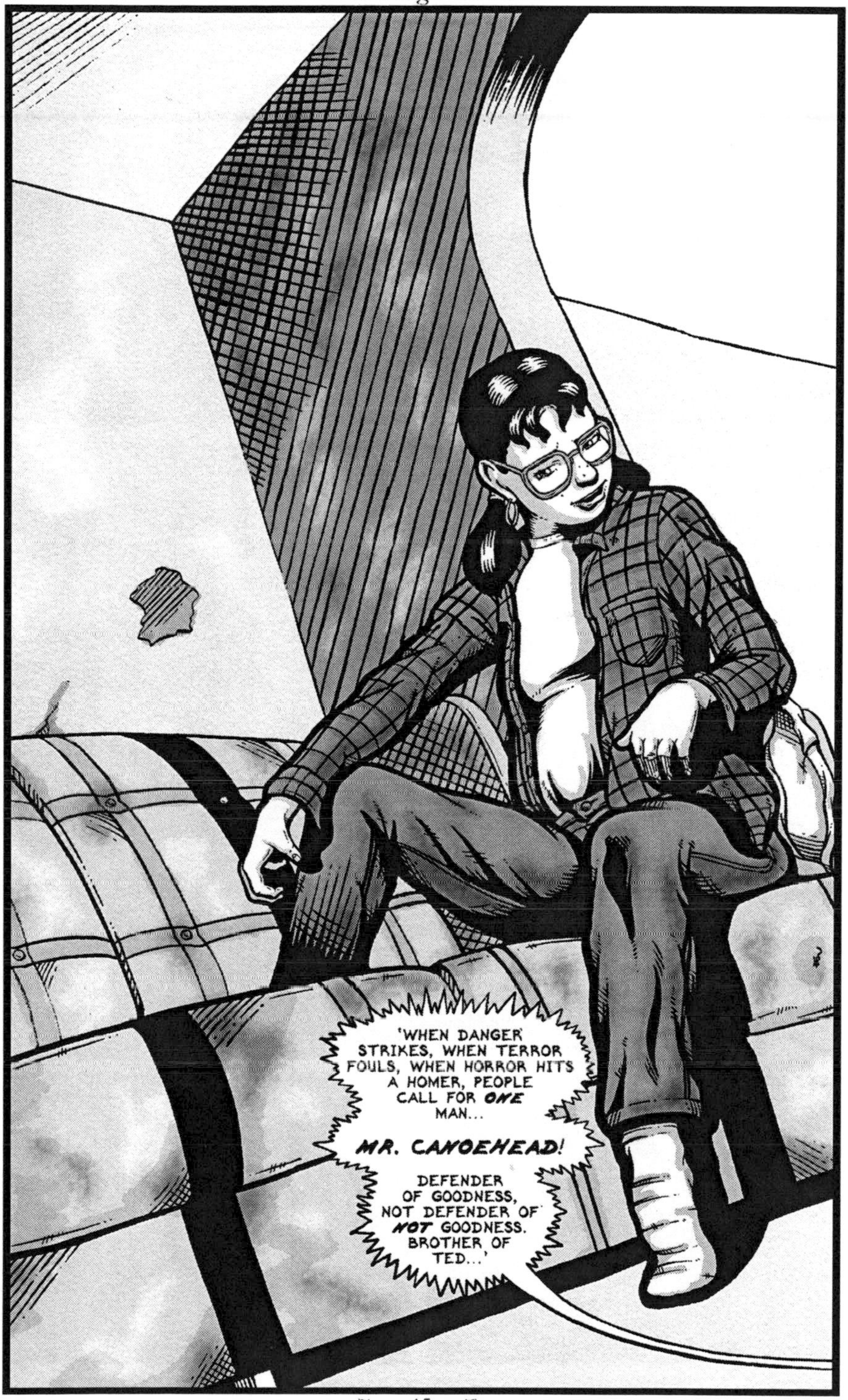
'WHEN DANGER STRIKES, WHEN TERROR FOULS, WHEN HORROR HITS A HOMER, PEOPLE CALL FOR ONE MAN...
MR. CANOEHEAD!
DEFENDER OF GOODNESS, NOT DEFENDER OF NOT GOODNESS. BROTHER OF TED...'

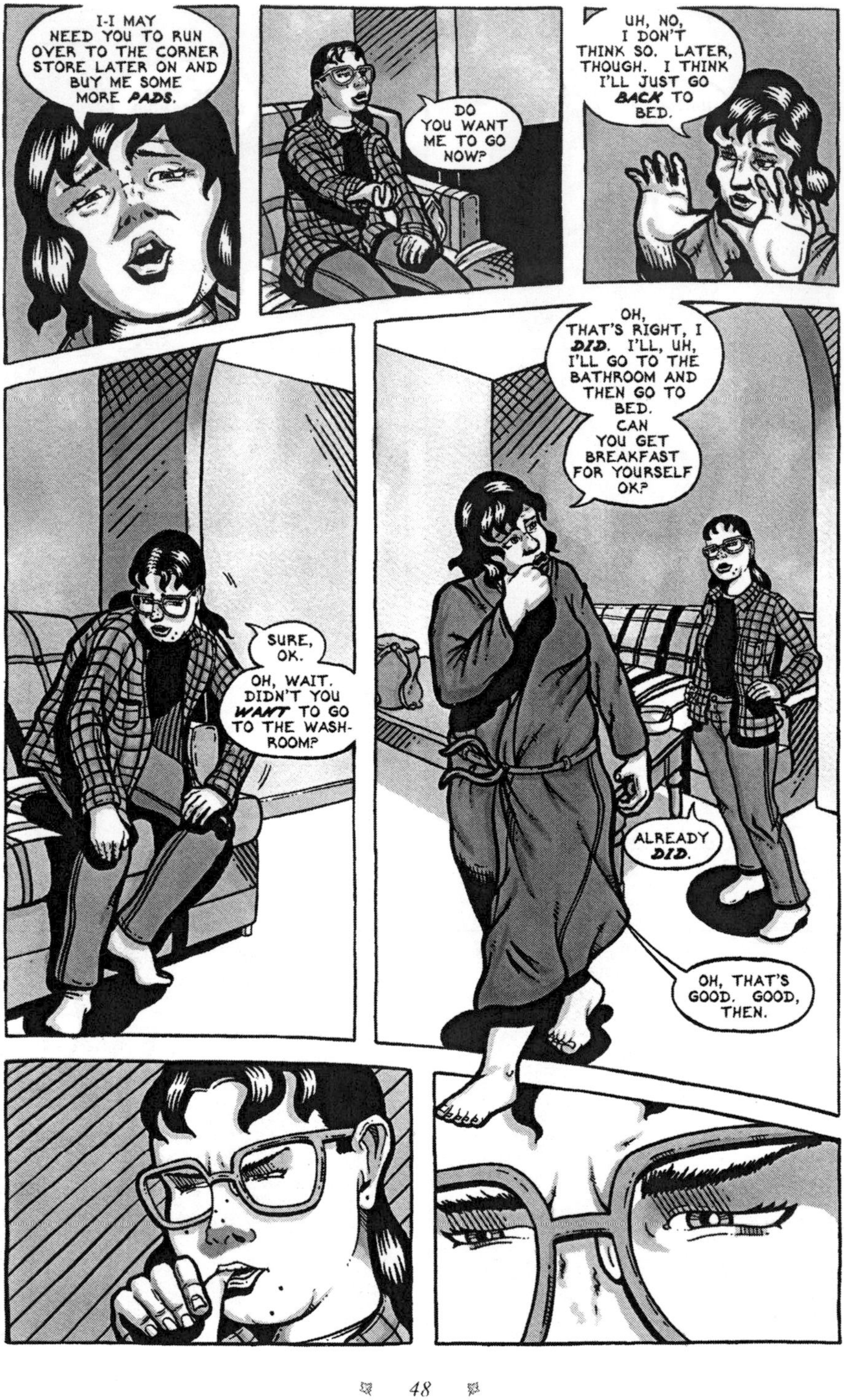
I-I MAY NEED YOU TO RUN OVER TO THE CORNER STORE LATER ON AND BUY ME SOME MORE PADS.
DO YOU WANT ME TO GO NOW?
UH, NO, I DON'T THINK SO. LATER, THOUGH. I THINK I'LL JUST GO BACK TO BED.
SURE, OK.
OH, WAIT. DIDN'T YOU WANT TO GO TO THE WASH-ROOM?
OH, THAT'S RIGHT, I DID. I'LL, UH, I'LL GO TO THE BATHROOM AND THEN GO TO BED.
CAN YOU GET BREAKFAST FOR YOURSELF OK?
ALREADY DID.
OH, THAT'S GOOD. GOOD, THEN.

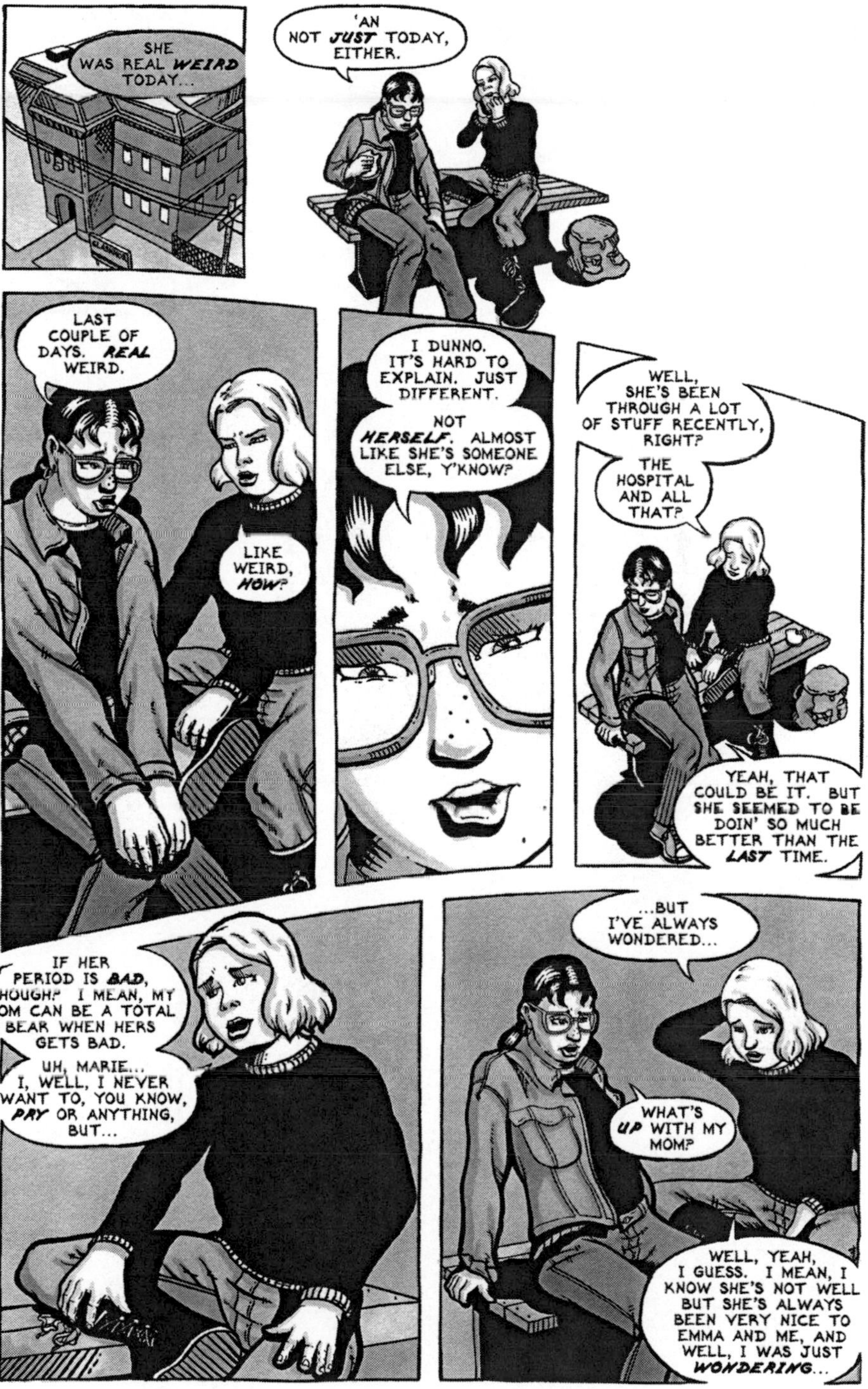
SHE WAS REAL WEIRD TODAY...
'AN NOT JUST TODAY, EITHER.
LAST COUPLE OF DAYS. REAL WEIRD.
LIKE WEIRD, HOW?
I DUNNO. IT'S HARD TO EXPLAIN. JUST DIFFERENT.
NOT HERSELF. ALMOST LIKE SHE'S SOMEONE ELSE, Y'KNOW?
WELL, SHE'S BEEN THROUGH A LOT OF STUFF RECENTLY, RIGHT?
THE HOSPITAL AND ALL THAT?
YEAH, THAT COULD BE IT. BUT SHE SEEMED TO BE DOIN' SO MUCH BETTER THAN THE LAST TIME.
IF HER PERIOD IS BAD, THOUGH? I MEAN, MY MOM CAN BE A TOTAL BEAR WHEN HERS GETS BAD.
UH, MARIE... I, WELL, I NEVER WANT TO, YOU KNOW, PRY OR ANYTHING, BUT...
...BUT I'VE ALWAYS WONDERED...
WHAT'S UP WITH MY MOM?
WELL, YEAH, I GUESS. I MEAN, I KNOW SHE'S NOT WELL BUT SHE'S ALWAYS BEEN VERY NICE TO EMMA AND ME, AND WELL, I WAS JUST WONDERING...

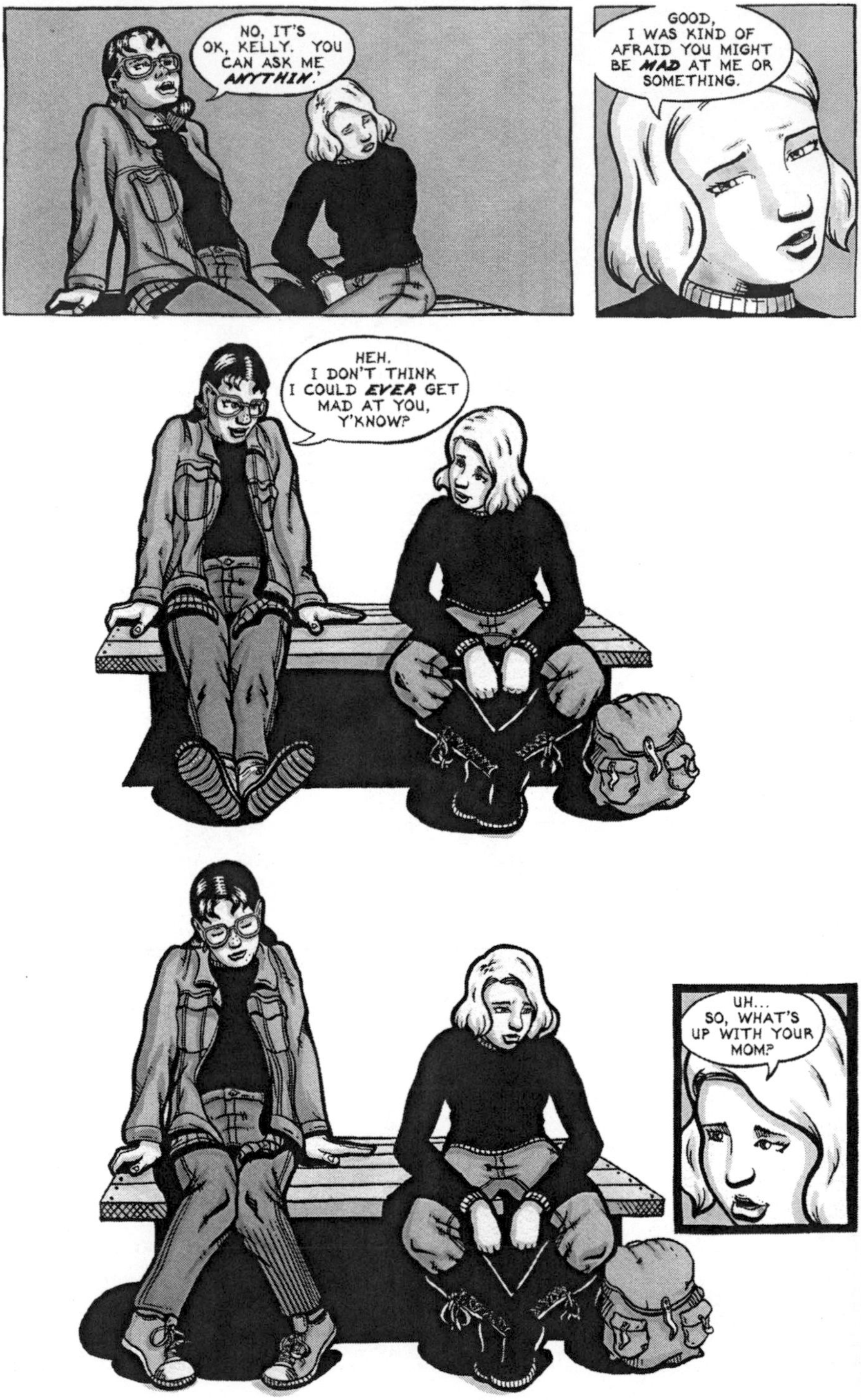
NO, IT'S OK, KELLY. YOU CAN ASK ME ANYTHIN.'
GOOD, I WAS KIND OF AFRAID YOU MIGHT BE MAD AT ME OR SOMETHING.
HEH. I DON'T THINK I COULD EVER GET MAD AT YOU, Y'KNOW?
UH... SO, WHAT'S UP WITH YOUR MOM?

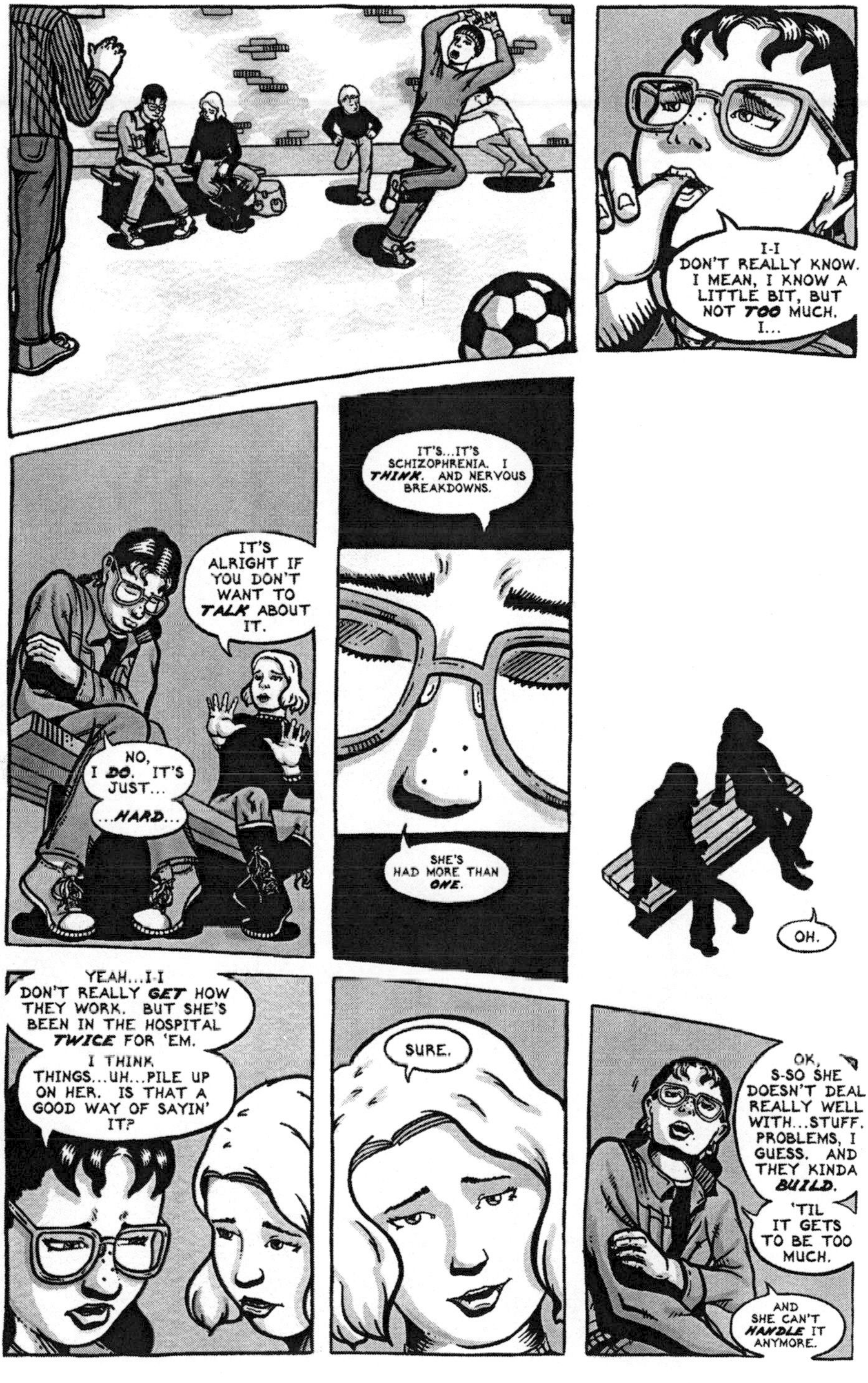
I-I DON'T REALLY KNOW. I MEAN, I KNOW A LITTLE BIT, BUT NOT TOO MUCH. I...
IT'S ALRIGHT IF YOU DON'T WANT TO TALK ABOUT IT.
NO, I DO. IT'S JUST...
...HARD...
IT'S...IT'S SCHIZOPHRENIA. I THINK. AND NERVOUS BREAKDOWNS.
SHE'S HAD MORE THAN ONE.
OH.
YEAH...I-I DON'T REALLY GET HOW THEY WORK. BUT SHE'S BEEN IN THE HOSPITAL TWICE FOR 'EM.
I THINK THINGS...UH...PILE UP ON HER. IS THAT A GOOD WAY OF SAYIN' IT?
SURE.
OK, S-SO SHE DOESN'T DEAL REALLY WELL WITH...STUFF. PROBLEMS, I GUESS. AND THEY KINDA BUILD.
'TIL IT GETS TO BE TOO MUCH.
AND SHE CAN'T HANDLE IT ANYMORE.

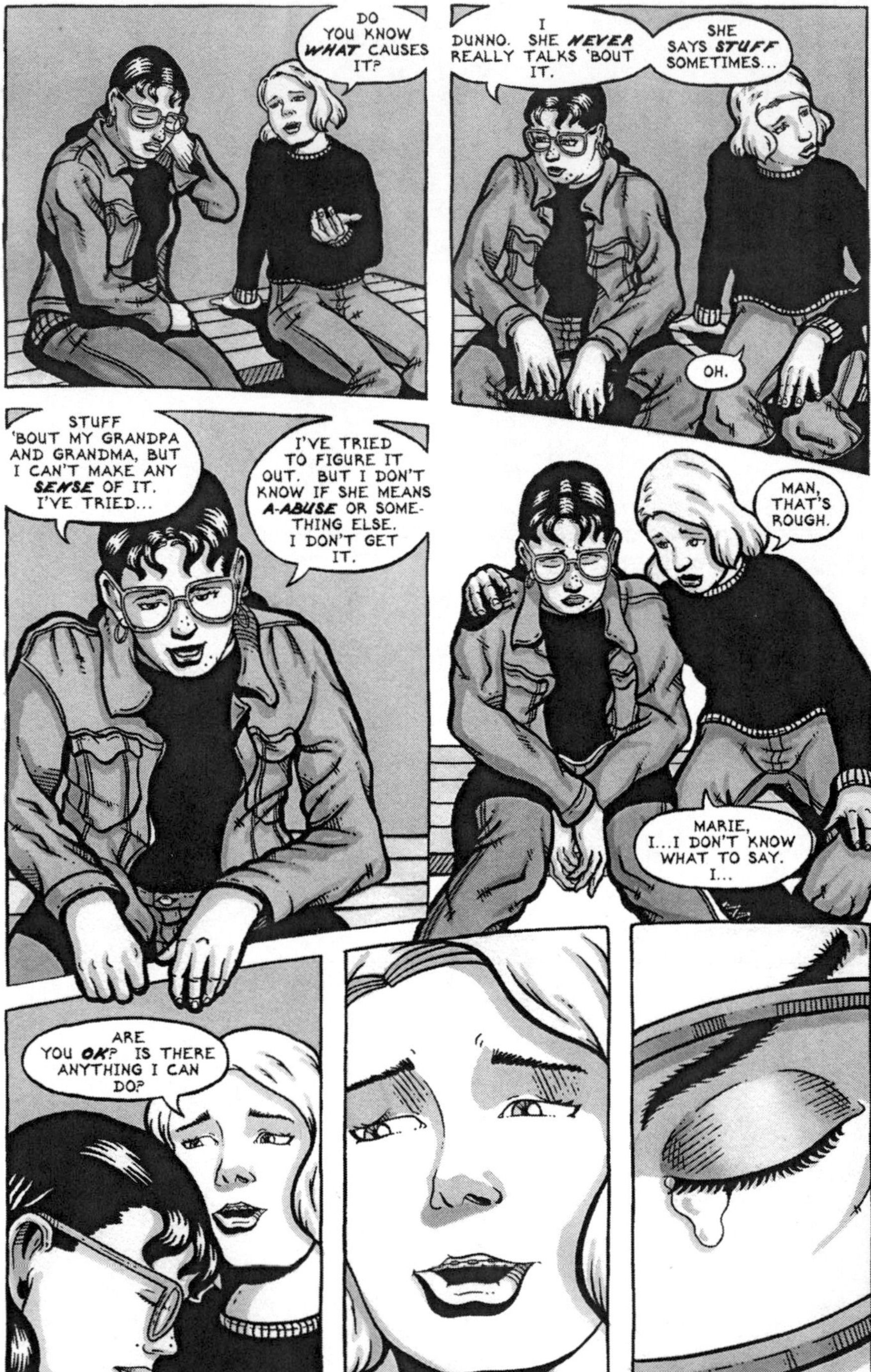
DO YOU KNOW WHAT CAUSES IT?
I DUNNO. SHE NEVER REALLY TALKS 'BOUT IT.
SHE SAYS STUFF SOMETIMES...
OH.
STUFF 'BOUT MY GRANDPA AND GRANDMA, BUT I CAN'T MAKE ANY SENSE OF IT. I'VE TRIED...
I'VE TRIED TO FIGURE IT OUT. BUT I DON'T KNOW IF SHE MEANS A-ABUSE OR SOMETHING ELSE. I DON'T GET IT.
MAN, THAT'S ROUGH.
MARIE, I...I DON'T KNOW WHAT TO SAY. I...
ARE YOU OK? IS THERE ANYTHING I CAN DO?

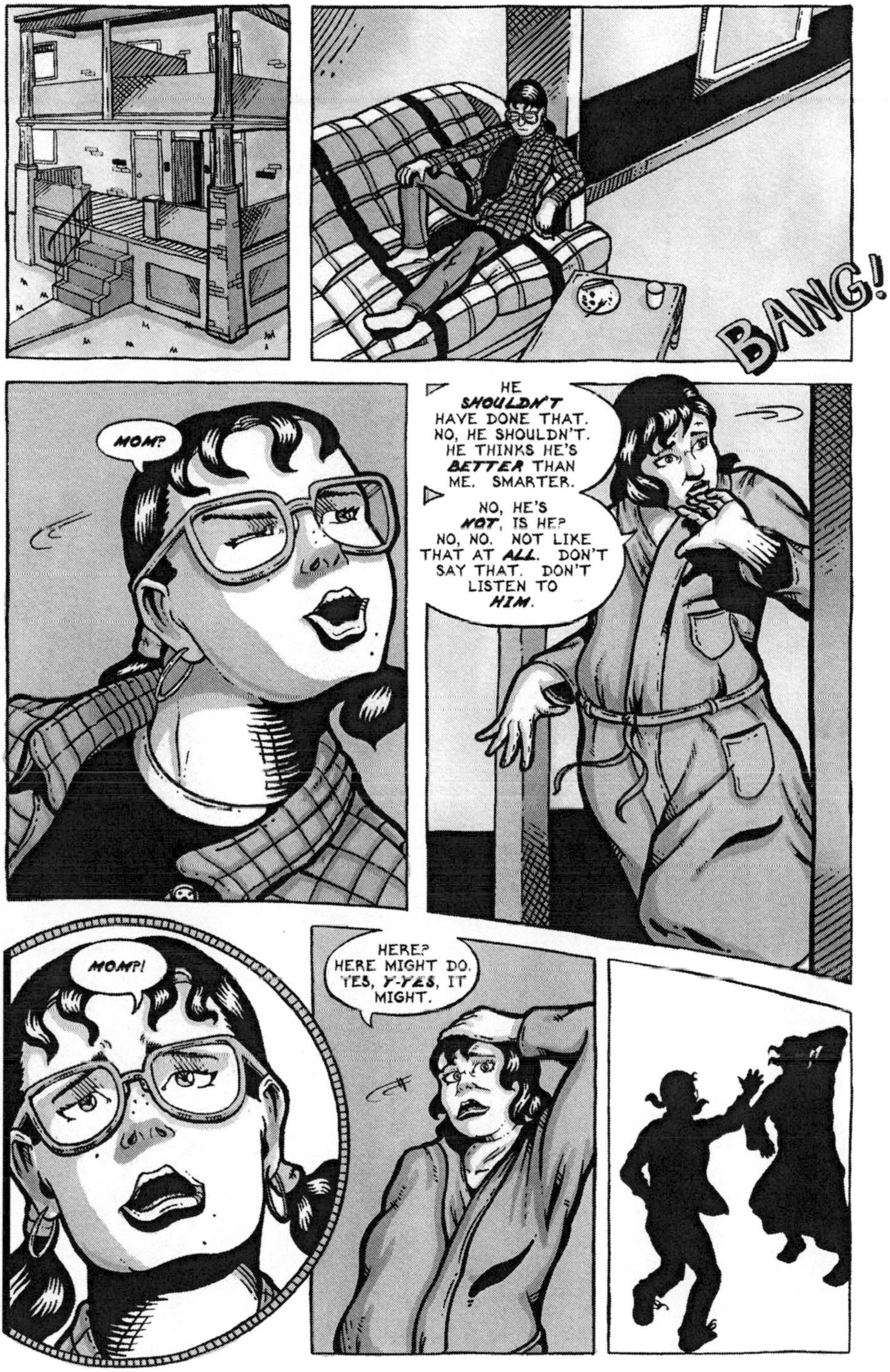
BANG!
MOM?
HE SHOULDN'T HAVE DONE THAT. NO, HE SHOULDN'T. HE THINKS HE'S BETTER THAN ME. SMARTER.
NO, HE'S NOT, IS HE? NO, NO. NOT LIKE THAT AT ALL. DON'T SAY THAT. DON'T LISTEN TO HIM.
MOM?!
HERE? HERE MIGHT DO. YES, Y-YES, IT MIGHT.

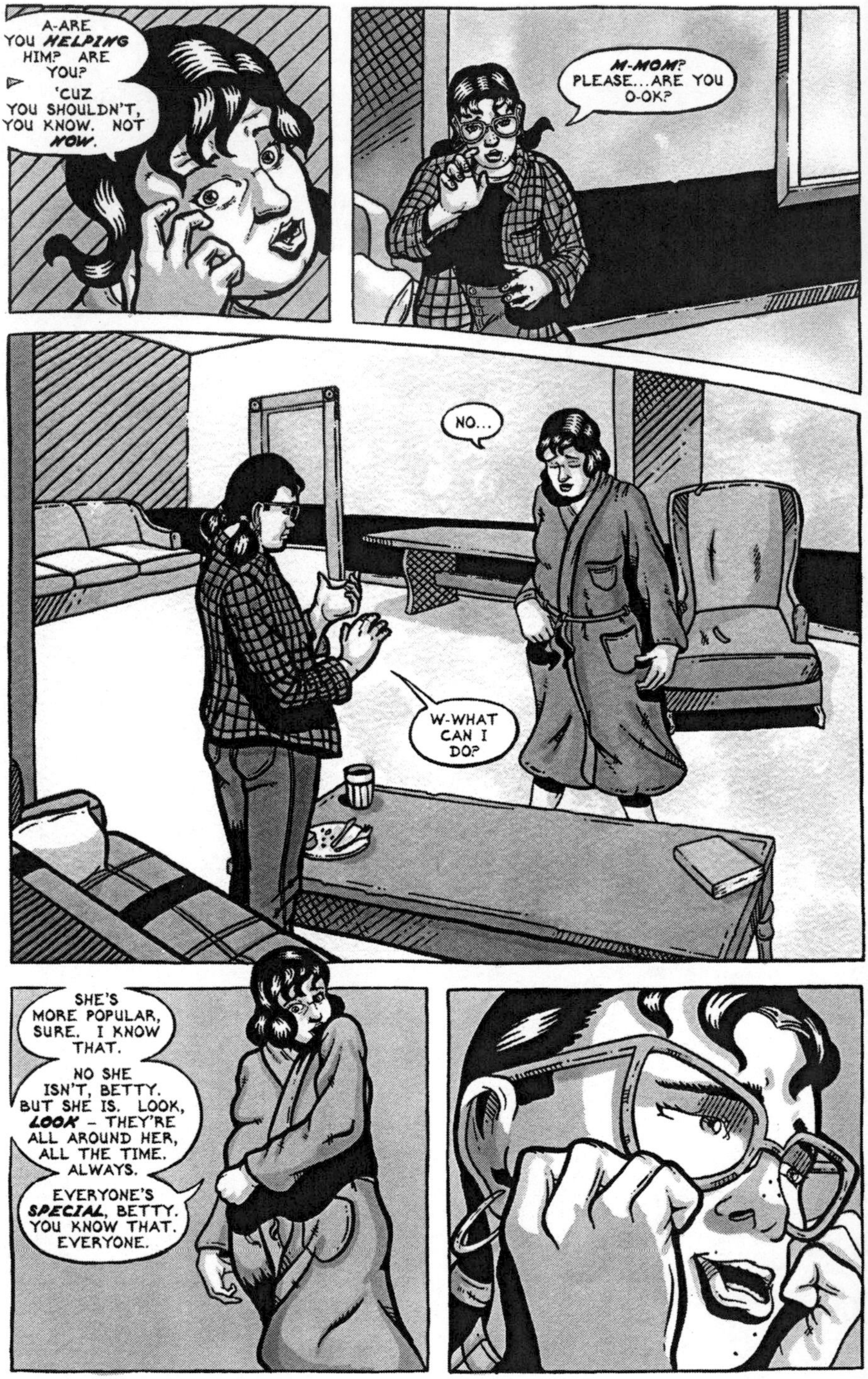
A-ARE YOU HELPING HIM? ARE YOU?
'CUZ YOU SHOULDN'T, YOU KNOW. NOT NOW.
M-MOM? PLEASE...ARE YOU O-OK?
NO...
W-WHAT CAN I DO?
SHE'S MORE POPULAR, SURE. I KNOW THAT.
NO SHE ISN'T, BETTY. BUT SHE IS. LOOK, LOOK - THEY'RE ALL AROUND HER, ALL THE TIME. ALWAYS.
EVERYONE'S SPECIAL, BETTY. YOU KNOW THAT. EVERYONE.

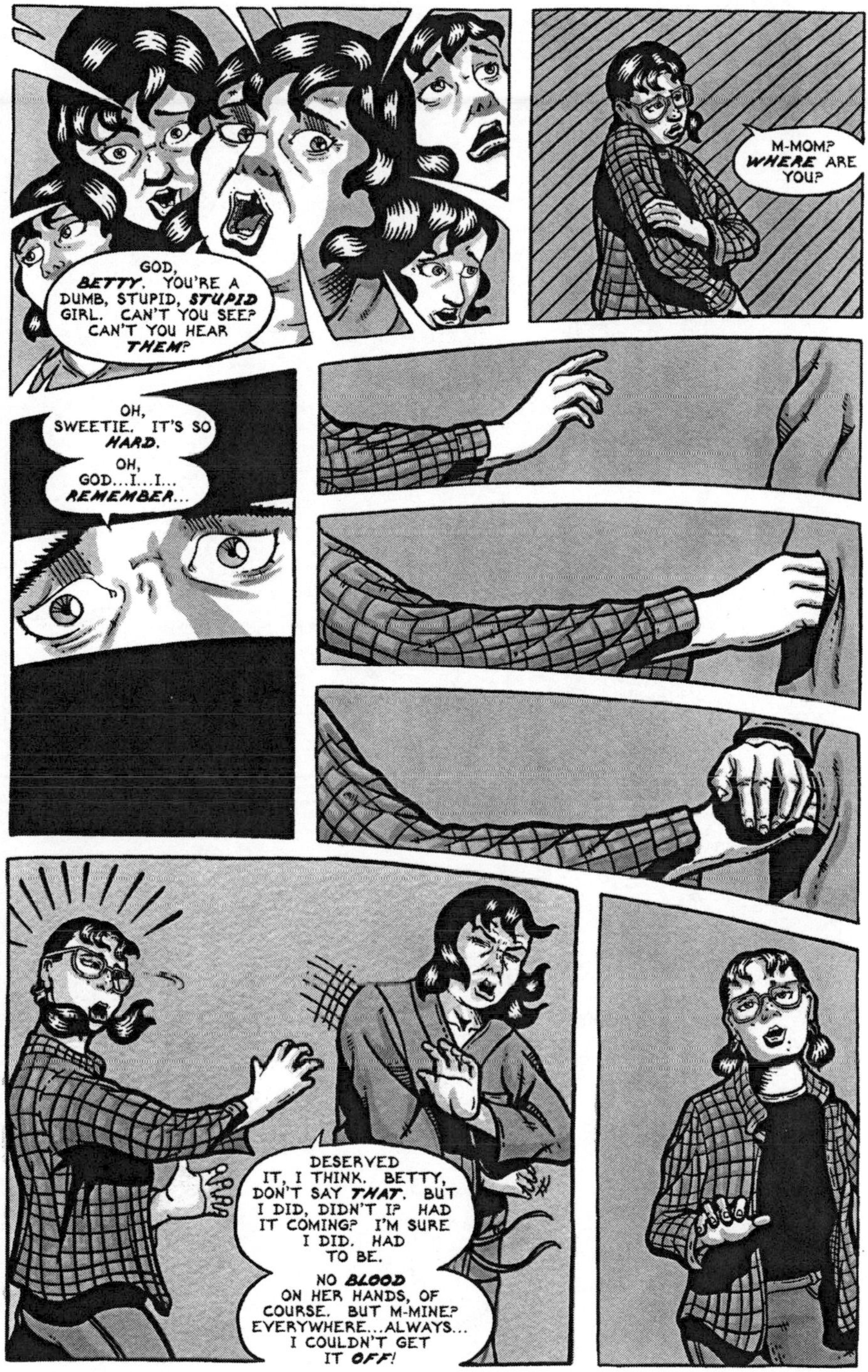
GOD, BETTY. YOU'RE A DUMB, STUPID, STUPID GIRL. CAN'T YOU SEE? CAN'T YOU HEAR THEM?
M-MOM? WHERE ARE YOU?
OH, SWEETIE. IT'S SO HARD.
OH, GOD...I...I... REMEMBER...
DESERVED IT, I THINK. BETTY, DON'T SAY THAT. BUT I DID, DIDN'T I? HAD IT COMING? I'M SURE I DID. HAD TO BE.
NO BLOOD ON HER HANDS, OF COURSE. BUT M-MINE? EVERYWHERE...ALWAYS... I COULDN'T GET IT OFF!

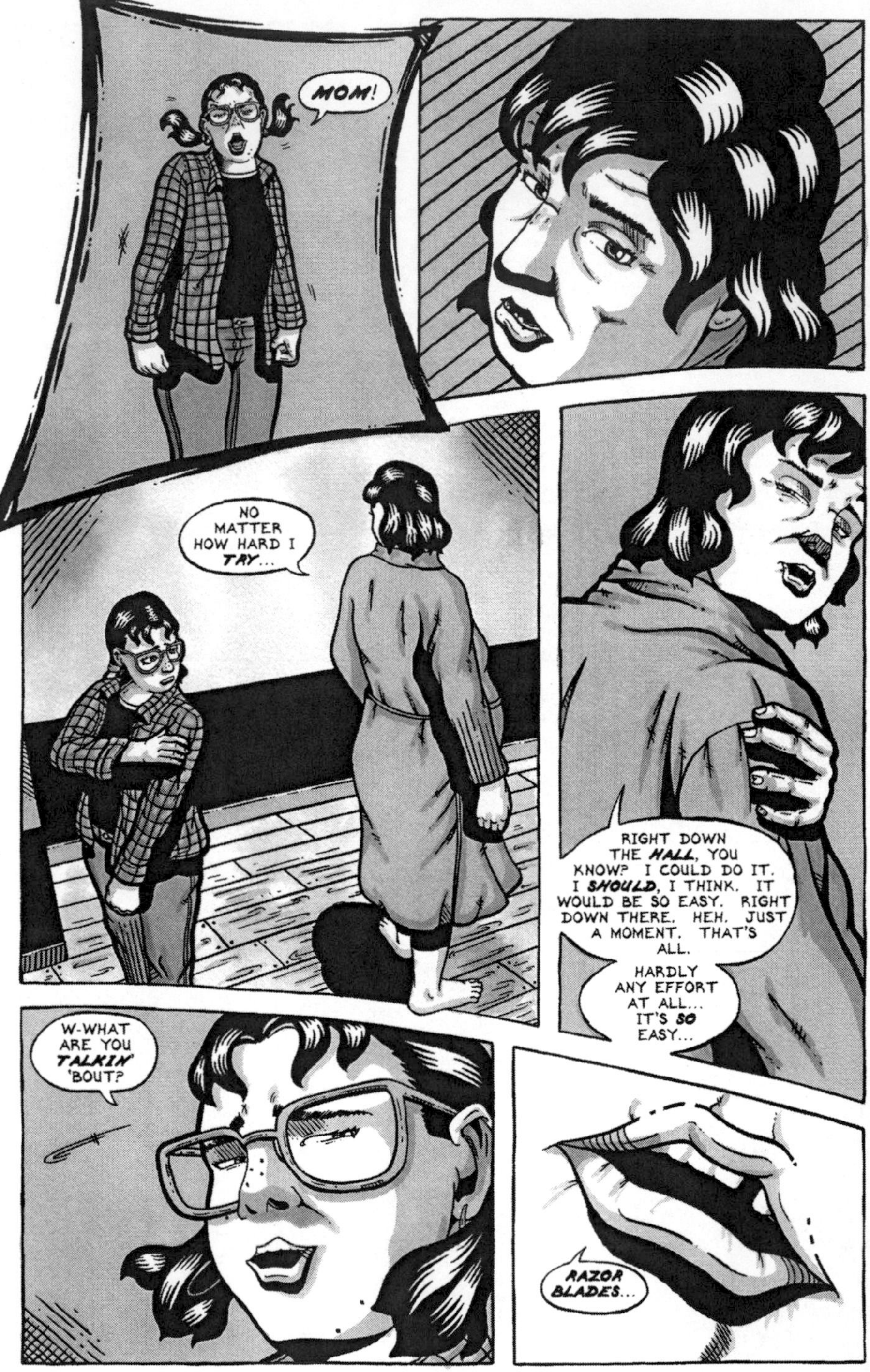
MOM!
NO MATTER HOW HARD I TRY...
RIGHT DOWN THE HALL, YOU KNOW? I COULD DO IT. I SHOULD, I THINK. IT WOULD BE SO EASY. RIGHT DOWN THERE. HEH. JUST A MOMENT. THAT'S ALL.
HARDLY ANY EFFORT AT ALL... IT'S SO EASY...
W-WHAT ARE YOU TALKIN' 'BOUT?
RAZOR BLADES...

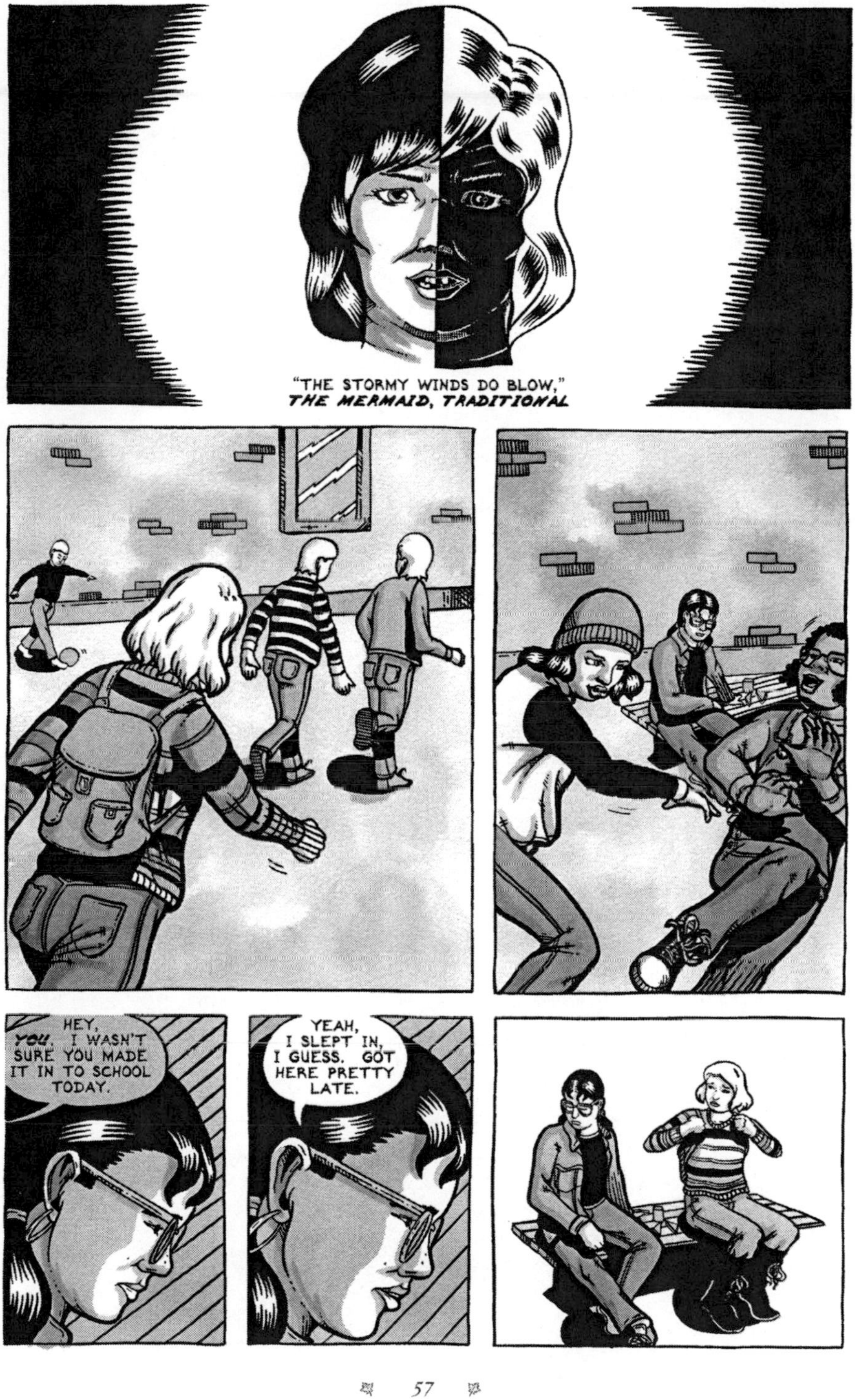
"THE STORMY WINDS DO BLOW,"
THE MERMAID, TRADITIONAL
HEY, YOU. I WASN'T SURE YOU MADE IT IN TO SCHOOL TODAY.
YEAH, I SLEPT IN, I GUESS. GOT HERE PRETTY LATE.

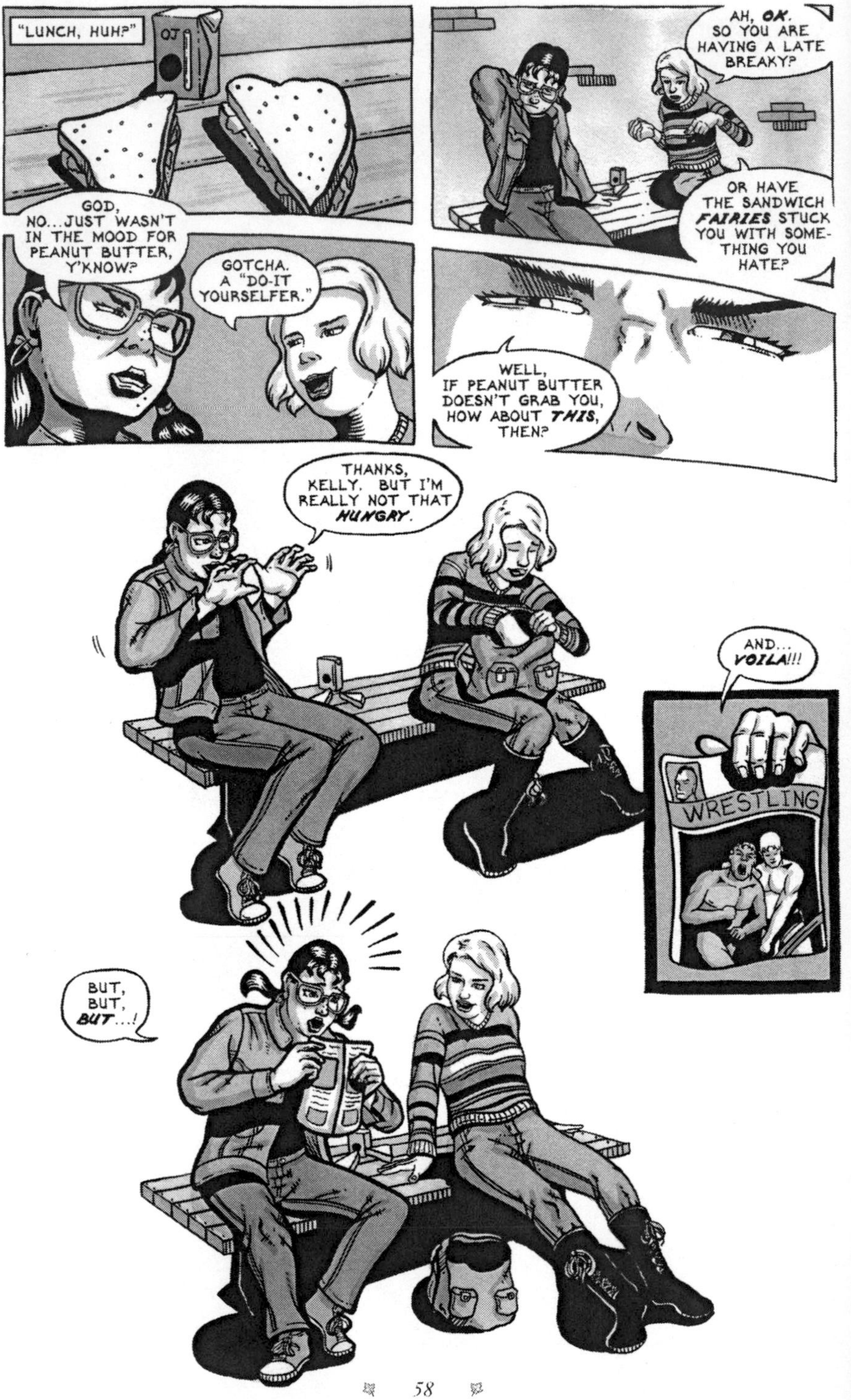
"LUNCH, HUH?"
OJ
AH, OK. SO YOU ARE HAVING A LATE BREAKY?
OR HAVE THE SANDWICH FAIRIES STUCK YOU WITH SOMETHING YOU HATE?
GOD, NO...JUST WASN'T IN THE MOOD FOR PEANUT BUTTER, Y'KNOW?
GOTCHA. A "DO-IT YOURSELFER."
WELL, IF PEANUT BUTTER DOESN'T GRAB YOU, HOW ABOUT THIS, THEN?
THANKS, KELLY. BUT I'M REALLY NOT THAT HUNGRY.
AND... VOILA!!!
WRESTLING
BUT, BUT, BUT...!

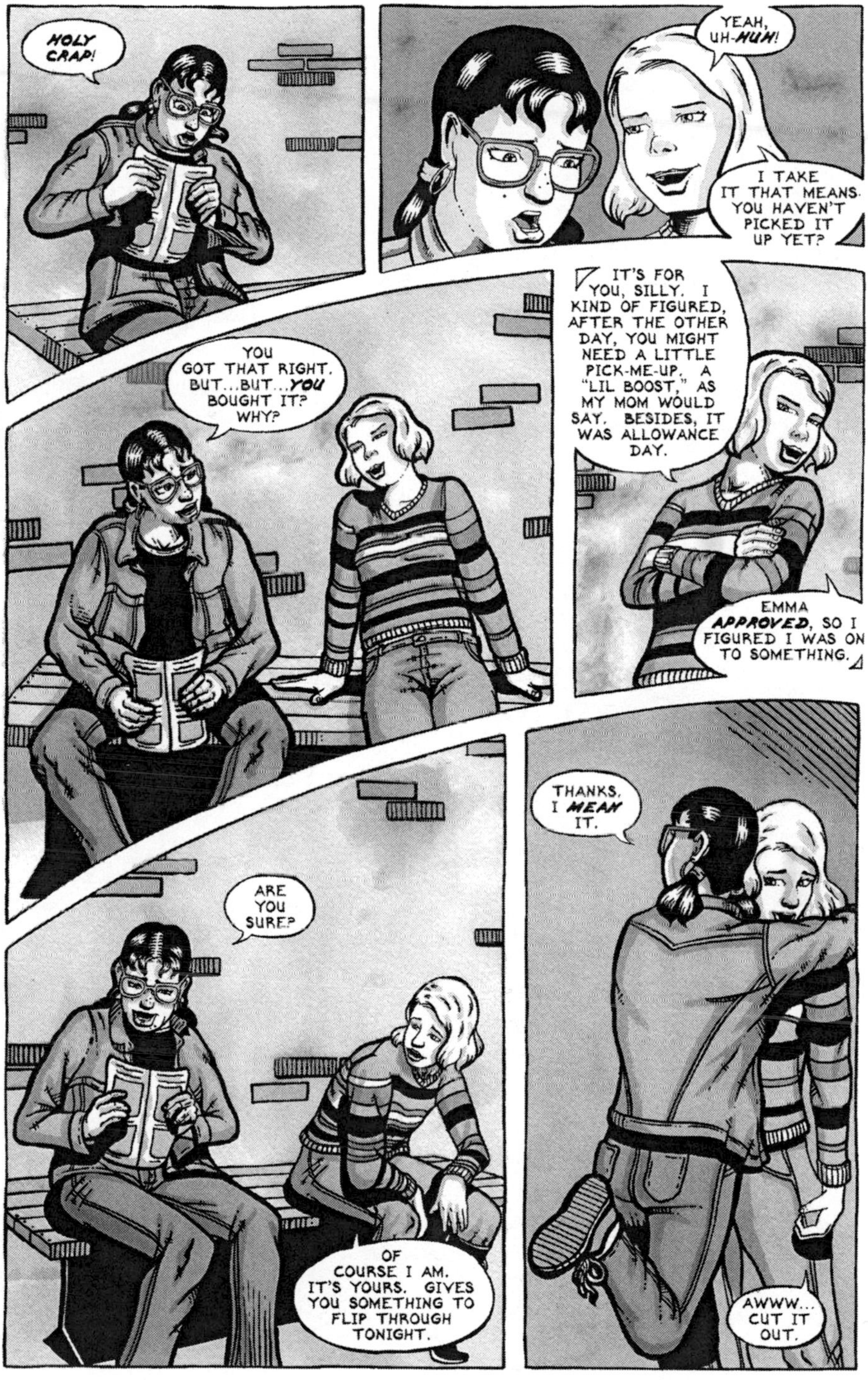
HOLY CRAP!
YEAH, UH-HUH!
I TAKE IT THAT MEANS YOU HAVEN'T PICKED IT UP YET?
YOU GOT THAT RIGHT. BUT...BUT...YOU BOUGHT IT? WHY?
IT'S FOR YOU, SILLY. I KIND OF FIGURED, AFTER THE OTHER DAY, YOU MIGHT NEED A LITTLE PICK-ME-UP. A "LIL BOOST," AS MY MOM WOULD SAY. BESIDES, IT WAS ALLOWANCE DAY.
EMMA APPROVED, SO I FIGURED I WAS ON TO SOMETHING.
ARE YOU SURE?
OF COURSE I AM. IT'S YOURS. GIVES YOU SOMETHING TO FLIP THROUGH TONIGHT.
THANKS. I MEAN IT.
AWWW... CUT IT OUT.

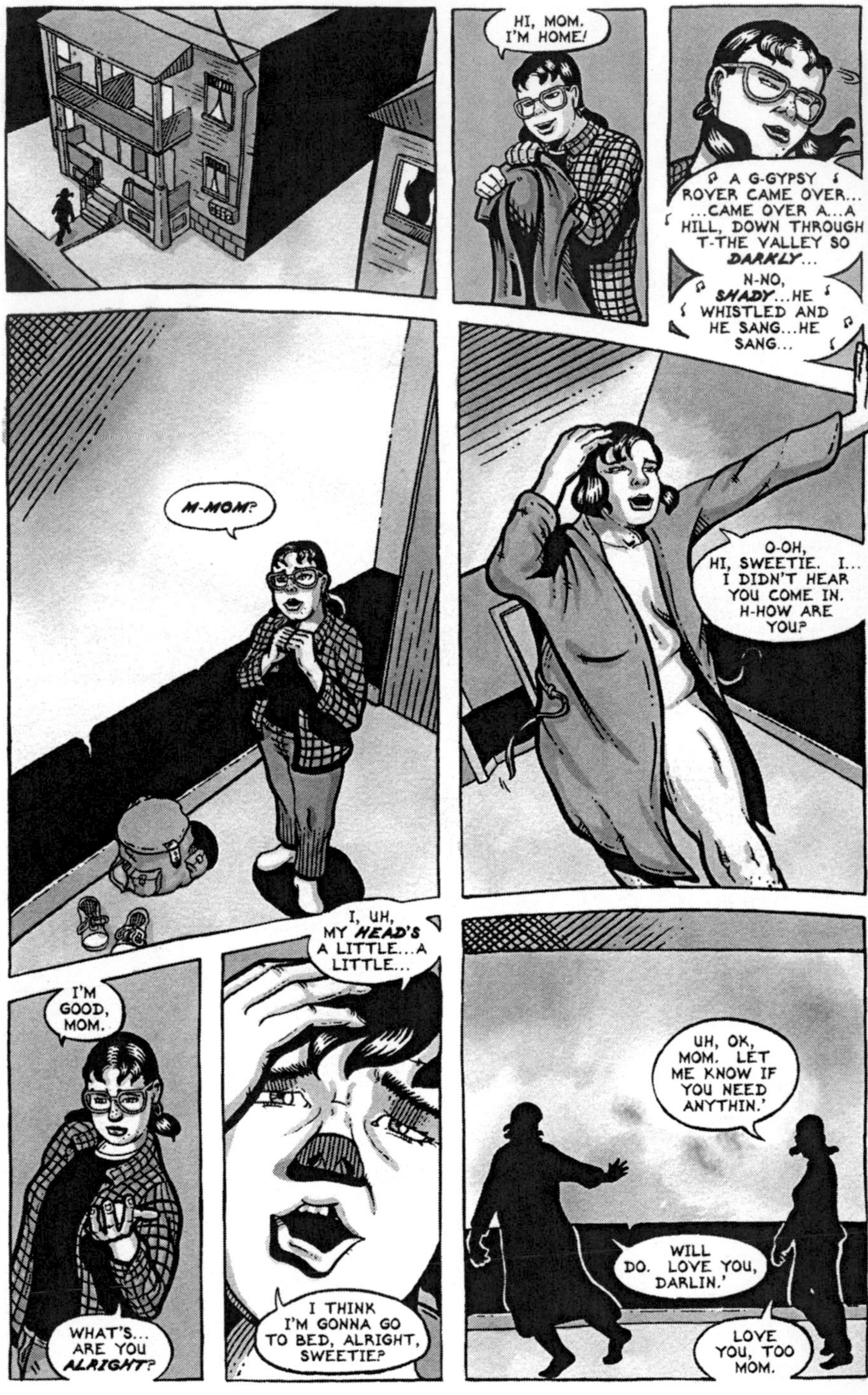

HI, MOM. I'M HOME!
A G-GYPSY ROVER CAME OVER... ...CAME OVER A...A HILL, DOWN THROUGH T-THE VALLEY SO DARKLY...
N-NO, SHADY...HE WHISTLED AND HE SANG...HE SANG...
M-MOM?
O-OH, HI, SWEETIE. I... I DIDN'T HEAR YOU COME IN. H-HOW ARE YOU?
I'M GOOD, MOM.
WHAT'S... ARE YOU ALRIGHT?
I, UH, MY HEAD'S A LITTLE...A LITTLE...
I THINK I'M GONNA GO TO BED, ALRIGHT, SWEETIE?
UH, OK, MOM. LET ME KNOW IF YOU NEED ANYTHIN.'
WILL DO. LOVE YOU, DARLIN.'
LOVE YOU, TOO MOM.

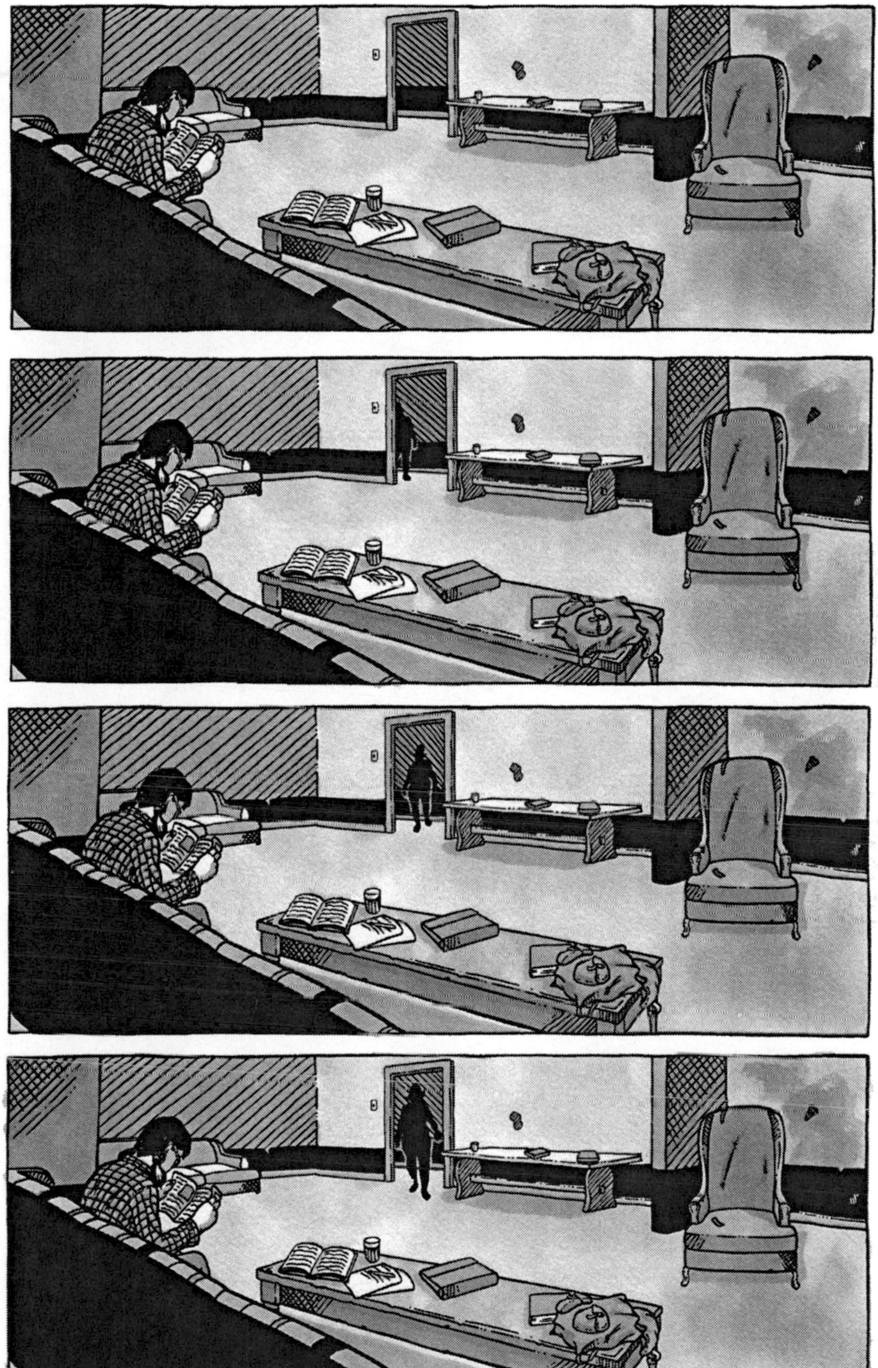

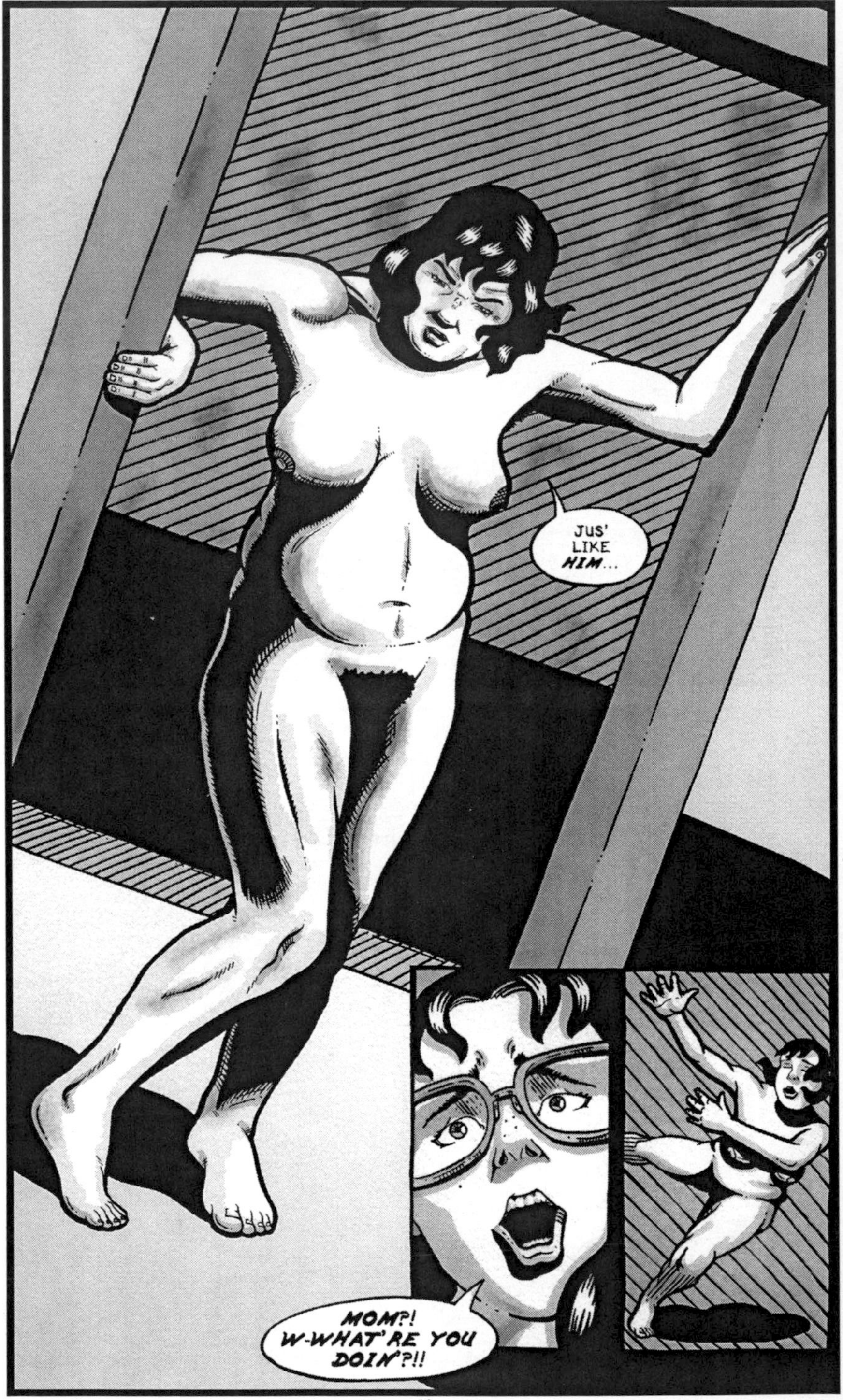
JUS' LIKE *HIM*...
MOM?! W-WHAT'RE YOU DOIN'?!!

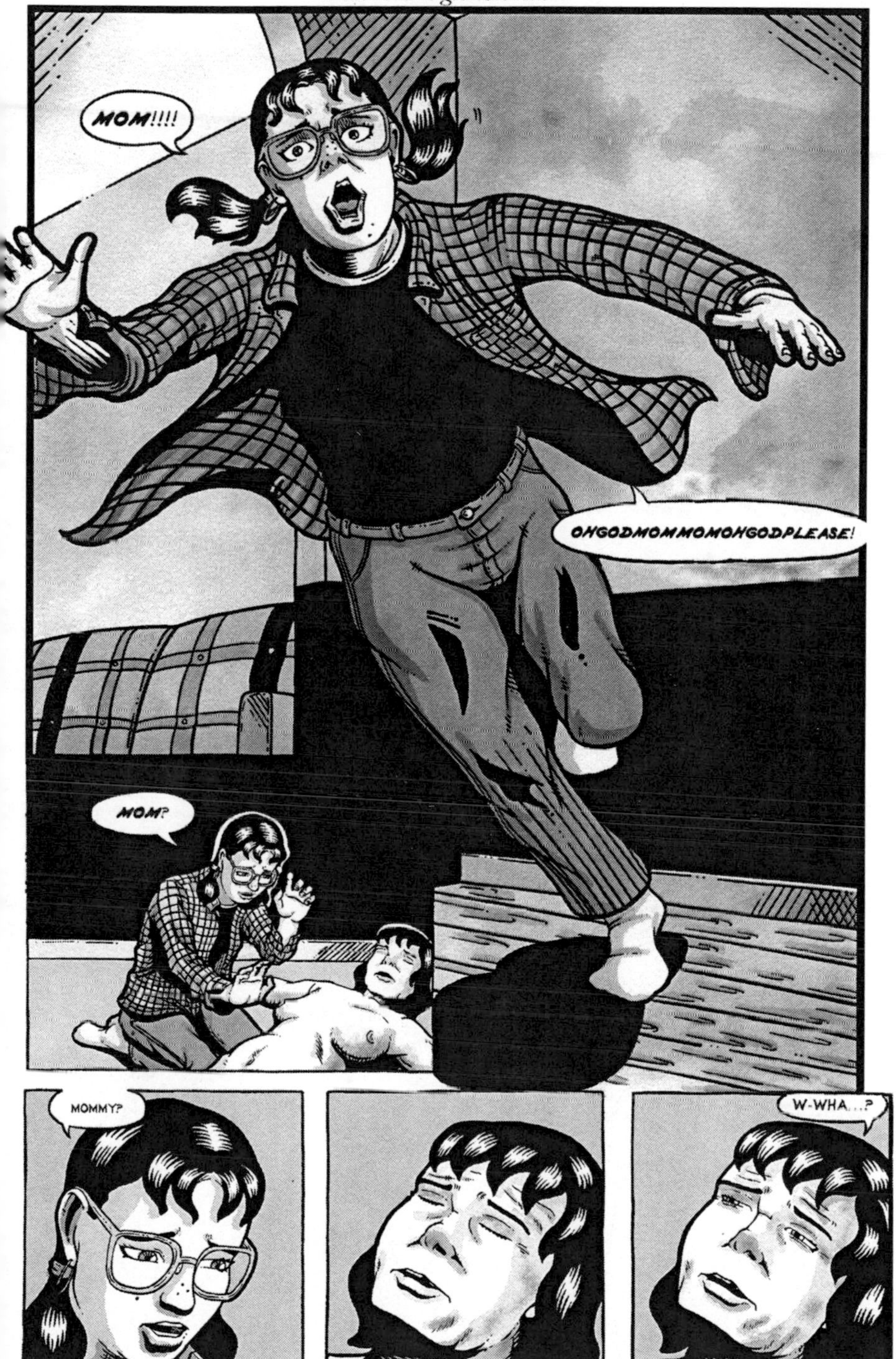
MOM!!!!
ОНGODMOMMOMOHGODPLEASE!
MOM?
MOMMY?
W-WHA...?

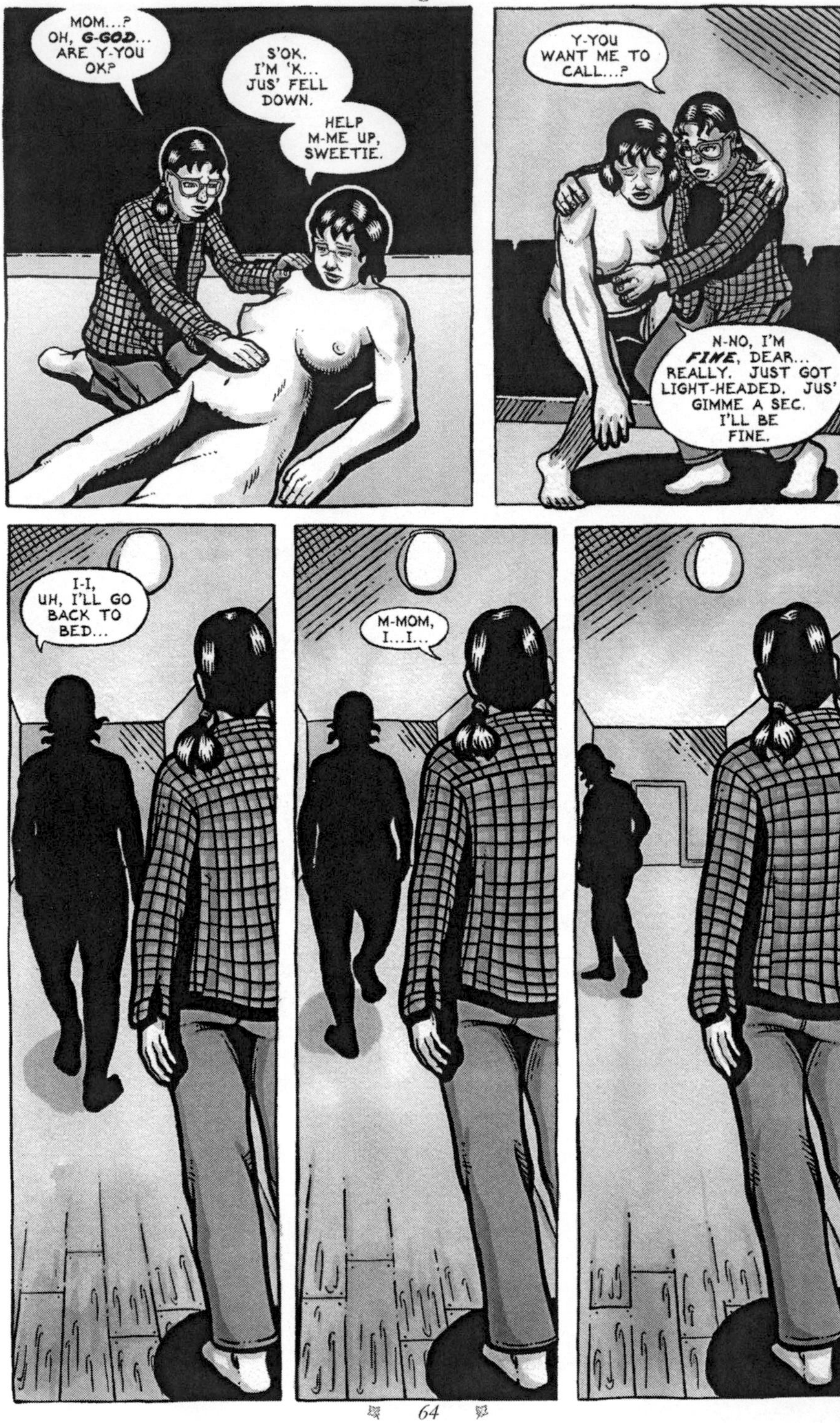
MOM...? OH, G-GOD... ARE Y-YOU OK?
S'OK. I'M 'K... JUS' FELL DOWN.
HELP M-ME UP, SWEETIE.
Y-YOU WANT ME TO CALL...?
N-NO, I'M FINE, DEAR... REALLY. JUST GOT LIGHT-HEADED. JUS' GIMME A SEC. I'LL BE FINE.
I-I, UH, I'LL GO BACK TO BED...
M-MOM, I...I...

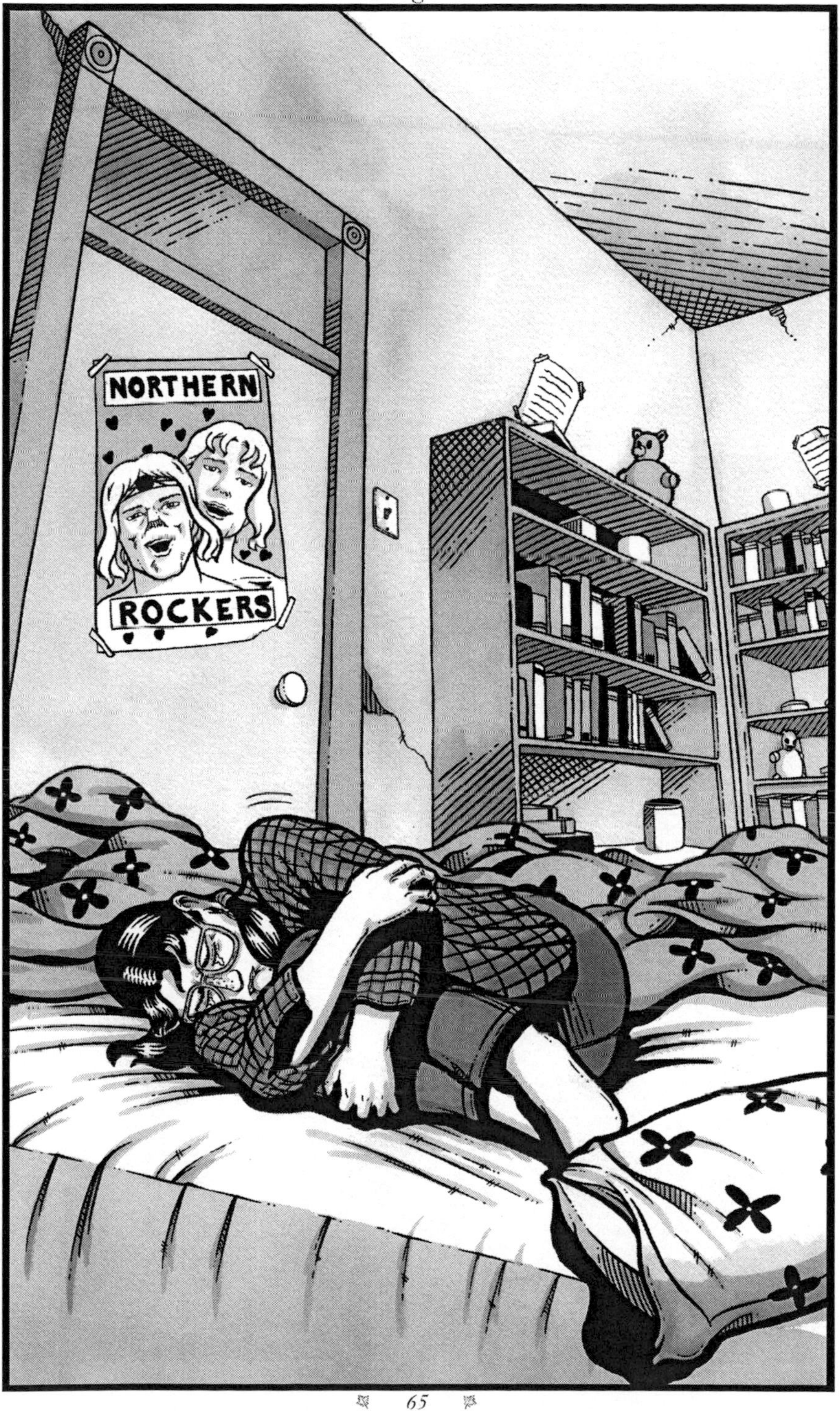
NORTHERN
ROCKERS

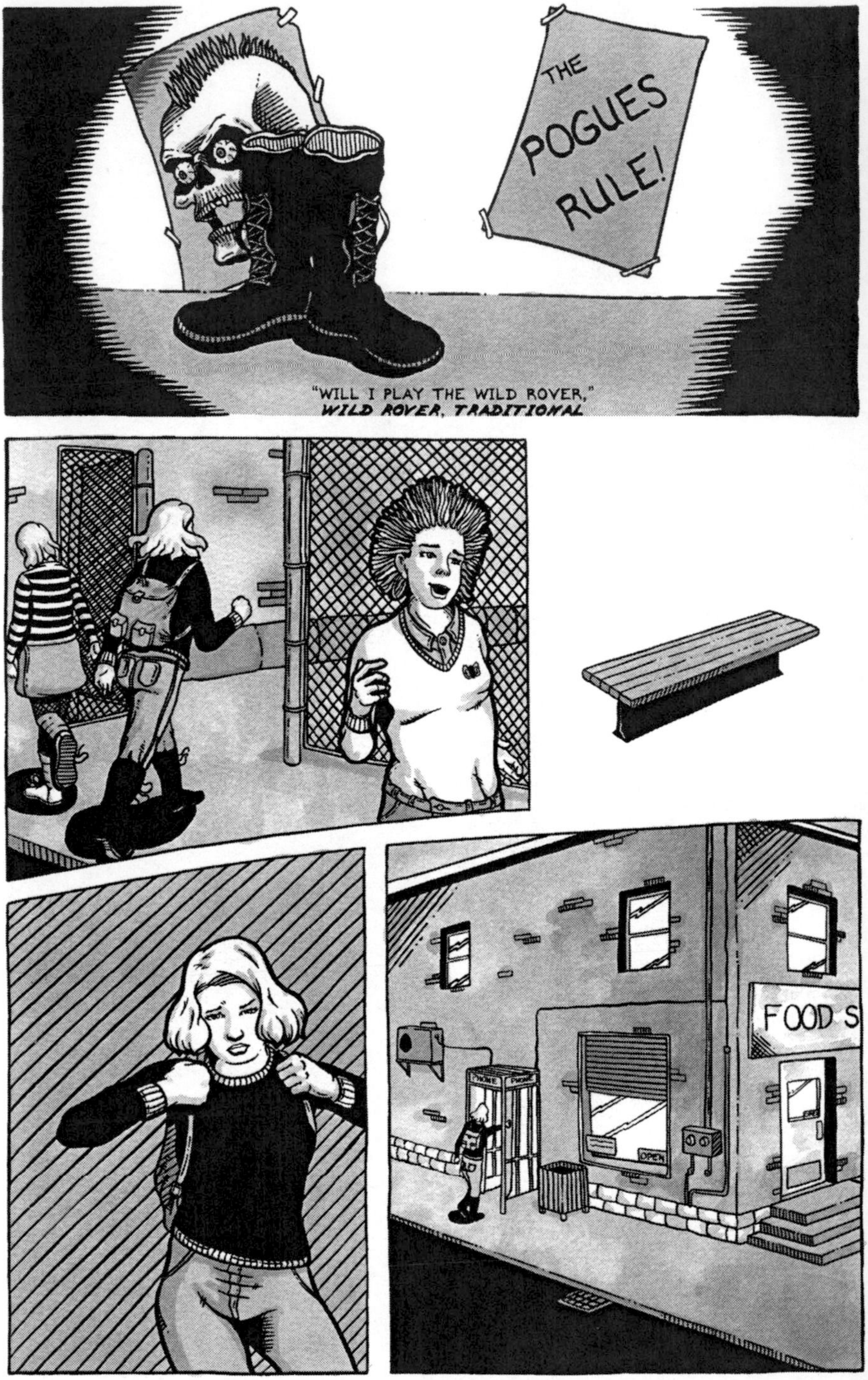
THE POGUES RULE!
"WILL I PLAY THE WILD ROVER,"
WILD ROVER, TRADITIONAL
FOOD S
OPEN

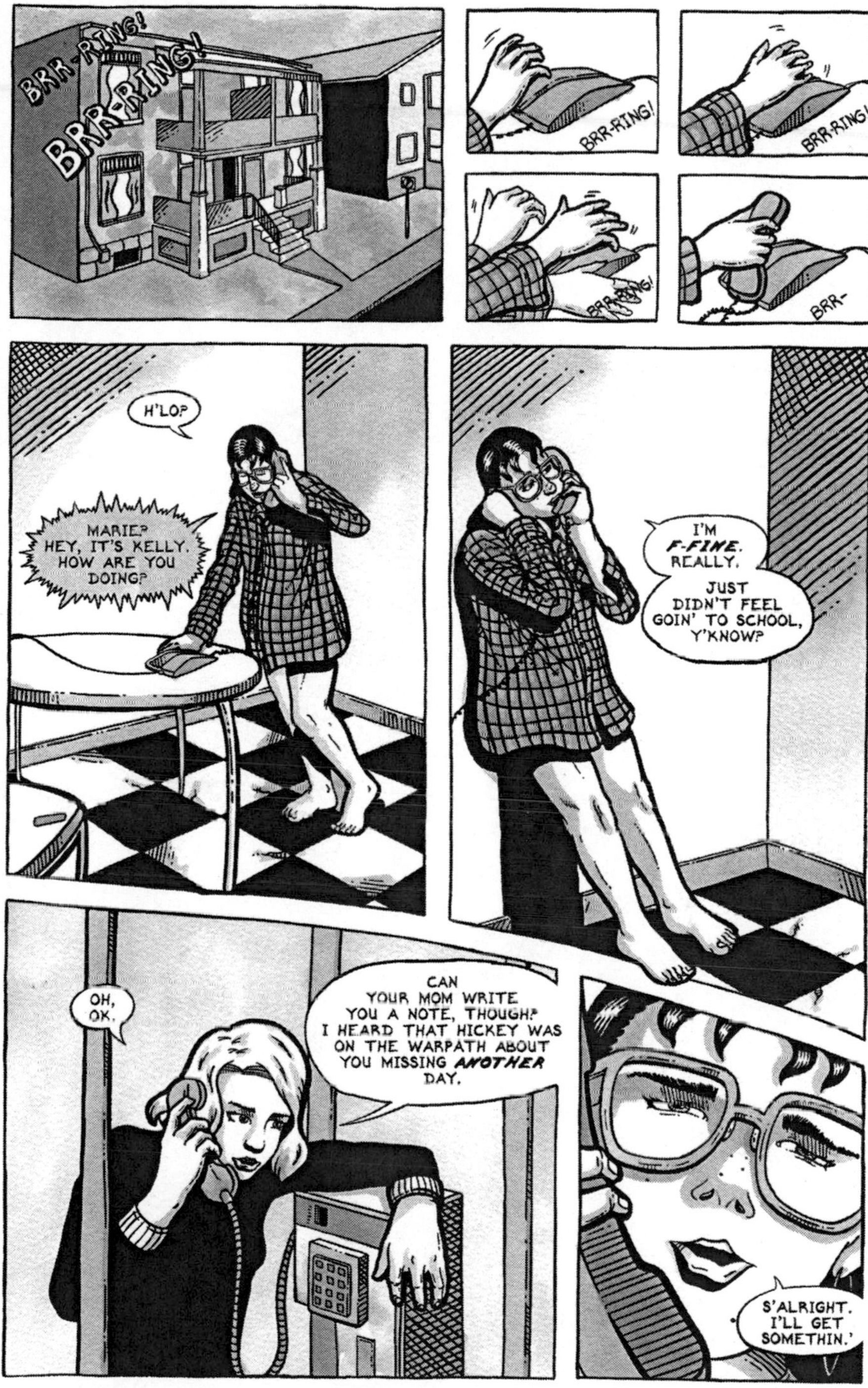
BRR-RING!
BRR-RING!
BRR-RING!
BRR-RING!
BRR-RING!
BRR-
H'LO?
MARIE? HEY, IT'S KELLY. HOW ARE YOU DOING?
I'M F-FINE. REALLY.
JUST DIDN'T FEEL GOIN' TO SCHOOL, Y'KNOW?
OH, OK.
CAN YOUR MOM WRITE YOU A NOTE, THOUGH? I HEARD THAT HICKEY WAS ON THE WARPATH ABOUT YOU MISSING ANOTHER DAY.
S'ALRIGHT. I'LL GET SOMETHIN.'

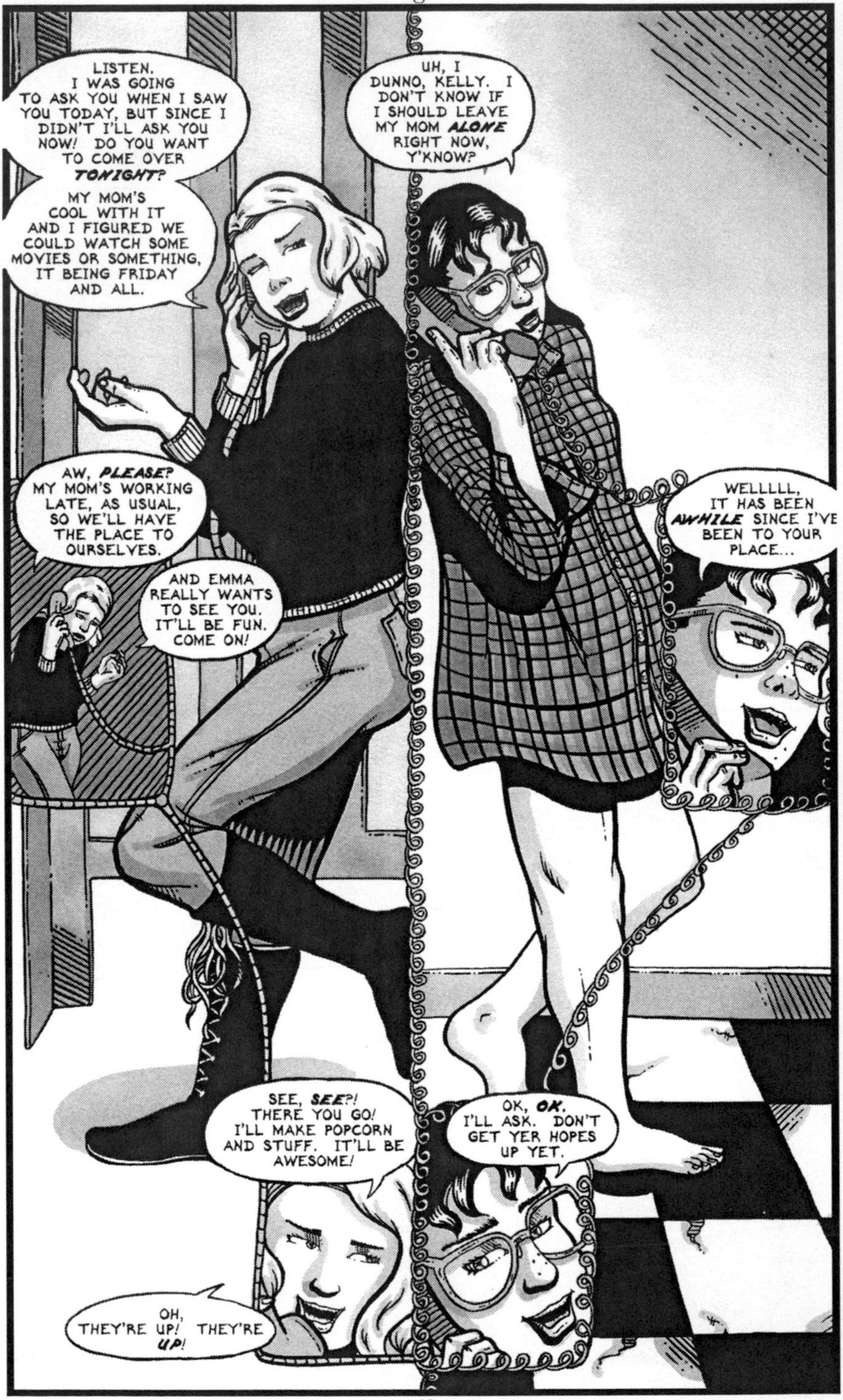
LISTEN. I WAS GOING TO ASK YOU WHEN I SAW YOU TODAY, BUT SINCE I DIDN'T I'LL ASK YOU NOW! DO YOU WANT TO COME OVER TONIGHT?
MY MOM'S COOL WITH IT AND I FIGURED WE COULD WATCH SOME MOVIES OR SOMETHING, IT BEING FRIDAY AND ALL.
UH, I DUNNO, KELLY. I DON'T KNOW IF I SHOULD LEAVE MY MOM ALONE RIGHT NOW, Y'KNOW?
AW, PLEASE? MY MOM'S WORKING LATE, AS USUAL, SO WE'LL HAVE THE PLACE TO OURSELVES.
AND EMMA REALLY WANTS TO SEE YOU. IT'LL BE FUN. COME ON!
WELLLLL, IT HAS BEEN AWHILE SINCE I'VE BEEN TO YOUR PLACE...
SEE, SEE?! THERE YOU GO! I'LL MAKE POPCORN AND STUFF. IT'LL BE AWESOME!
OK, OK. I'LL ASK. DON'T GET YER HOPES UP YET.
OH, THEY'RE UP! THEY'RE UP!

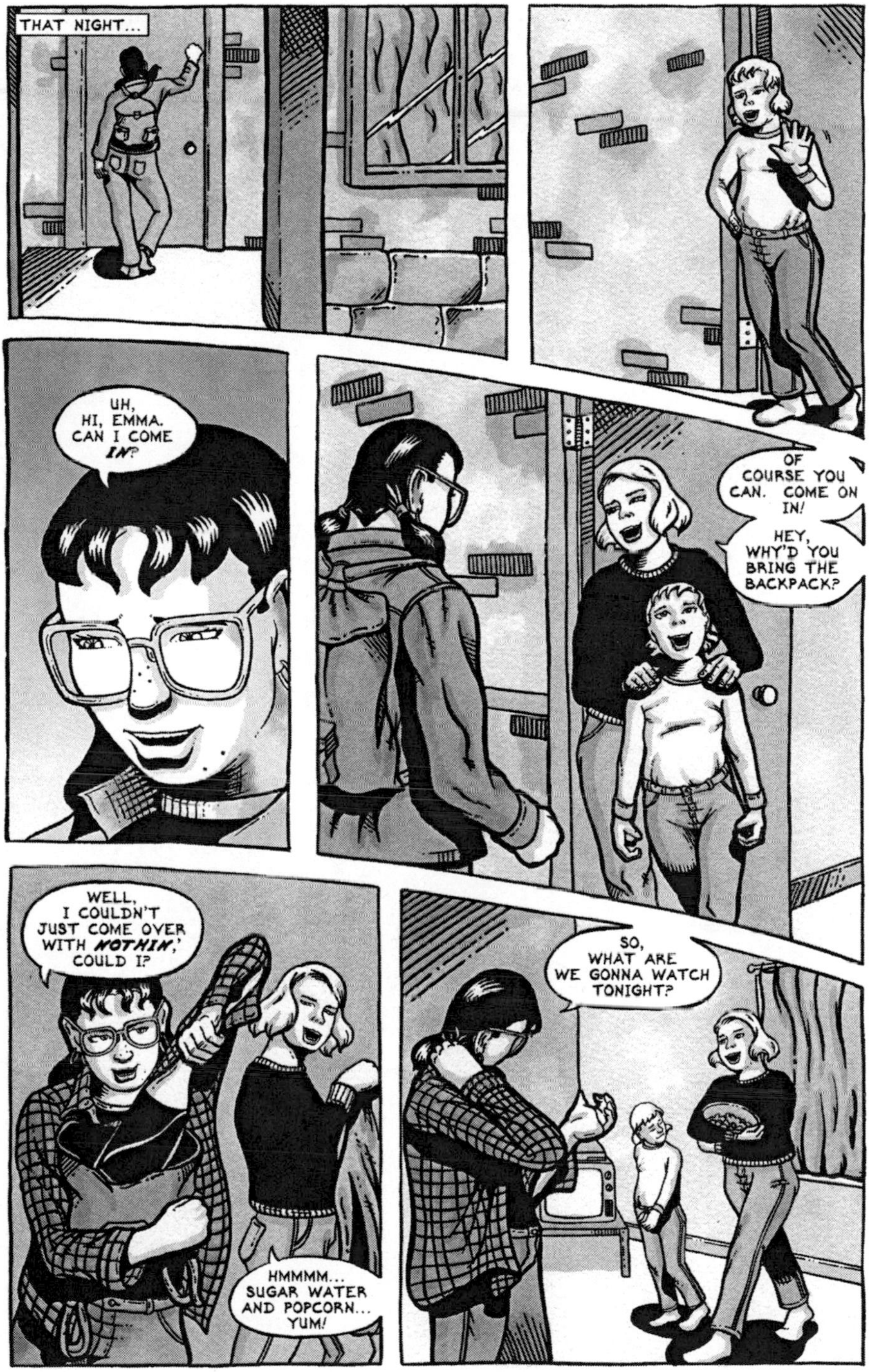
THAT NIGHT...
UH, HI, EMMA. CAN I COME IN?
OF COURSE YOU CAN. COME ON IN!
HEY, WHY'D YOU BRING THE BACKPACK?
WELL, I COULDN'T JUST COME OVER WITH NOTHIN,' COULD I?
HMMMM... SUGAR WATER AND POPCORN... YUM!
SO, WHAT ARE WE GONNA WATCH TONIGHT?

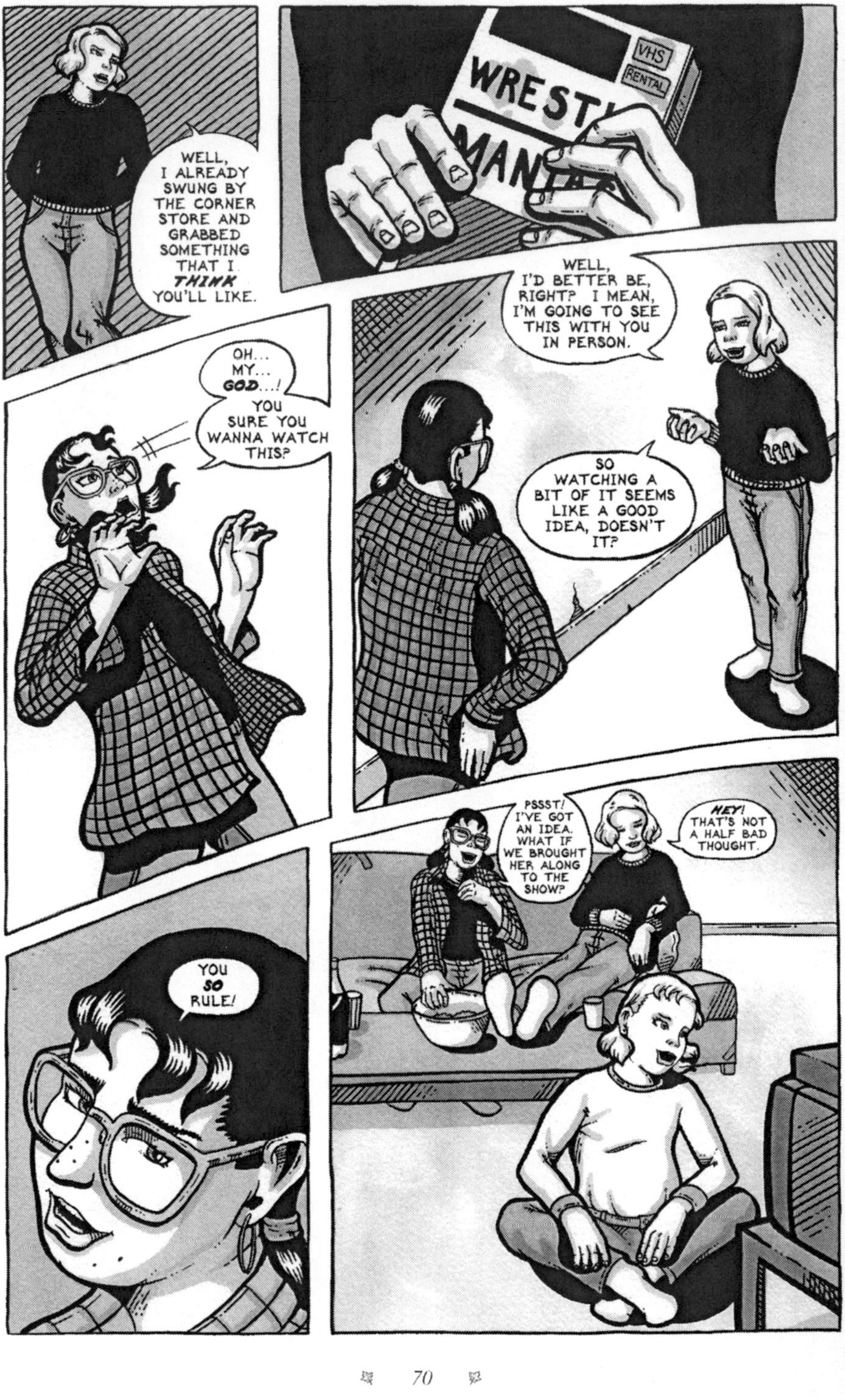
WELL, I ALREADY SWUNG BY THE CORNER STORE AND GRABBED SOMETHING THAT I. THINK YOU'LL LIKE.
WRESTL MANIA
VHS
RENTAL
WELL, I'D BETTER BE, RIGHT? I MEAN, I'M GOING TO SEE THIS WITH YOU IN PERSON.
OH... MY... GOD...!
YOU SURE YOU WANNA WATCH THIS?
SO WATCHING A BIT OF IT SEEMS LIKE A GOOD IDEA, DOESN'T IT?
PSSST! I'VE GOT AN IDEA. WHAT IF WE BROUGHT HER ALONG TO THE SHOW?
HEY! THAT'S NOT A HALF BAD THOUGHT.
YOU SO RULE!

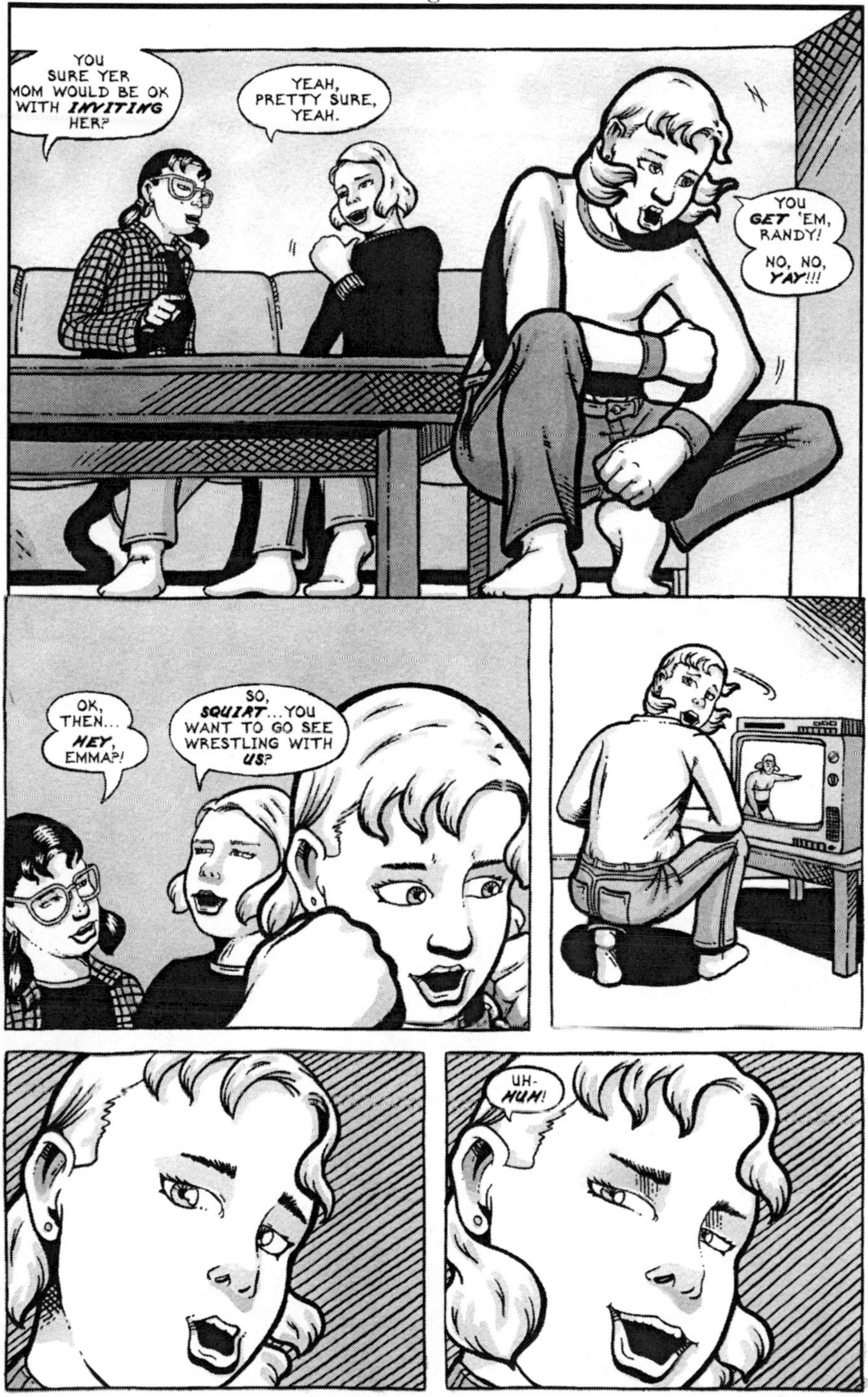
YOU SURE YER MOM WOULD BE OK WITH INVITING HER?
YEAH, PRETTY SURE, YEAH.
YOU GET 'EM, RANDY!
NO, NO, YAY!!!
OK, THEN... HEY, EMMA?!
SO, SQUIRT...YOU WANT TO GO SEE WRESTLING WITH US?
UH-HUH!

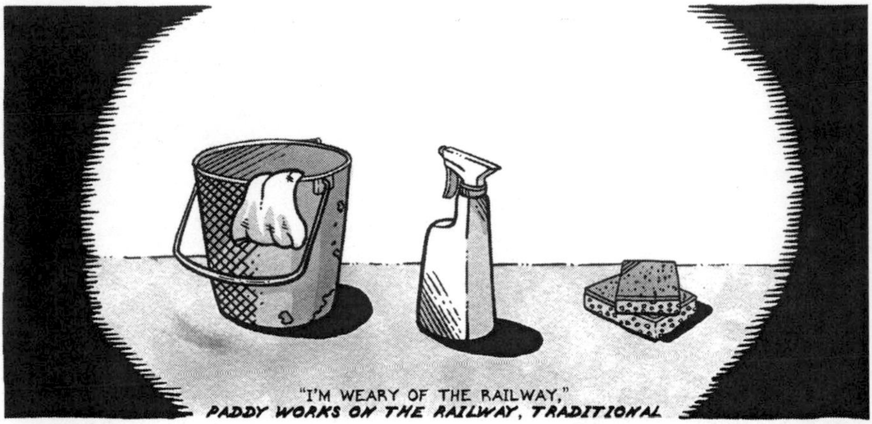
"I'M WEARY OF THE RAILWAY,"
PADDY WORKS ON THE RAILWAY, TRADITIONAL

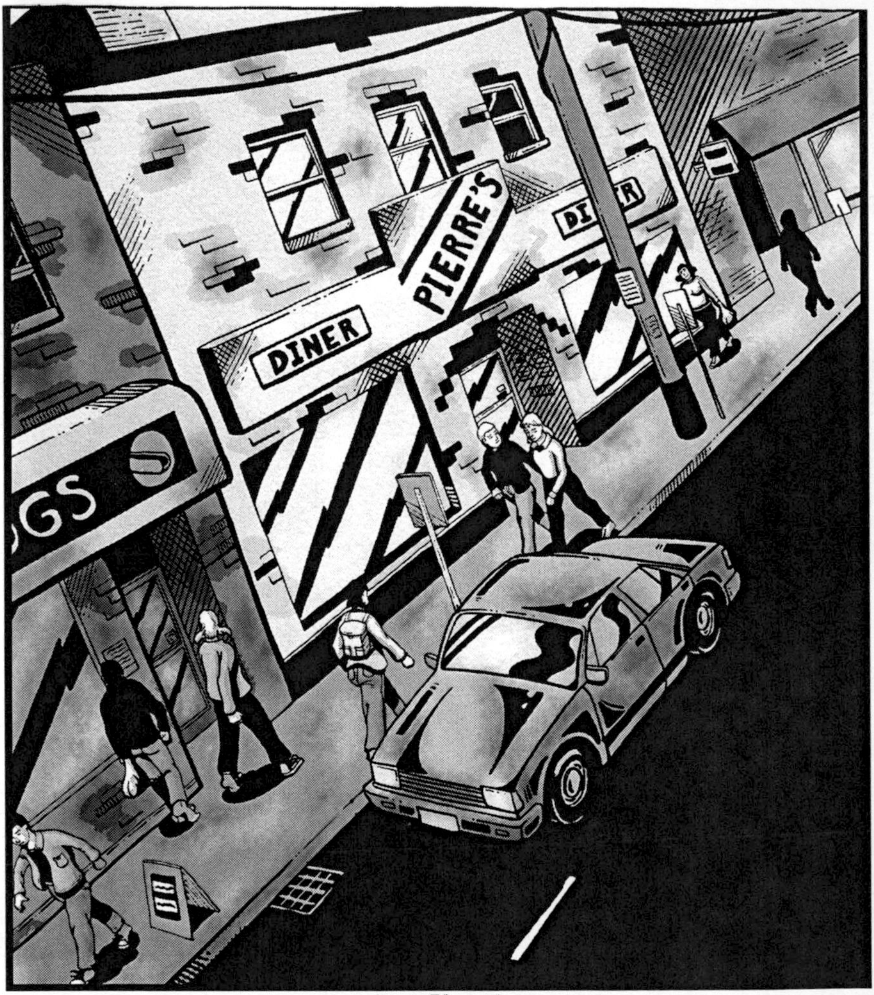
PIERRE'S
DINER
GS

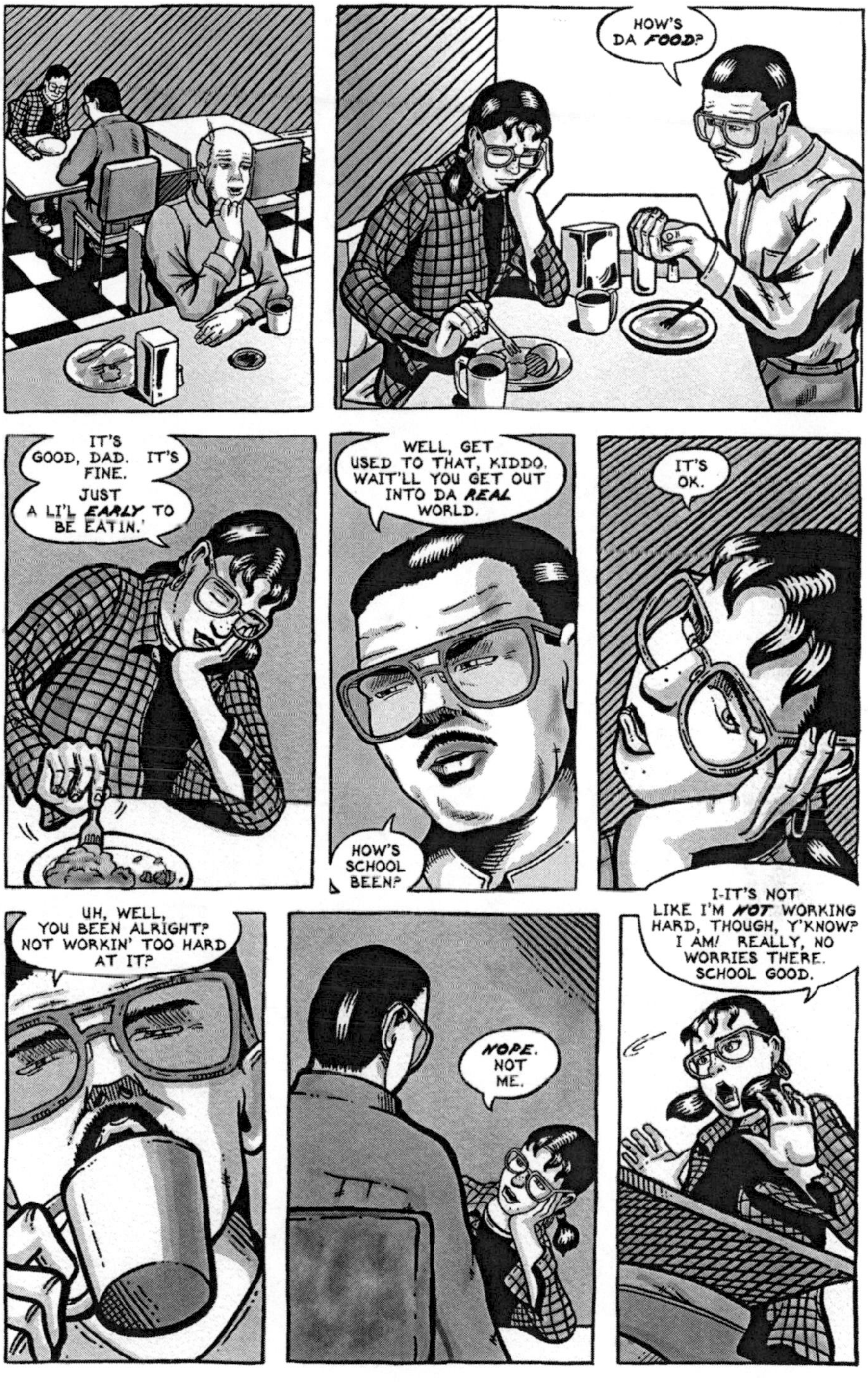
HOW'S DA FOOD?
IT'S GOOD, DAD. IT'S FINE.
JUST A LI'L EARLY TO BE EATIN.'
WELL, GET USED TO THAT, KIDDO. WAIT'LL YOU GET OUT INTO DA REAL WORLD.
HOW'S SCHOOL BEEN?
IT'S OK.
UH, WELL, YOU BEEN ALRIGHT? NOT WORKIN' TOO HARD AT IT?
NOPE. NOT ME.
I-IT'S NOT LIKE I'M NOT WORKING HARD, THOUGH, Y'KNOW? I AM! REALLY, NO WORRIES THERE. SCHOOL GOOD.

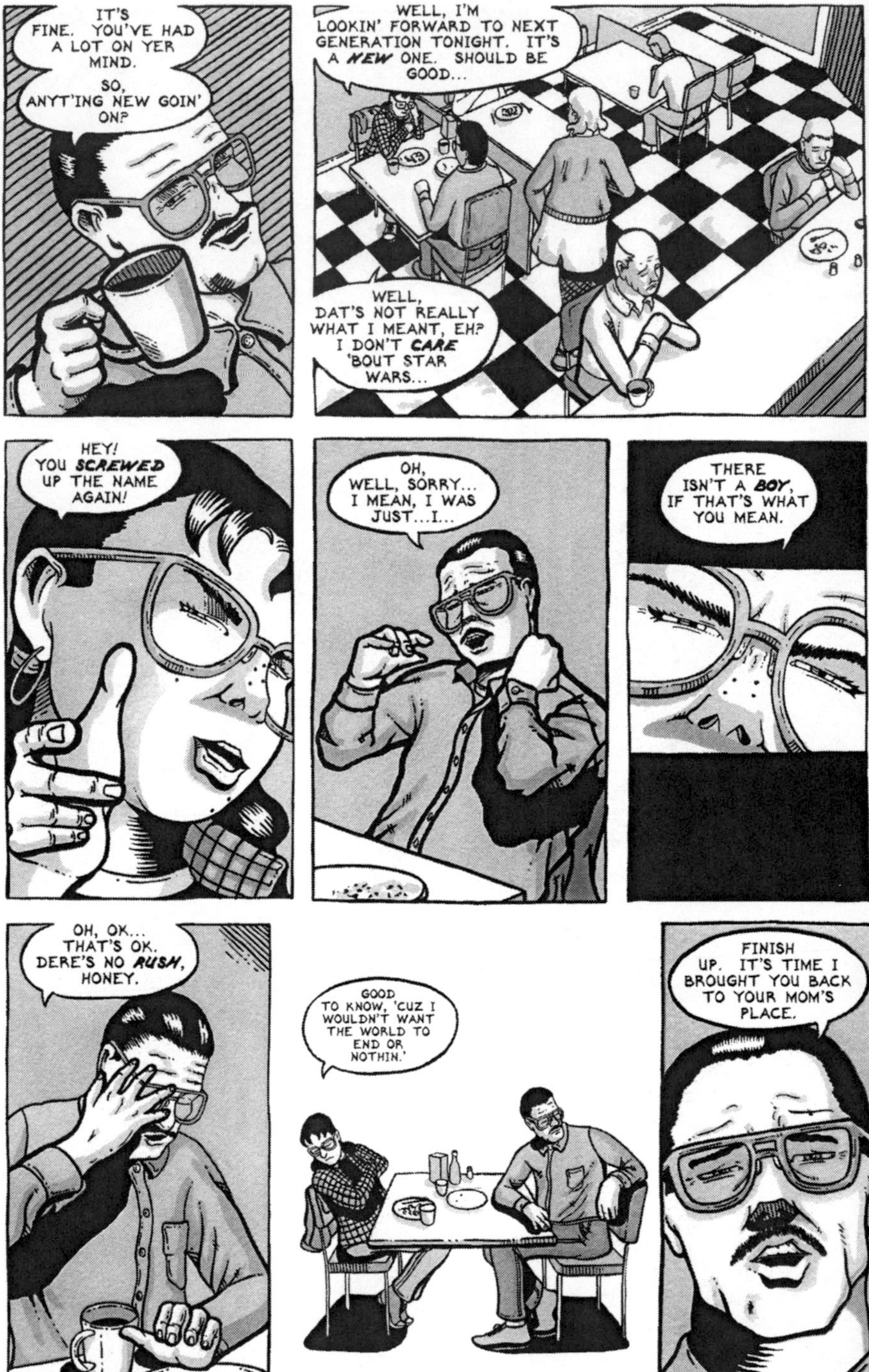
IT'S FINE. YOU'VE HAD A LOT ON YER MIND.
SO, ANYT'ING NEW GOIN' ON?
WELL, I'M LOOKIN' FORWARD TO NEXT GENERATION TONIGHT. IT'S A NEW ONE. SHOULD BE GOOD...
WELL, DAT'S NOT REALLY WHAT I MEANT, EH? I DON'T CARE 'BOUT STAR WARS...
HEY! YOU SCREWED UP THE NAME AGAIN!
OH, WELL, SORRY... I MEAN, I WAS JUST...I...
THERE ISN'T A BOY, IF THAT'S WHAT YOU MEAN.
OH, OK... THAT'S OK. DERE'S NO RUSH, HONEY.
GOOD TO KNOW, 'CUZ I WOULDN'T WANT THE WORLD TO END OR NOTHIN.'
FINISH UP. IT'S TIME I BROUGHT YOU BACK TO YOUR MOM'S PLACE.

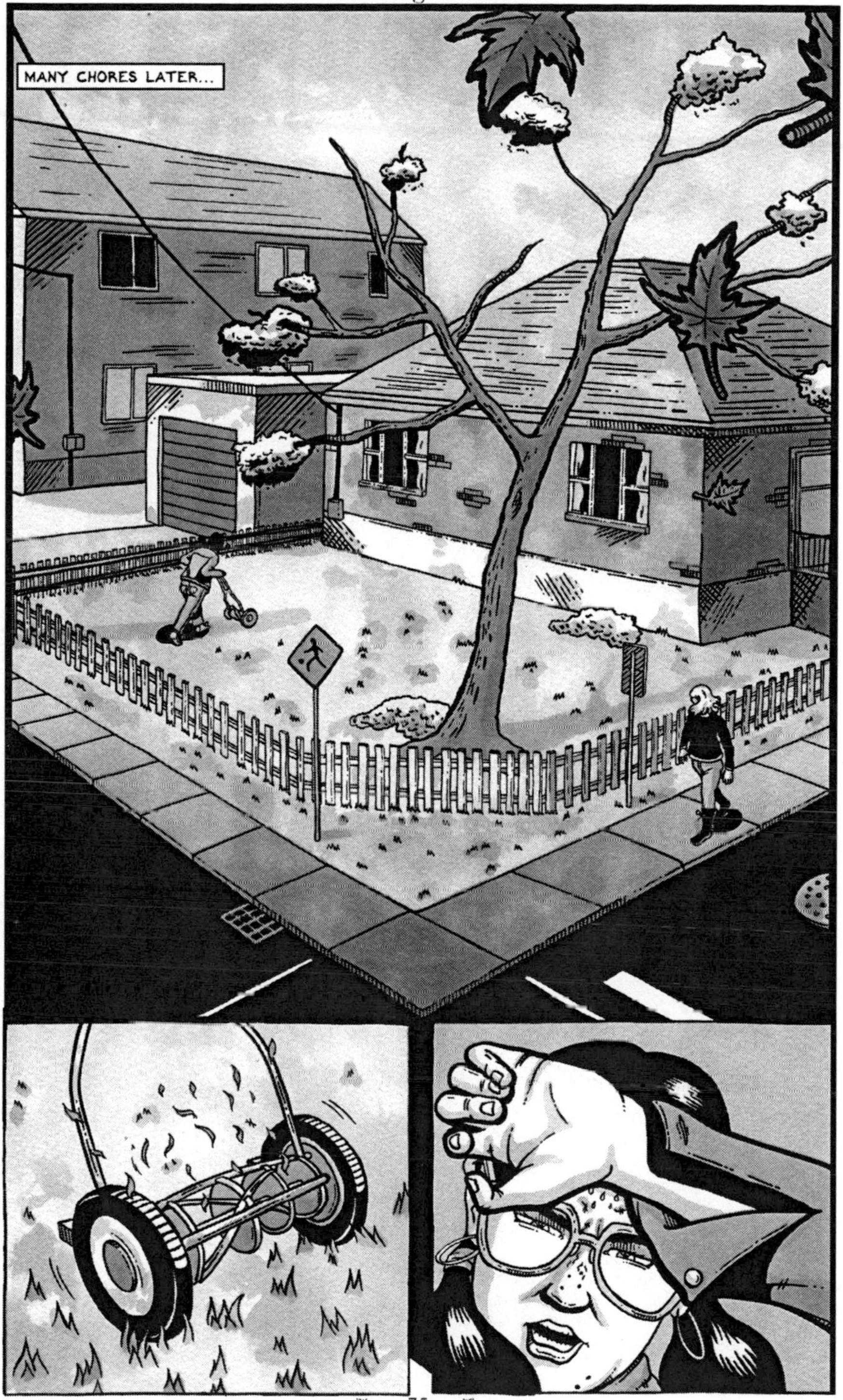
MANY CHORES LATER...

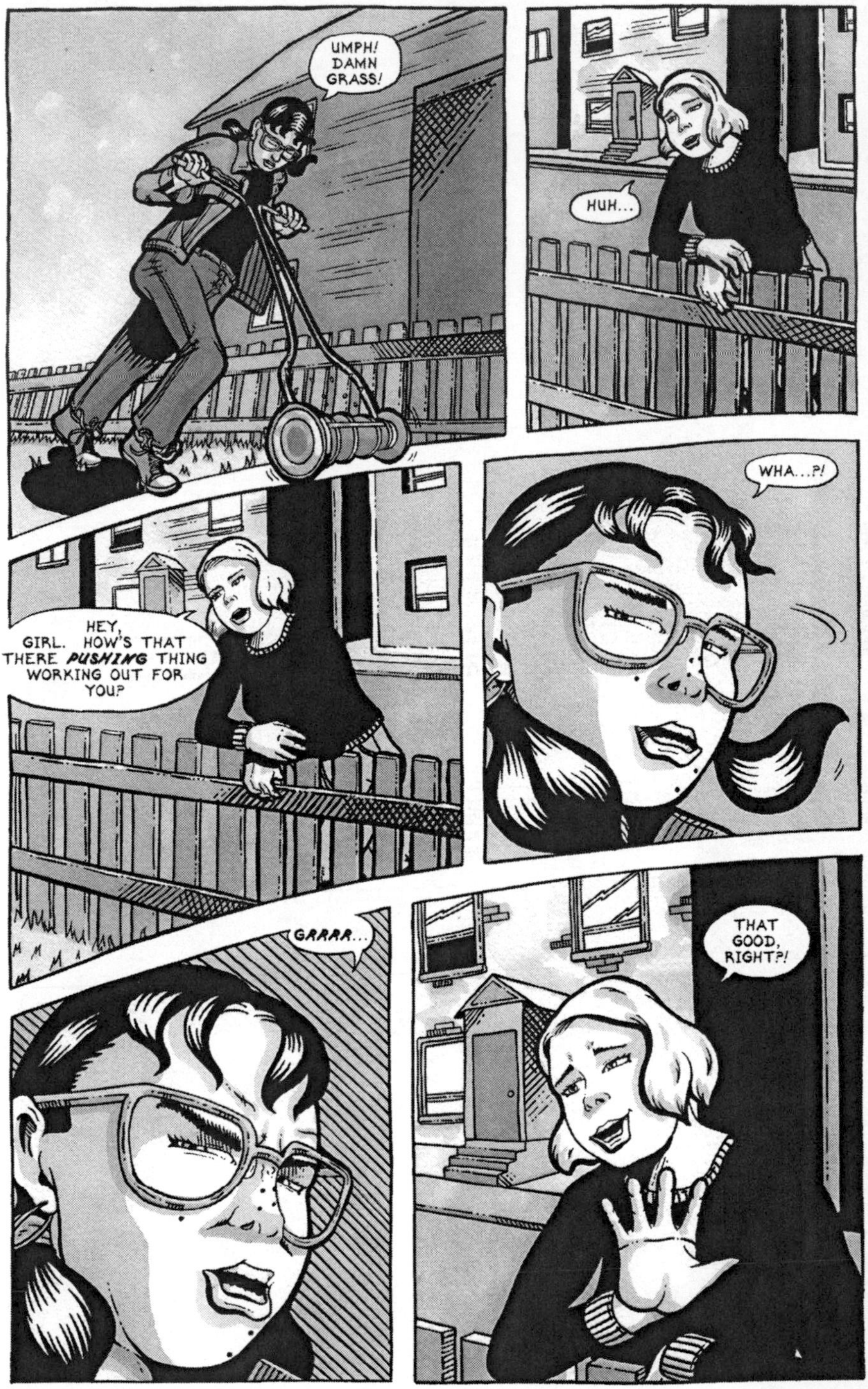
UMPH! DAMN GRASS!
HUH...
HEY, GIRL. HOW'S THAT THERE PUSHING THING WORKING OUT FOR YOU?
WHA...?!
GRRRR...
THAT GOOD, RIGHT?!

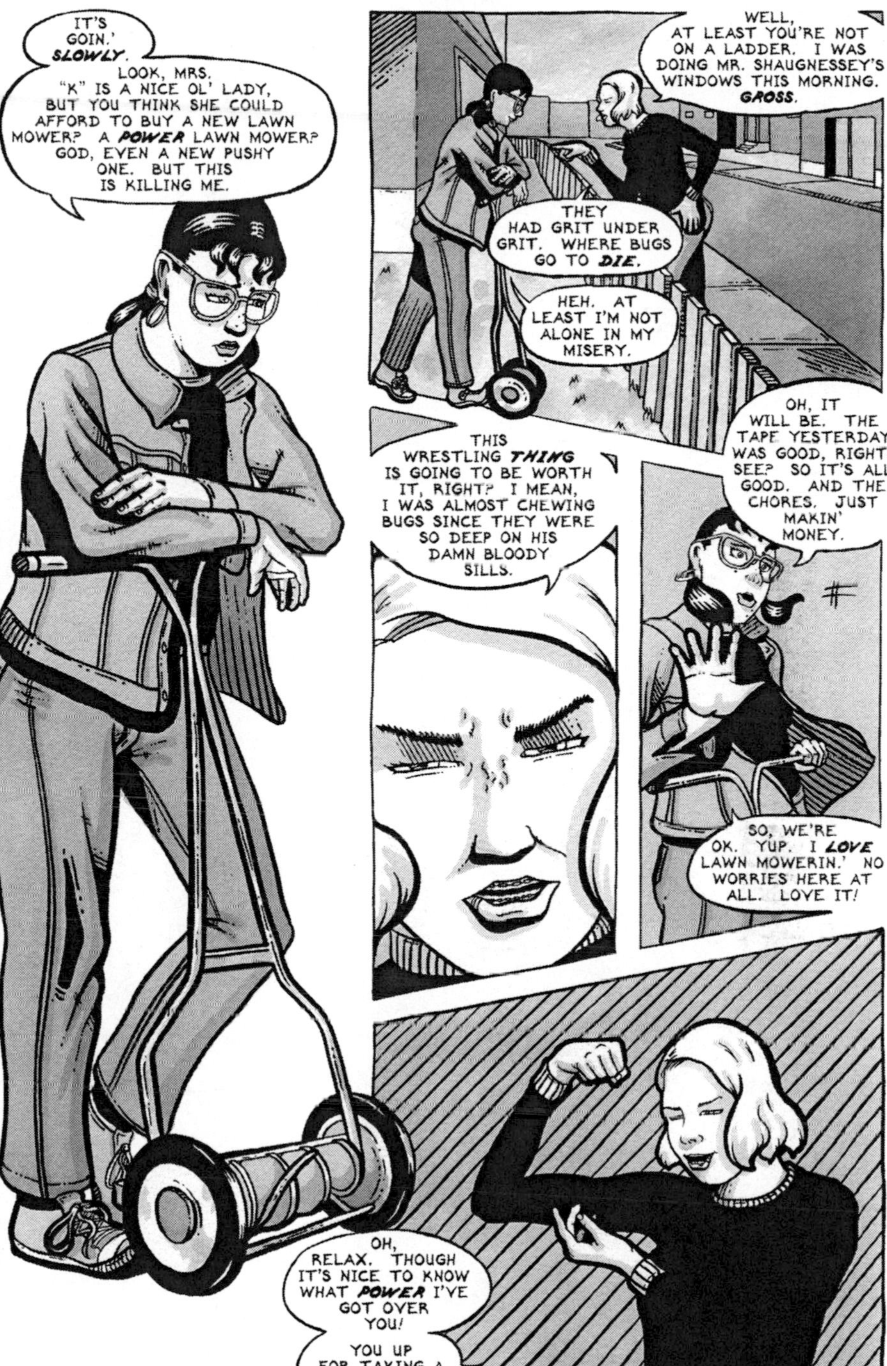
IT'S GOIN.' SLOWLY.
LOOK, MRS. "K" IS A NICE OL' LADY, BUT YOU THINK SHE COULD AFFORD TO BUY A NEW LAWN MOWER? A POWER LAWN MOWER? GOD, EVEN A NEW PUSHY ONE. BUT THIS IS KILLING ME.
WELL, AT LEAST YOU'RE NOT ON A LADDER. I WAS DOING MR. SHAUGNESSEY'S WINDOWS THIS MORNING. GROSS.
THEY HAD GRIT UNDER GRIT. WHERE BUGS GO TO DIE.
HEH. AT LEAST I'M NOT ALONE IN MY MISERY.
THIS WRESTLING THING IS GOING TO BE WORTH IT, RIGHT? I MEAN, I WAS ALMOST CHEWING BUGS SINCE THEY WERE SO DEEP ON HIS DAMN BLOODY SILLS.
OH, IT WILL BE. THE TAPE YESTERDAY WAS GOOD, RIGHT? SEE? SO IT'S ALL GOOD. AND THE CHORES. JUST MAKIN' MONEY.
SO, WE'RE OK. YUP. I LOVE LAWN MOWERIN.' NO WORRIES HERE AT ALL. LOVE IT!
OH, RELAX. THOUGH IT'S NICE TO KNOW WHAT POWER I'VE GOT OVER YOU!
YOU UP FOR TAKING A BREAK?

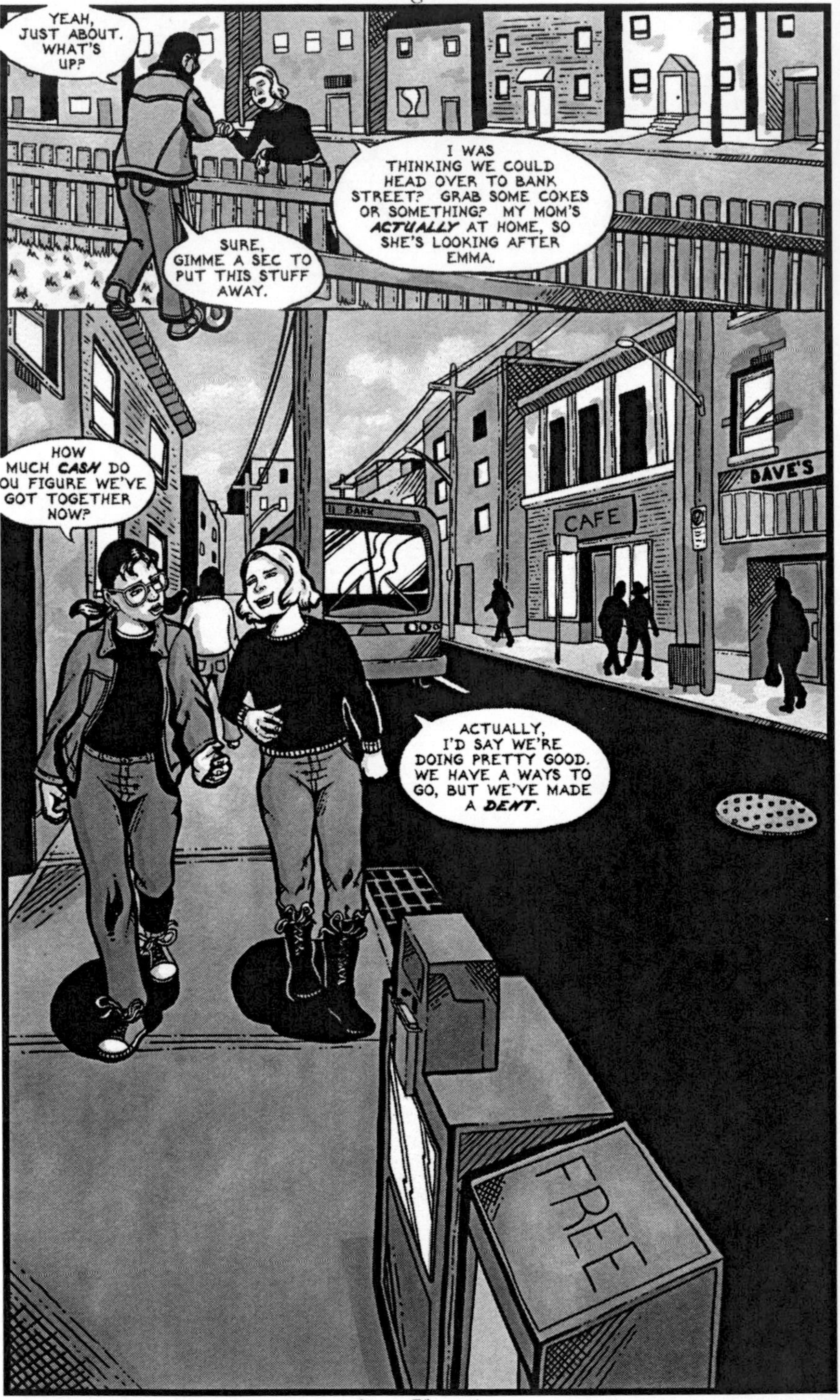
YEAH, JUST ABOUT. WHAT'S UP?
I WAS THINKING WE COULD HEAD OVER TO BANK STREET? GRAB SOME COKES OR SOMETHING? MY MOM'S ACTUALLY AT HOME, SO SHE'S LOOKING AFTER EMMA.
SURE, GIMME A SEC TO PUT THIS STUFF AWAY.
HOW MUCH CASH DO YOU FIGURE WE'VE GOT TOGETHER NOW?
ACTUALLY, I'D SAY WE'RE DOING PRETTY GOOD. WE HAVE A WAYS TO GO, BUT WE'VE MADE A DENT.
CAFE
DAVE'S
FREE

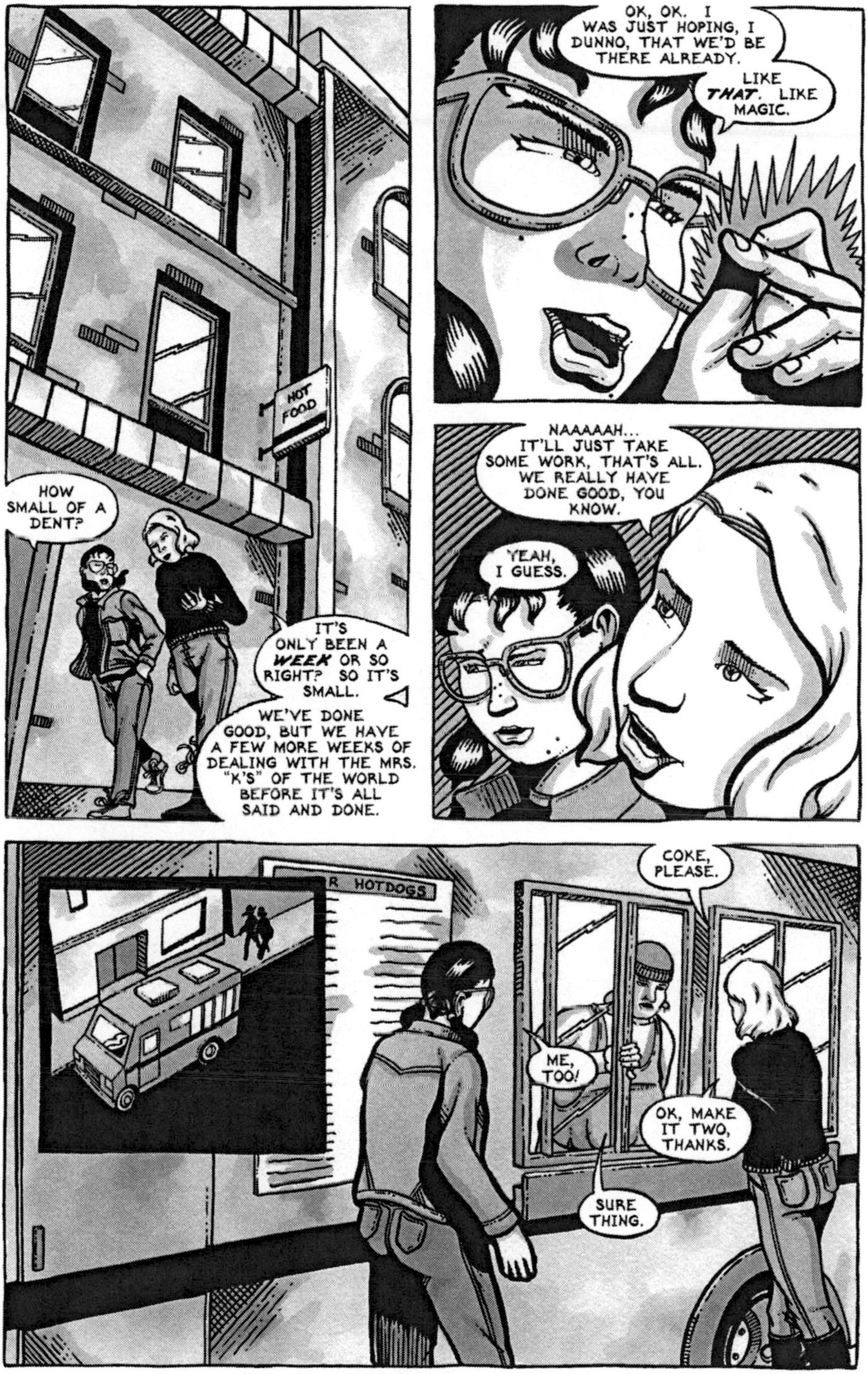
OK, OK. I WAS JUST HOPING, I DUNNO, THAT WE'D BE THERE ALREADY.
LIKE THAT. LIKE MAGIC.
HOT FOOD
HOW SMALL OF A DENT?
IT'S ONLY BEEN A WEEK OR SO RIGHT? SO IT'S SMALL.
WE'VE DONE GOOD, BUT WE HAVE A FEW MORE WEEKS OF DEALING WITH THE MRS. "K'S" OF THE WORLD BEFORE IT'S ALL SAID AND DONE.
NAAAAAH... IT'LL JUST TAKE SOME WORK, THAT'S ALL. WE REALLY HAVE DONE GOOD, YOU KNOW.
YEAH, I GUESS.
HOTDOGS
COKE, PLEASE.
ME, TOO!
OK, MAKE IT TWO, THANKS.
SURE THING.

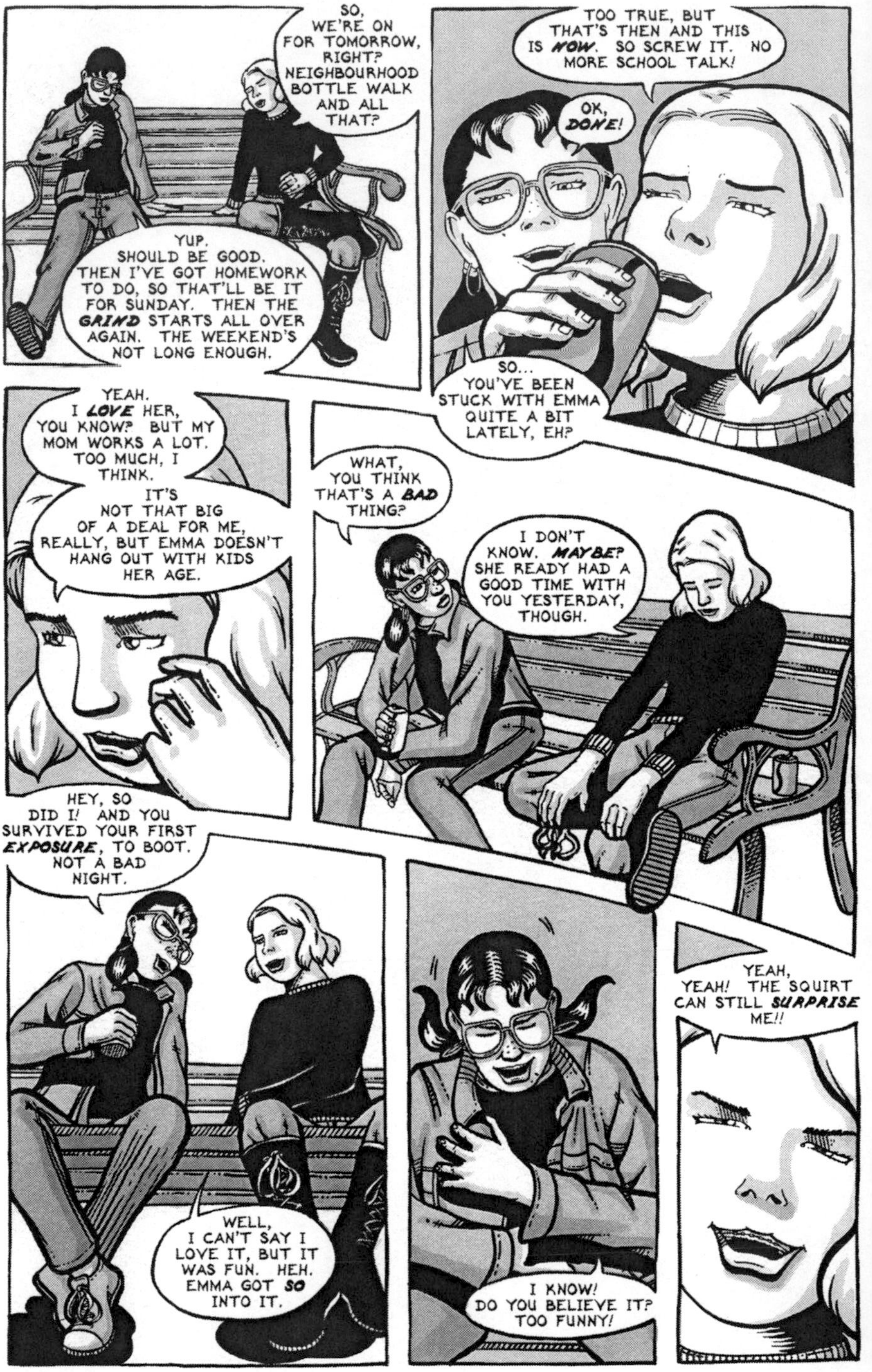
SO, WE'RE ON FOR TOMORROW, RIGHT? NEIGHBOURHOOD BOTTLE WALK AND ALL THAT?
YUP. SHOULD BE GOOD. THEN I'VE GOT HOMEWORK TO DO, SO THAT'LL BE IT FOR SUNDAY. THEN THE GRIND STARTS ALL OVER AGAIN. THE WEEKEND'S NOT LONG ENOUGH.
TOO TRUE, BUT THAT'S THEN AND THIS IS NOW. SO SCREW IT. NO MORE SCHOOL TALK!
OK, DONE!
SO... YOU'VE BEEN STUCK WITH EMMA QUITE A BIT LATELY, EH?
YEAH. I LOVE HER, YOU KNOW? BUT MY MOM WORKS A LOT. TOO MUCH, I THINK.
IT'S NOT THAT BIG OF A DEAL FOR ME, REALLY, BUT EMMA DOESN'T HANG OUT WITH KIDS HER AGE.
WHAT, YOU THINK THAT'S A BAD THING?
I DON'T KNOW. MAYBE? SHE READY HAD A GOOD TIME WITH YOU YESTERDAY, THOUGH.
HEY, SO DID I! AND YOU SURVIVED YOUR FIRST EXPOSURE, TO BOOT. NOT A BAD NIGHT.
WELL, I CAN'T SAY I LOVE IT, BUT IT WAS FUN. HEH. EMMA GOT SO INTO IT.
I KNOW! DO YOU BELIEVE IT? TOO FUNNY!
YEAH, YEAH! THE SQUIRT CAN STILL SURPRISE ME!!

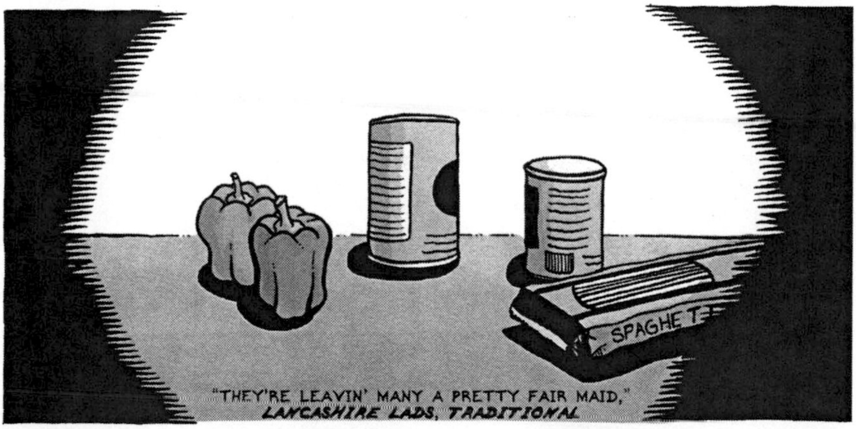
SPAGHET
"THEY'RE LEAVIN' MANY A PRETTY FAIR MAID,"
LANCASHIRE LADS, TRADITIONAL

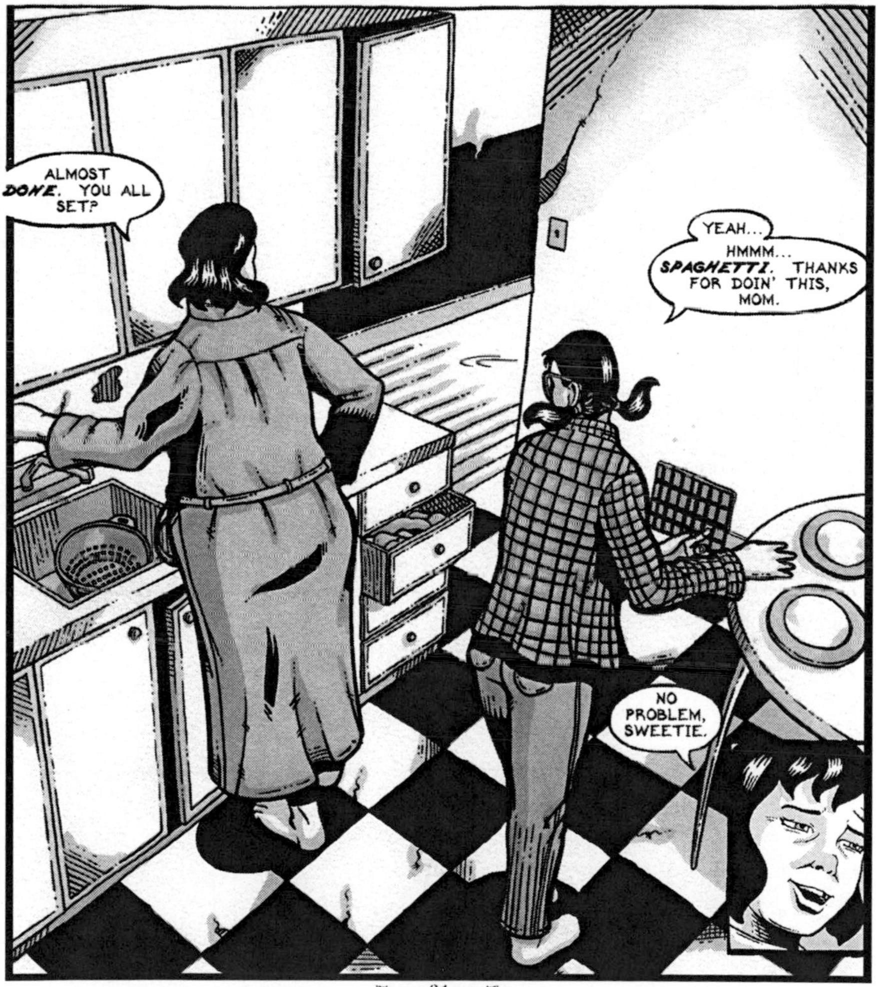
ALMOST DONE. YOU ALL SET?
YEAH...
HMMM... SPAGHETTI. THANKS FOR DOIN' THIS, MOM.
NO PROBLEM, SWEETIE.

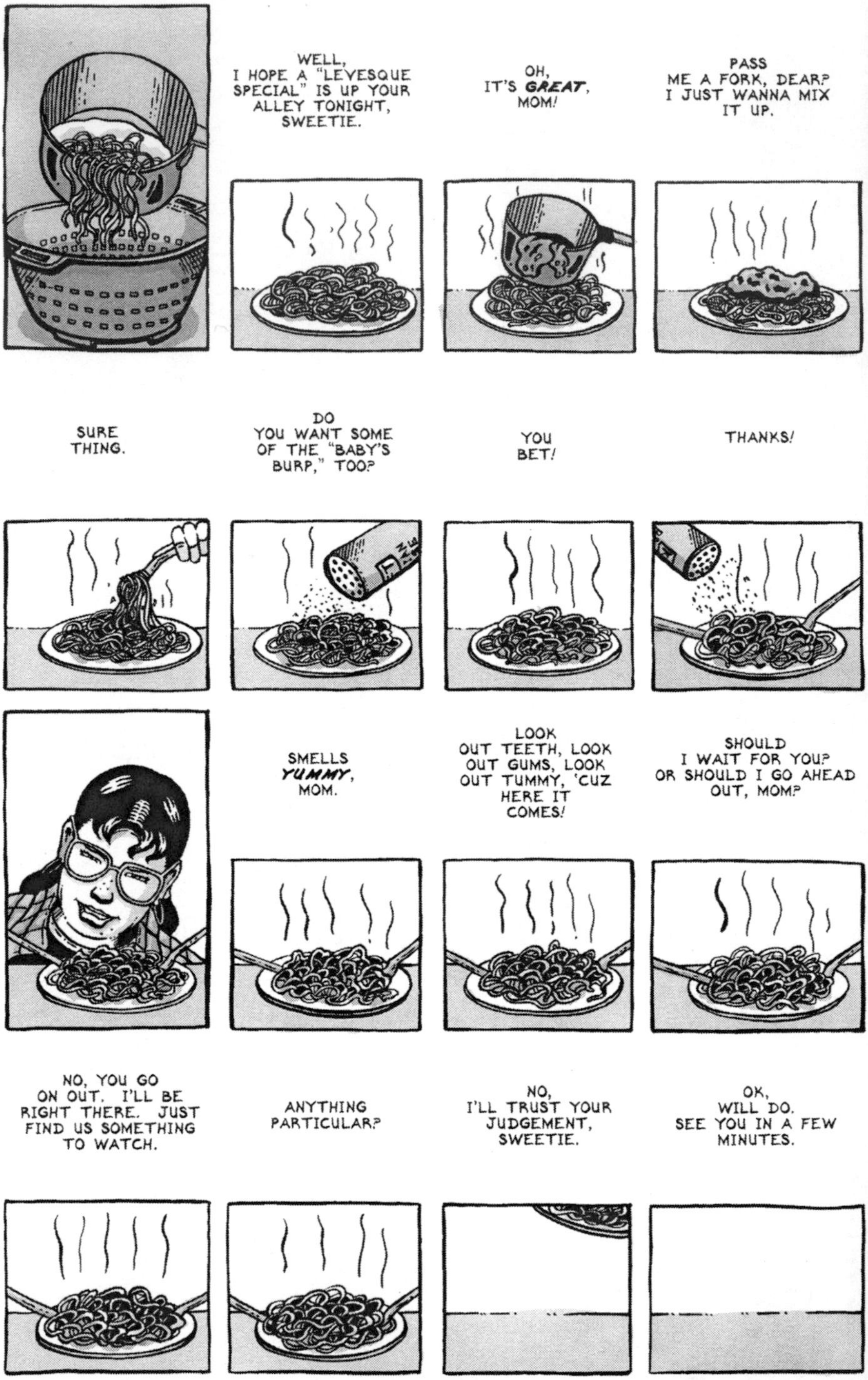
WELL, I HOPE A "LEVESQUE SPECIAL" IS UP YOUR ALLEY TONIGHT, SWEETIE.
OH, IT'S GREAT, MOM!
PASS ME A FORK, DEAR? I JUST WANNA MIX IT UP.
SURE THING.
DO YOU WANT SOME OF THE "BABY'S BURP," TOO?
YOU BET!
THANKS!
SMELLS YUMMY, MOM.
LOOK OUT TEETH, LOOK OUT GUMS, LOOK OUT TUMMY, 'CUZ HERE IT COMES!
SHOULD I WAIT FOR YOU? OR SHOULD I GO AHEAD OUT, MOM?
NO, YOU GO ON OUT. I'LL BE RIGHT THERE. JUST FIND US SOMETHING TO WATCH.
ANYTHING PARTICULAR?
NO, I'LL TRUST YOUR JUDGEMENT, SWEETIE.
OK, WILL DO. SEE YOU IN A FEW MINUTES.

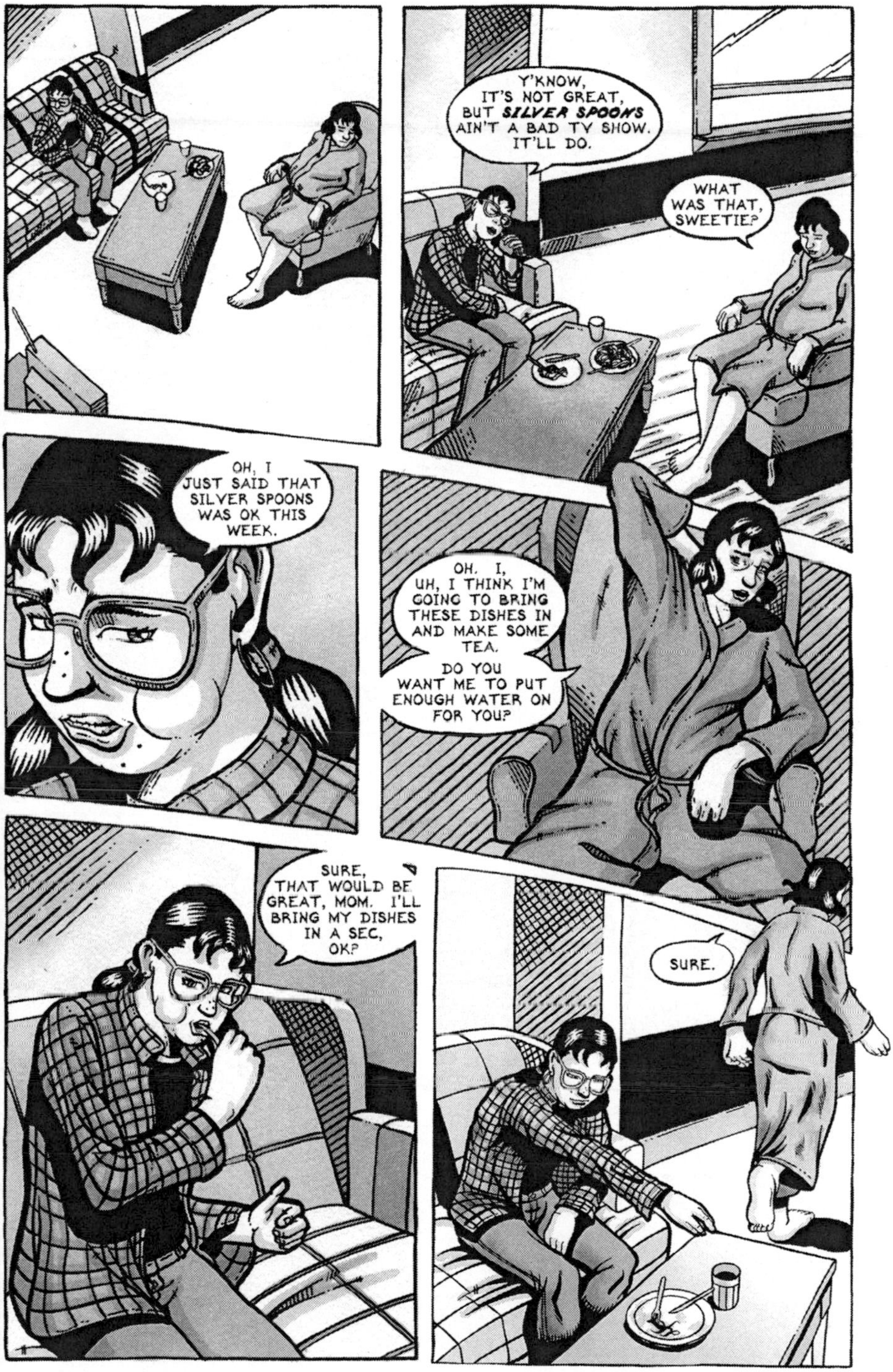
Y'KNOW, IT'S NOT GREAT, BUT SILVER SPOONS AIN'T A BAD TV SHOW. IT'LL DO.
WHAT WAS THAT, SWEETIE?
OH, I JUST SAID THAT SILVER SPOONS WAS OK THIS WEEK.
OH. I, UH, I THINK I'M GOING TO BRING THESE DISHES IN AND MAKE SOME TEA.
DO YOU WANT ME TO PUT ENOUGH WATER ON FOR YOU?
SURE, THAT WOULD BE GREAT, MOM. I'LL BRING MY DISHES IN A SEC, OK?
SURE.

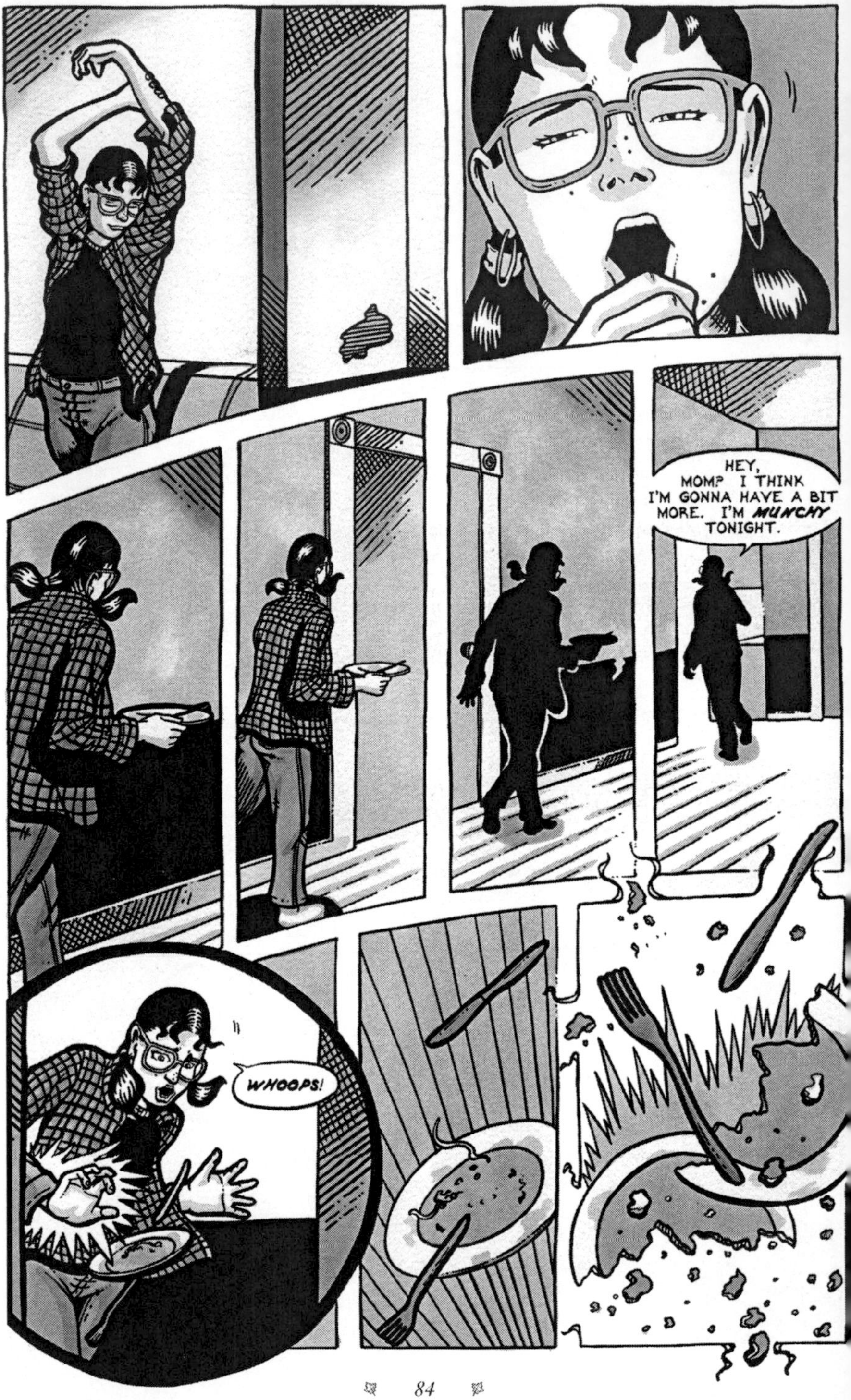
HEY, MOM? I THINK I'M GONNA HAVE A BIT MORE. I'M MUNCHY TONIGHT.
WHOOPS!

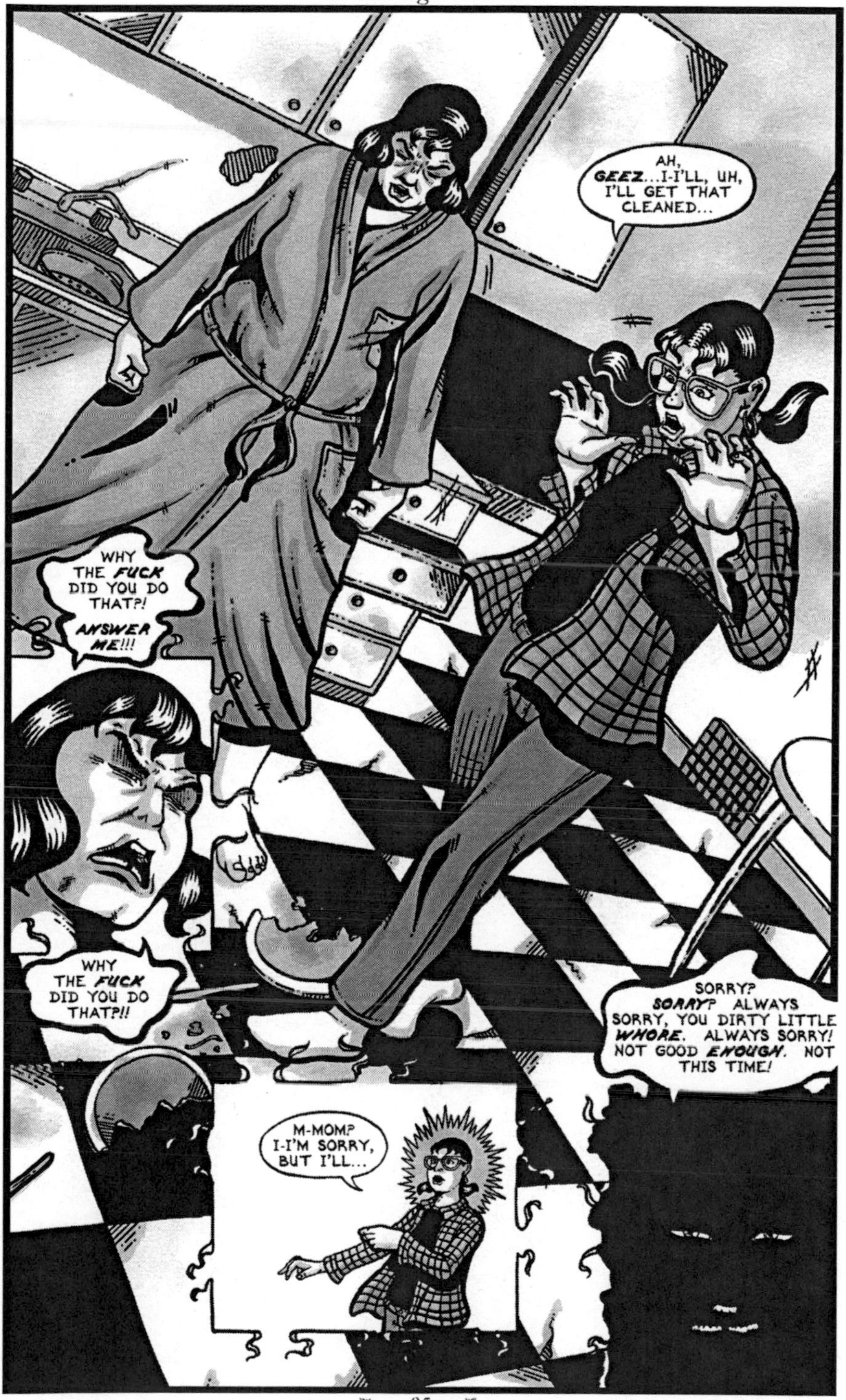
AH, GEEZ...I-I'LL, UH, I'LL GET THAT CLEANED...
WHY THE FUCK DID YOU DO THAT?!
ANSWER ME!!!
WHY THE FUCK DID YOU DO THAT?!!
SORRY? SORRY? ALWAYS SORRY, YOU DIRTY LITTLE WHORE. ALWAYS SORRY! NOT GOOD ENOUGH. NOT THIS TIME!
M-MOM? I-I'M SORRY, BUT I'LL...

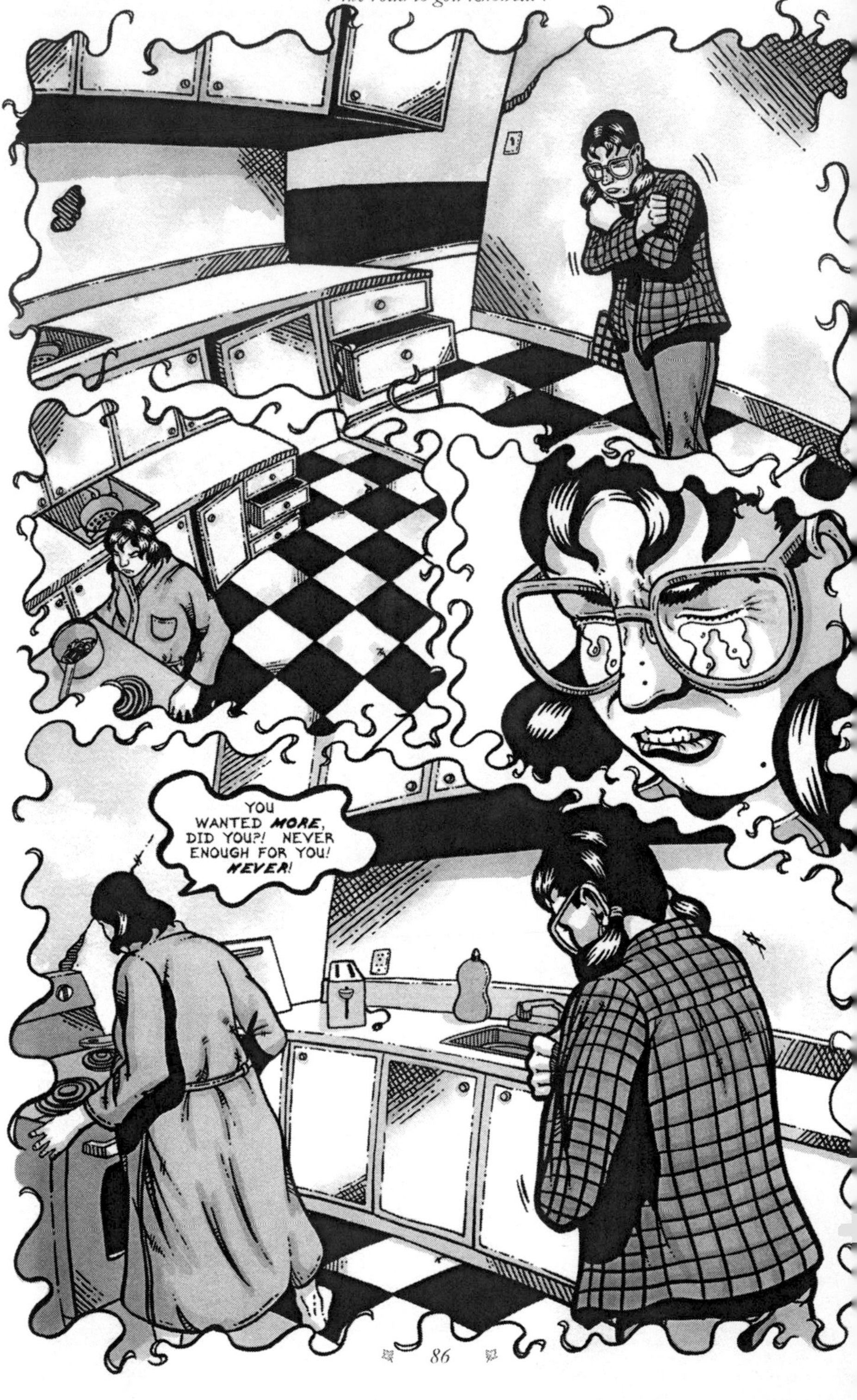
YOU WANTED **MORE**, DID YOU?! NEVER ENOUGH FOR YOU! **NEVER**!

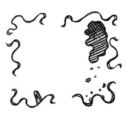

I'MSORRYI'MSORRYI'M
SORRYI'MSORRYI'MSORRY
I'MSORRYI'MSORRYI'M
SORRYI'MSORRYI'MSORRYI'M
SORRYI'MSORRYI'MSORRYI'M
SORRYI'MSORRYI'MSORRY

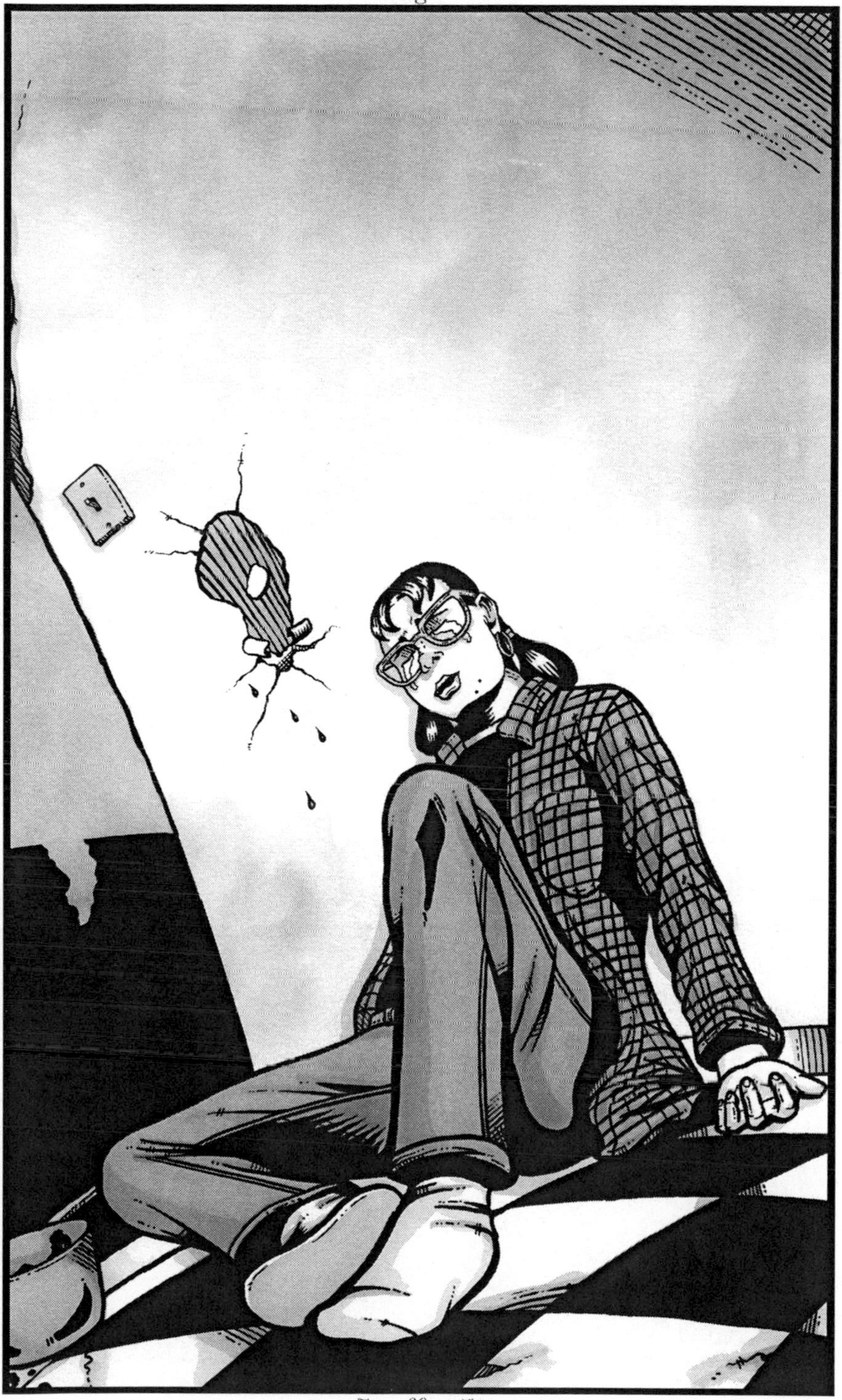

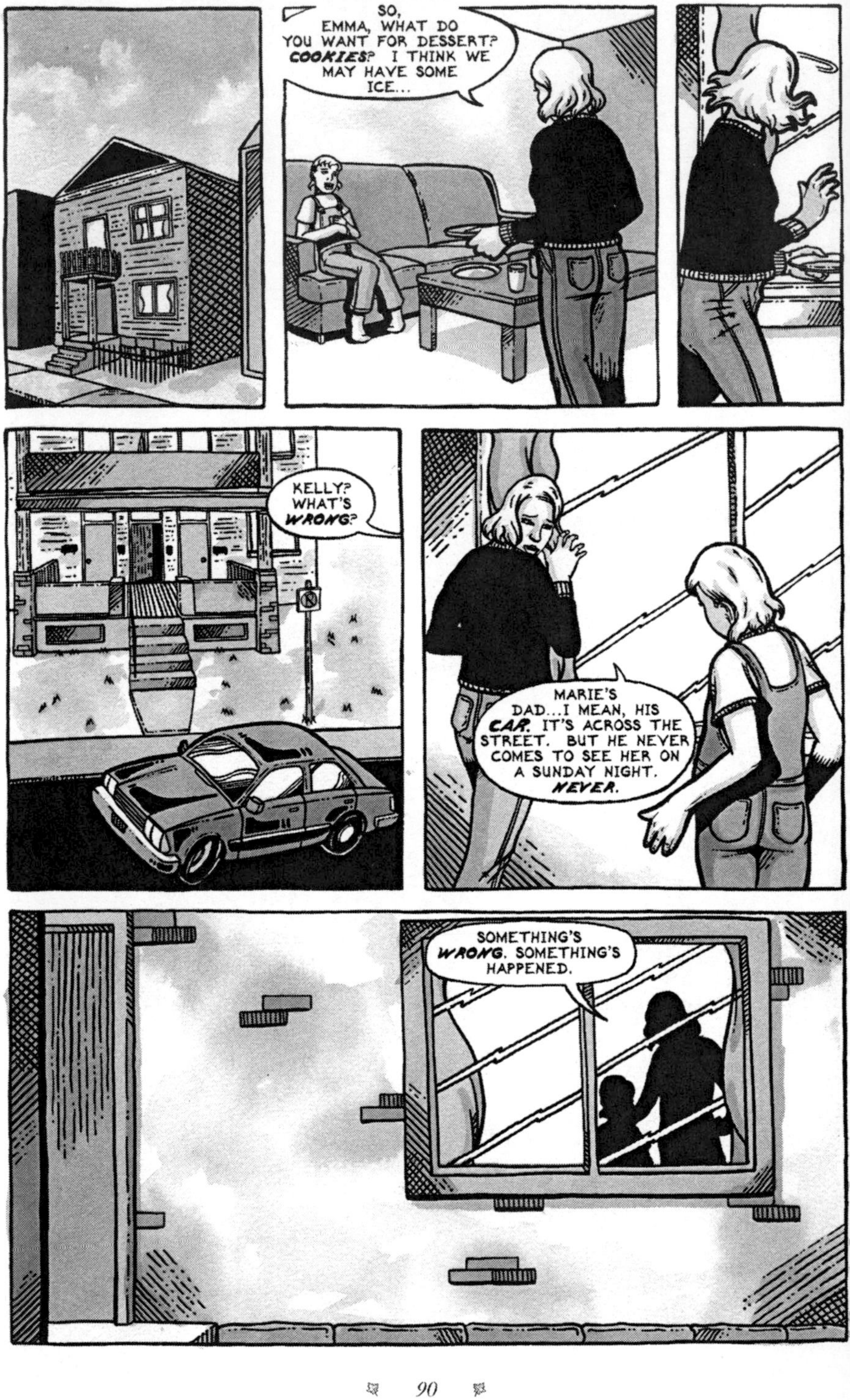
SO, EMMA, WHAT DO YOU WANT FOR DESSERT? COOKIES? I THINK WE MAY HAVE SOME ICE...
KELLY? WHAT'S WRONG?
MARIE'S DAD...I MEAN, HIS CAR. IT'S ACROSS THE STREET. BUT HE NEVER COMES TO SEE HER ON A SUNDAY NIGHT. NEVER.
SOMETHING'S WRONG. SOMETHING'S HAPPENED.

"OH, SHE'S LEAVING."
"WITHOUT HER MOM."
"OH, NO. NOT AGAIN."

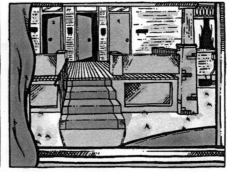

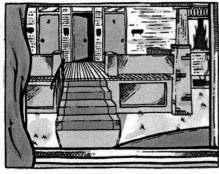

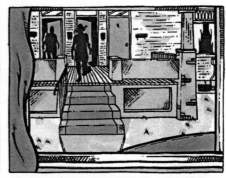

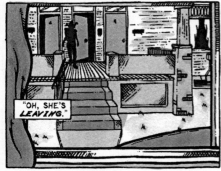

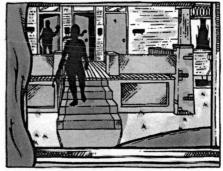

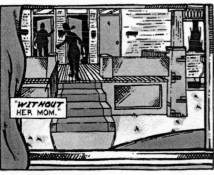

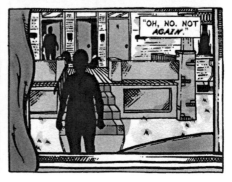

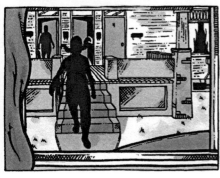

POOR MARIE...

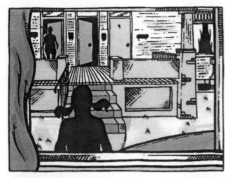

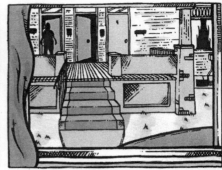

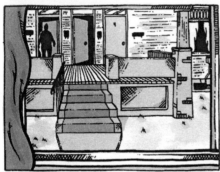

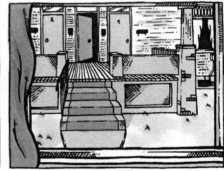

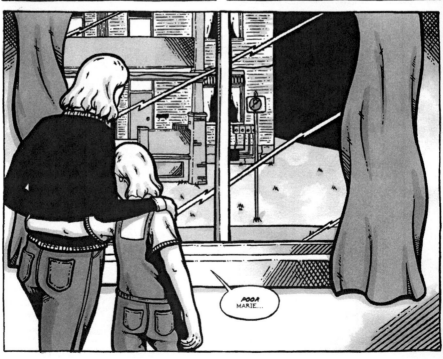

"AND THE DAYLIGHT'S SELDOM SEEN,"
GREENLAND WHALE FISHERIES, TRADITIONAL

"STAY *WITH* ME, GUYS..."

$\left(\frac{1}{8} \div \frac{3}{5}\right)$

THERE'LL BE A *TEST* ON THIS!

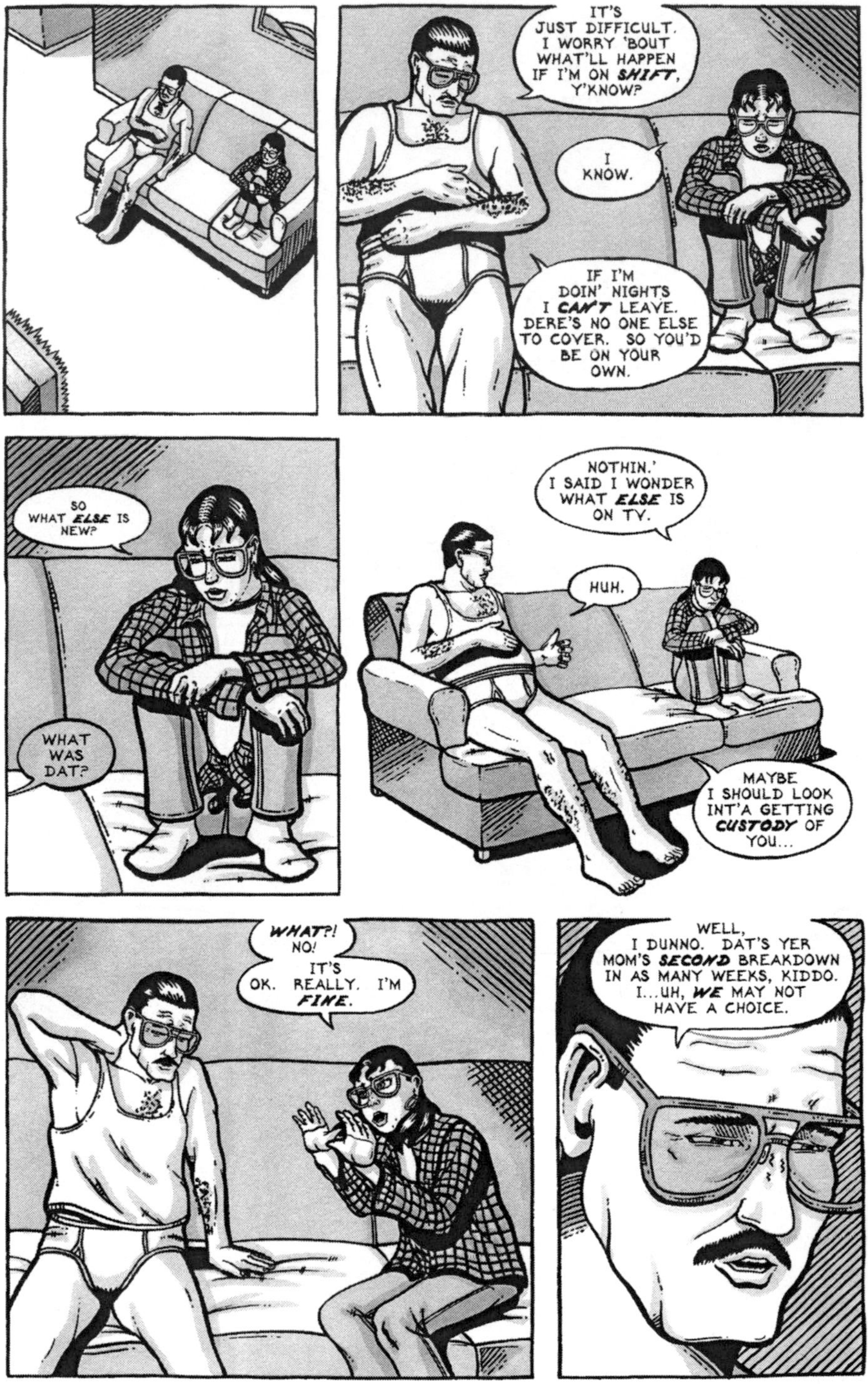
IT'S JUST DIFFICULT. I WORRY 'BOUT WHAT'LL HAPPEN IF I'M ON SHIFT, Y'KNOW?
I KNOW.
IF I'M DOIN' NIGHTS I CAN'T LEAVE. DERE'S NO ONE ELSE TO COVER. SO YOU'D BE ON YOUR OWN.
SO WHAT ELSE IS NEW?
WHAT WAS DAT?
NOTHIN.' I SAID I WONDER WHAT ELSE IS ON TV.
HUH.
MAYBE I SHOULD LOOK INT'A GETTING CUSTODY OF YOU...
WHAT?! NO!
IT'S OK. REALLY. I'M FINE.
WELL, I DUNNO. DAT'S YER MOM'S SECOND BREAKDOWN IN AS MANY WEEKS, KIDDO. I...UH, WE MAY NOT HAVE A CHOICE.

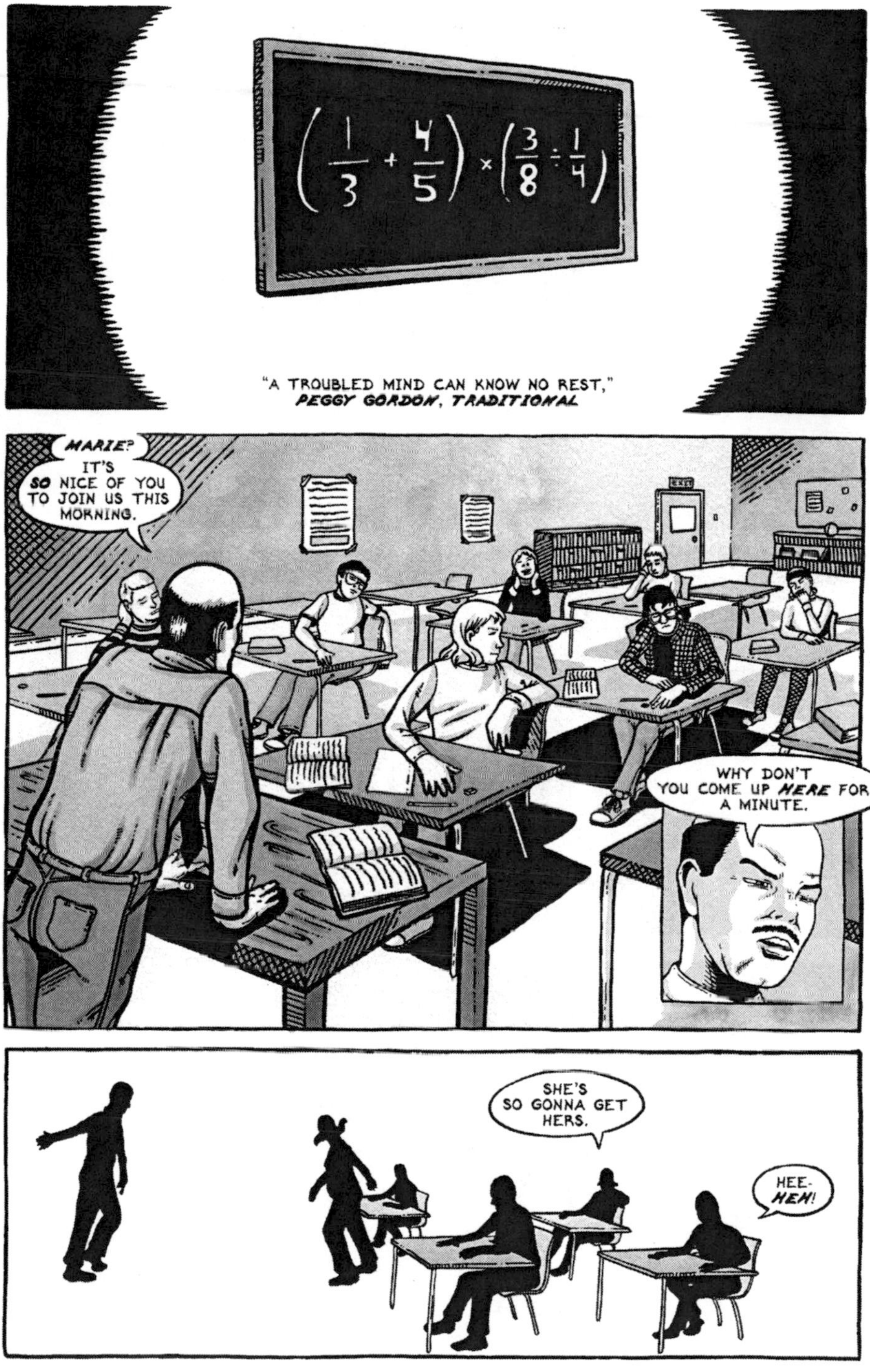
$\left(\frac{1}{3}+\frac{4}{5}\right)\times\left(\frac{3}{8}\div\frac{1}{4}\right)$
"A TROUBLED MIND CAN KNOW NO REST,"
PEGGY GORDON, TRADITIONAL
MARIE? IT'S SO NICE OF YOU TO JOIN US THIS MORNING.
WHY DON'T YOU COME UP HERE FOR A MINUTE.
SHE'S SO GONNA GET HERS.
HEE-HEH!

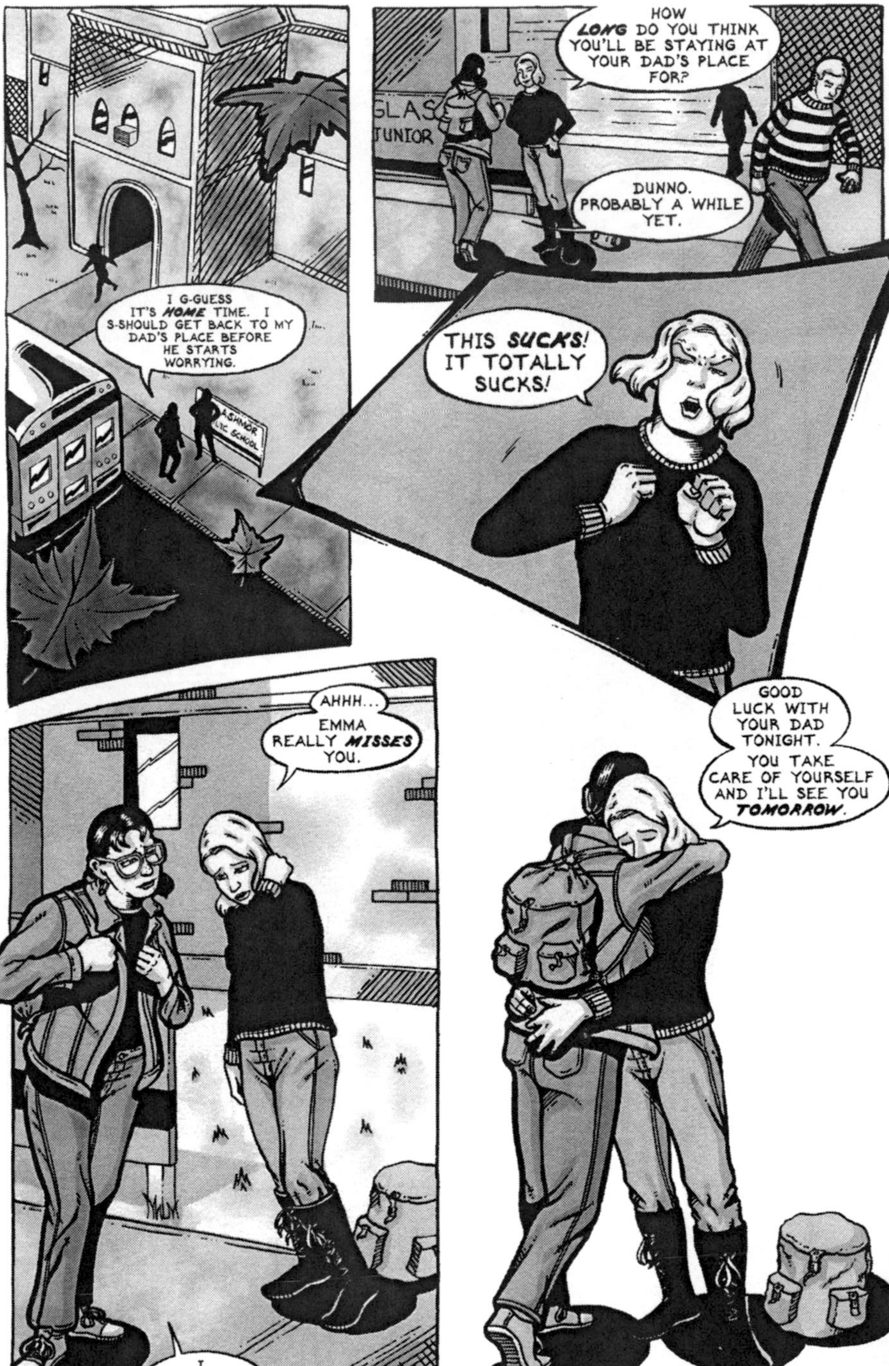
I G-GUESS IT'S HOME TIME. I S-SHOULD GET BACK TO MY DAD'S PLACE BEFORE HE STARTS WORRYING.
HOW LONG DO YOU THINK YOU'LL BE STAYING AT YOUR DAD'S PLACE FOR?
DUNNO. PROBABLY A WHILE YET.
THIS SUCKS! IT TOTALLY SUCKS!
AHHH... EMMA REALLY MISSES YOU.
I MISS HER, TOO.
GOOD LUCK WITH YOUR DAD TONIGHT.
YOU TAKE CARE OF YOURSELF AND I'LL SEE YOU TOMORROW.

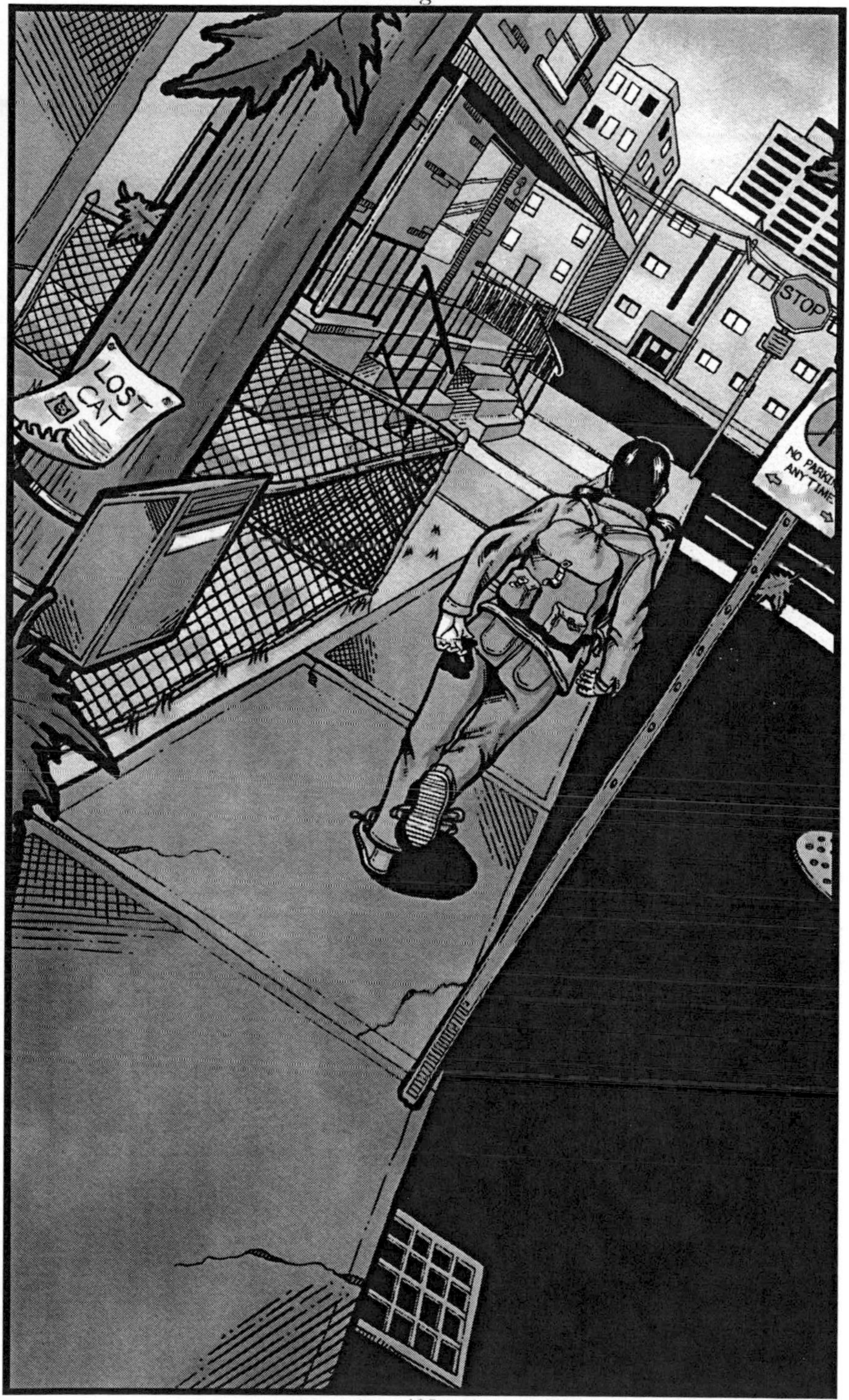
LOST
CAT
STOP
NO PARKI
ANYTIME

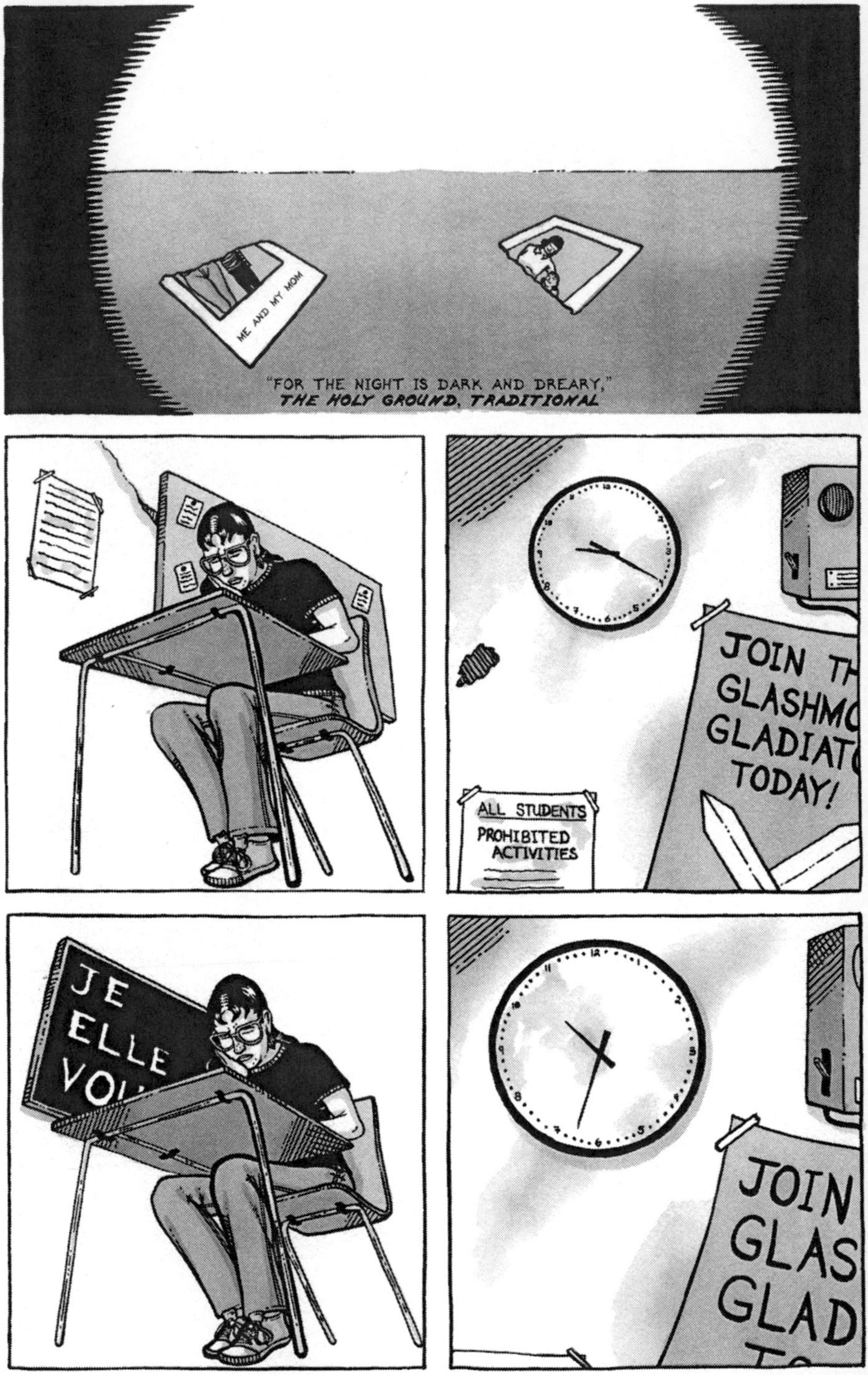
ME AND MY MOM
"FOR THE NIGHT IS DARK AND DREARY,"
THE HOLY GROUND, TRADITIONAL
JOIN TH
GLASHMO
GLADIATO
TODAY!
ALL STUDENTS
PROHIBITED
ACTIVITIES
JE
ELLE
VOU
JOIN
GLAS
GLAD

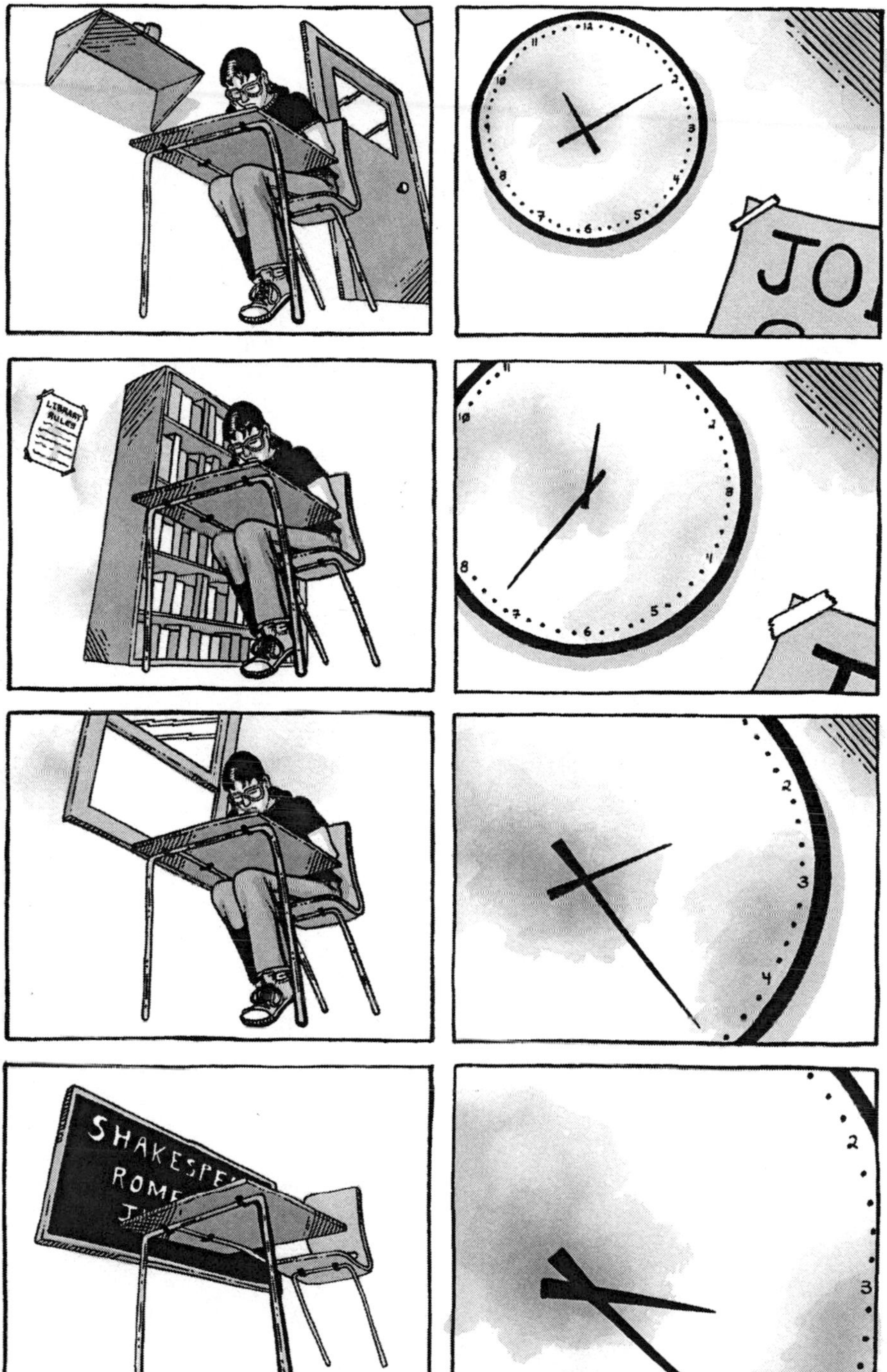
JO
LIBRARY RULES
SHAKESPE
ROME

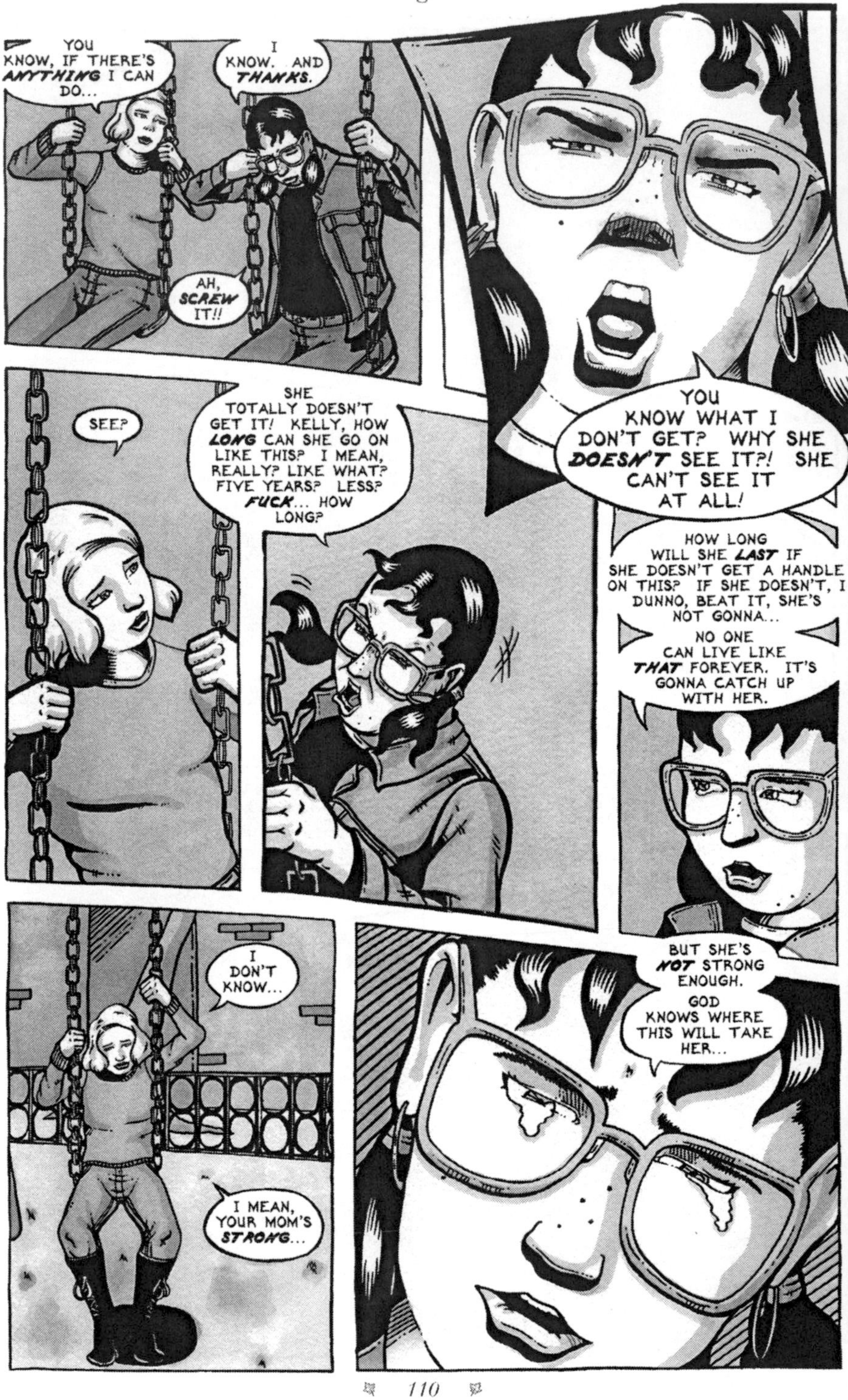
YOU KNOW, IF THERE'S ANYTHING I CAN DO...
I KNOW. AND THANKS.
AH, SCREW IT!!
YOU KNOW WHAT I DON'T GET? WHY SHE DOESN'T SEE IT?! SHE CAN'T SEE IT AT ALL!
SEE?
SHE TOTALLY DOESN'T GET IT! KELLY, HOW LONG CAN SHE GO ON LIKE THIS? I MEAN, REALLY? LIKE WHAT? FIVE YEARS? LESS? FUCK... HOW LONG?
HOW LONG WILL SHE LAST IF SHE DOESN'T GET A HANDLE ON THIS? IF SHE DOESN'T, I DUNNO, BEAT IT, SHE'S NOT GONNA...
NO ONE CAN LIVE LIKE THAT FOREVER. IT'S GONNA CATCH UP WITH HER.
I DON'T KNOW...
I MEAN, YOUR MOM'S STRONG...
BUT SHE'S NOT STRONG ENOUGH.
GOD KNOWS WHERE THIS WILL TAKE HER...

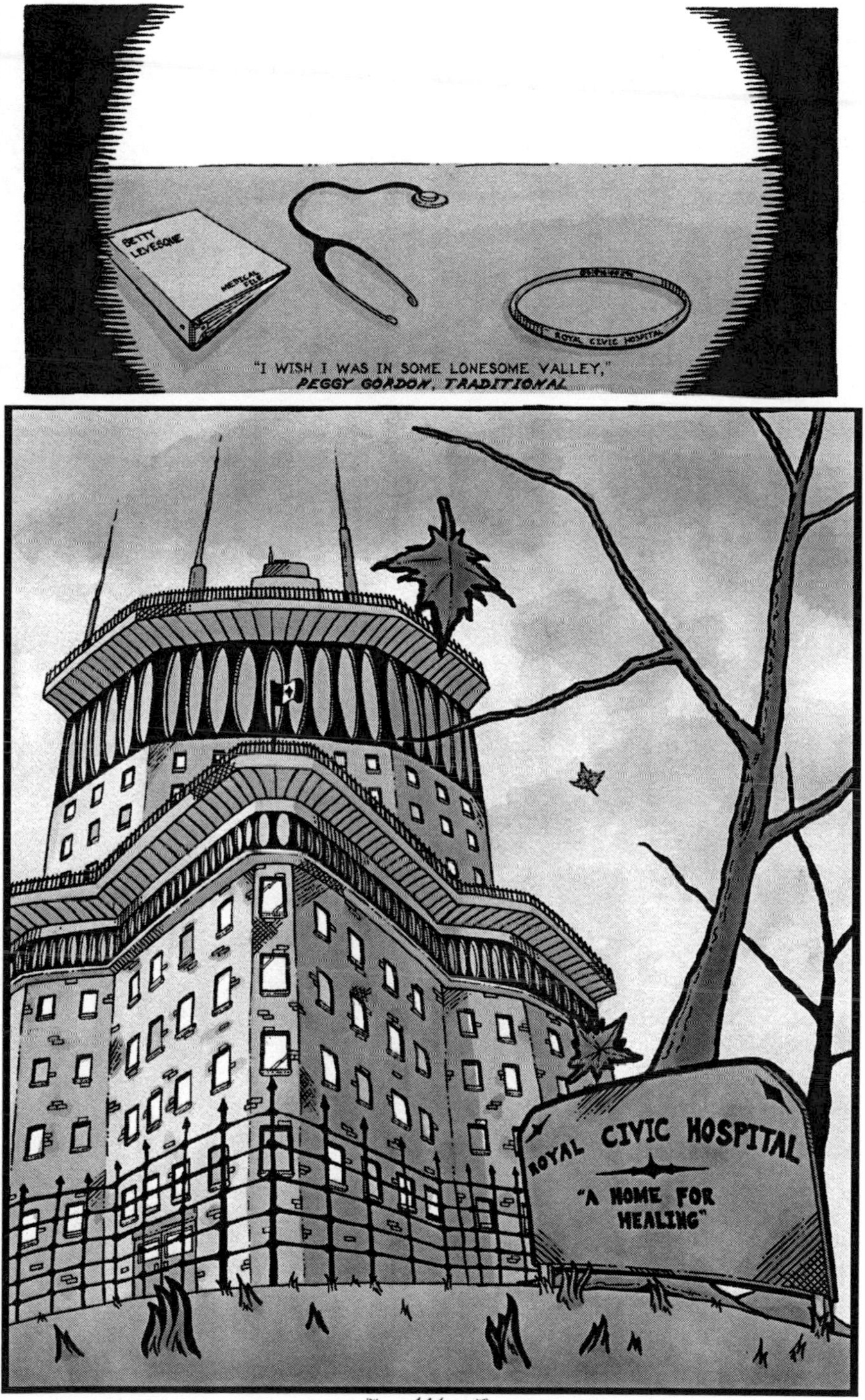
BETTY LEVESQUE
MEDICAL FILE
ROYAL CIVIC HOSPITAL
"I WISH I WAS IN SOME LONESOME VALLEY,"
PEGGY GORDON, TRADITIONAL
ROYAL CIVIC HOSPITAL
"A HOME FOR HEALING"

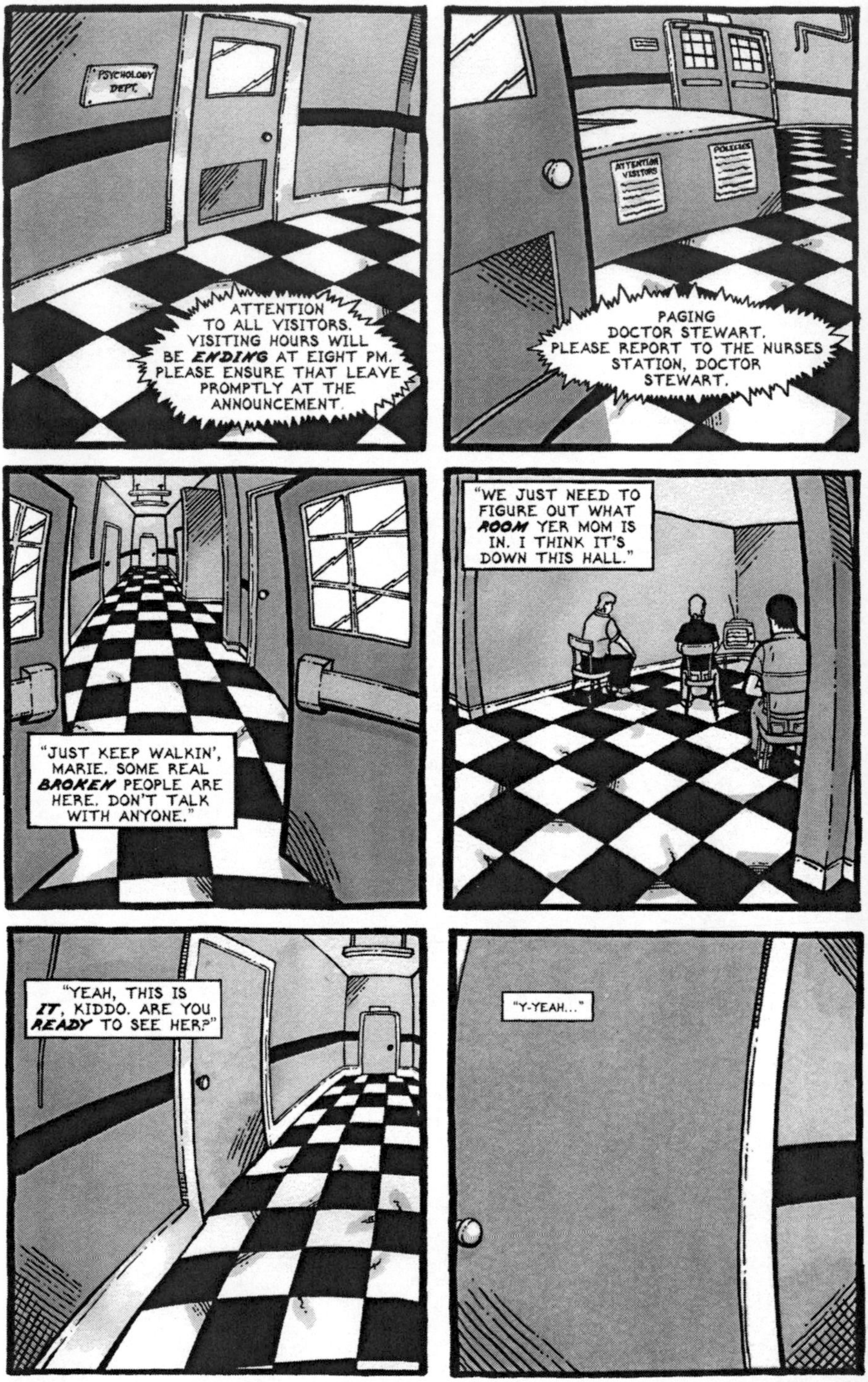
PSYCHOLOGY DEPT.
ATTENTION TO ALL VISITORS. VISITING HOURS WILL BE ENDING AT EIGHT PM. PLEASE ENSURE THAT LEAVE PROMPTLY AT THE ANNOUNCEMENT.
ATTENTION VISITORS
POLICIES
PAGING DOCTOR STEWART. PLEASE REPORT TO THE NURSES STATION, DOCTOR STEWART.
"JUST KEEP WALKIN', MARIE. SOME REAL BROKEN PEOPLE ARE HERE. DON'T TALK WITH ANYONE."
"WE JUST NEED TO FIGURE OUT WHAT ROOM YER MOM IS IN. I THINK IT'S DOWN THIS HALL."
"YEAH, THIS IS IT, KIDDO. ARE YOU READY TO SEE HER?"
"Y-YEAH..."

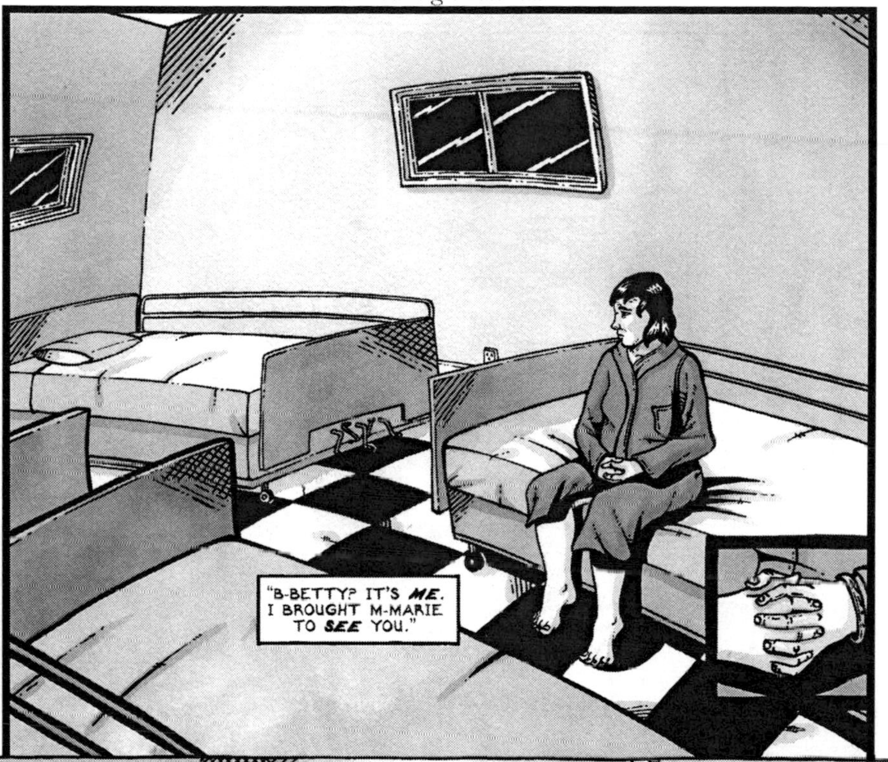
"B-BETTY? IT'S ME. I BROUGHT M-MARIE TO SEE YOU."

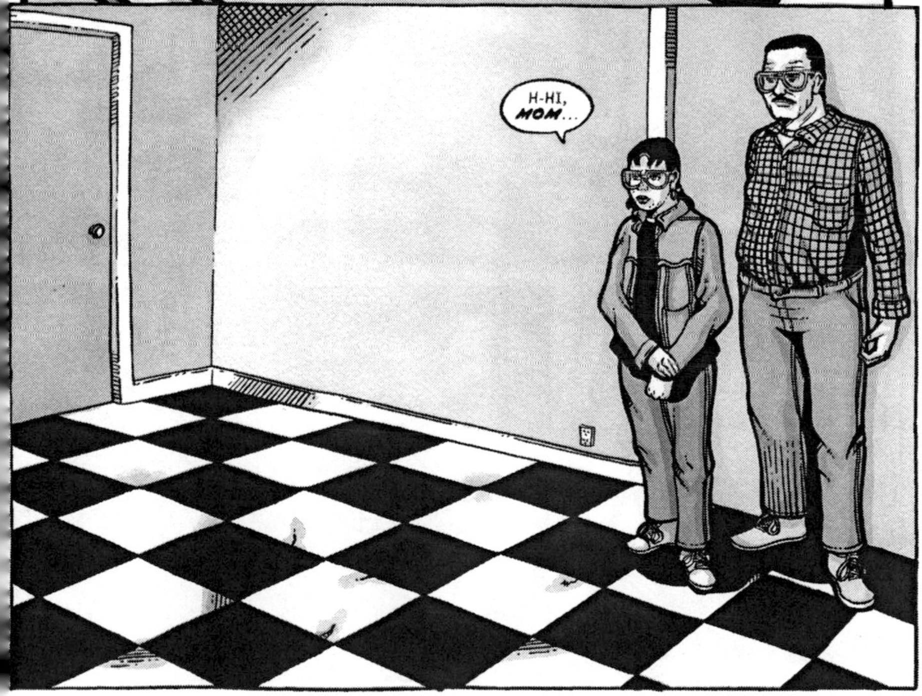
H-HI, MOM...

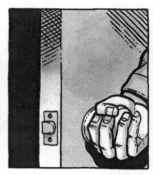

OH, H-HI, SWEETIE.

Y-YOU PROBABLY WANNA *TALK* WITH YER MOM, EH? I'LL, AH, I'LL JUST GO GET A DRINK MYSELF.

I'LL BE IN THE HALL WHEN YER *DONE*, KIDDO.

M-MOM, I...I...

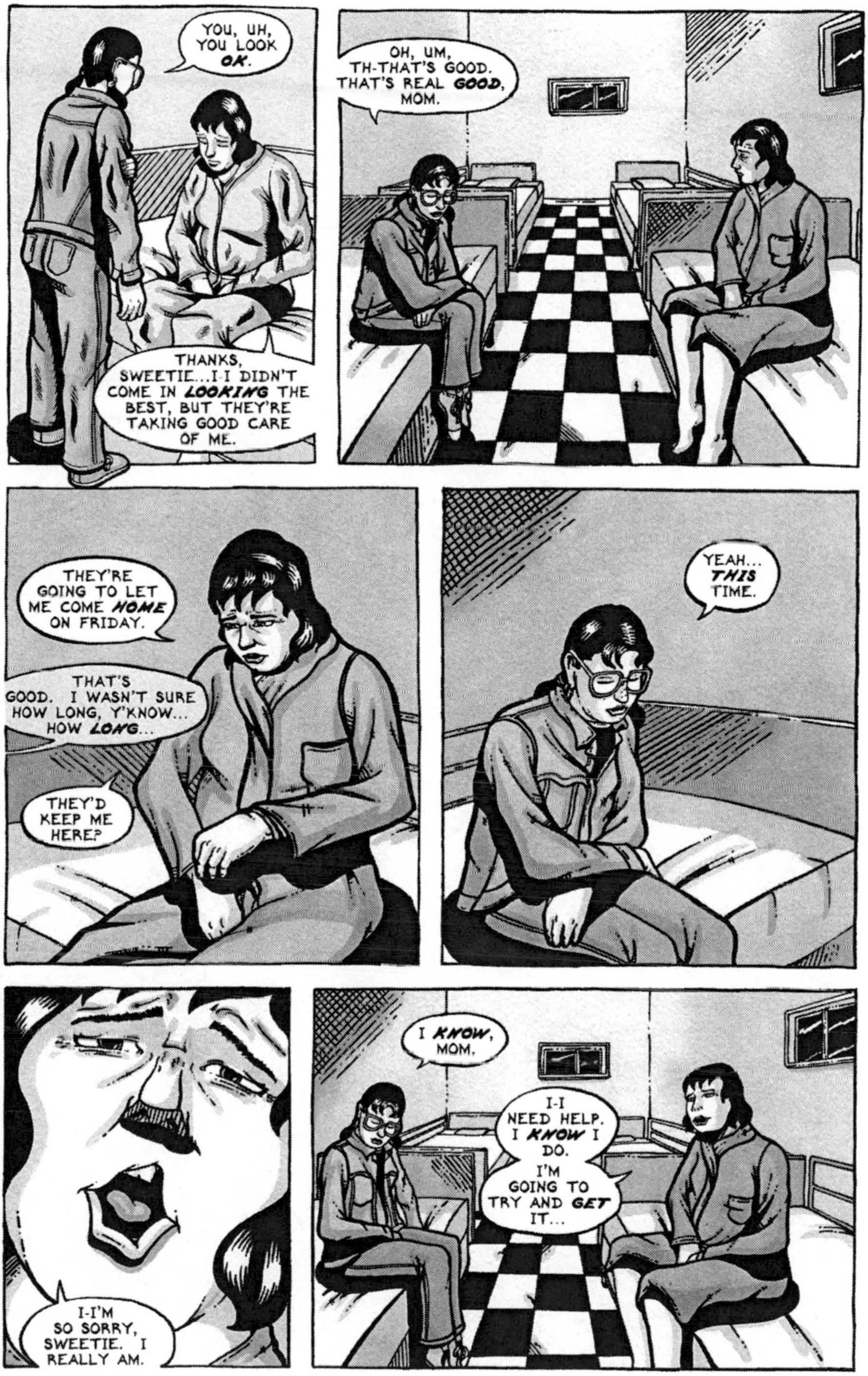
YOU, UH, YOU LOOK OK.
THANKS, SWEETIE...I-I DIDN'T COME IN LOOKING THE BEST, BUT THEY'RE TAKING GOOD CARE OF ME.
OH, UM, TH-THAT'S GOOD. THAT'S REAL GOOD, MOM.
THEY'RE GOING TO LET ME COME HOME ON FRIDAY.
THAT'S GOOD. I WASN'T SURE HOW LONG, Y'KNOW... HOW LONG...
THEY'D KEEP ME HERE?
YEAH... THIS TIME.
I-I'M SO SORRY, SWEETIE. I REALLY AM.
I KNOW, MOM.
I-I NEED HELP. I KNOW I DO.
I'M GOING TO TRY AND GET IT...

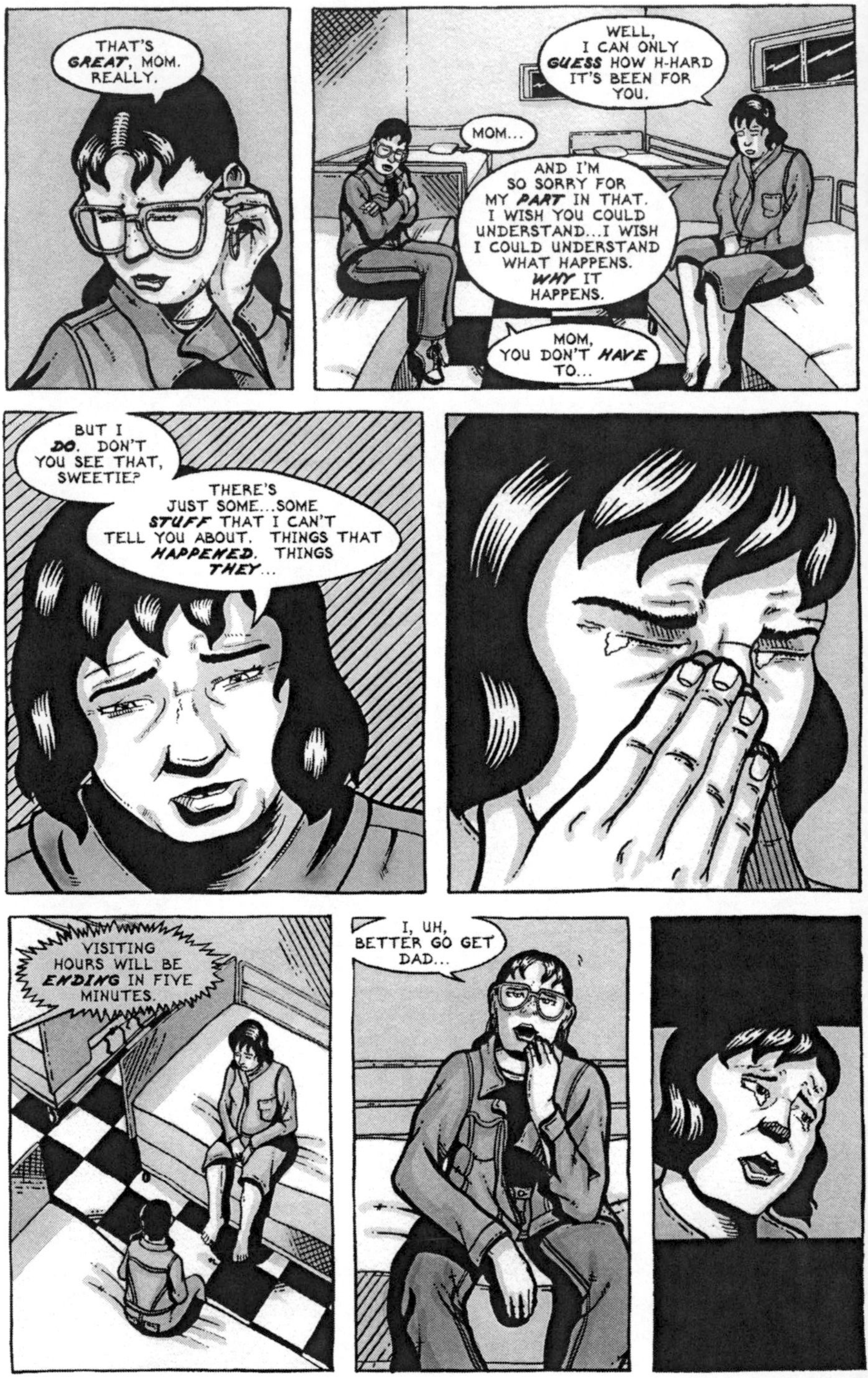
THAT'S GREAT, MOM. REALLY.
WELL, I CAN ONLY GUESS HOW H-HARD IT'S BEEN FOR YOU.
MOM...
AND I'M SO SORRY FOR MY PART IN THAT. I WISH YOU COULD UNDERSTAND...I WISH I COULD UNDERSTAND WHAT HAPPENS. WHY IT HAPPENS.
MOM, YOU DON'T HAVE TO...
BUT I DO. DON'T YOU SEE THAT, SWEETIE?
THERE'S JUST SOME...SOME STUFF THAT I CAN'T TELL YOU ABOUT. THINGS THAT HAPPENED. THINGS THEY...
VISITING HOURS WILL BE ENDING IN FIVE MINUTES.
I, UH, BETTER GO GET DAD...

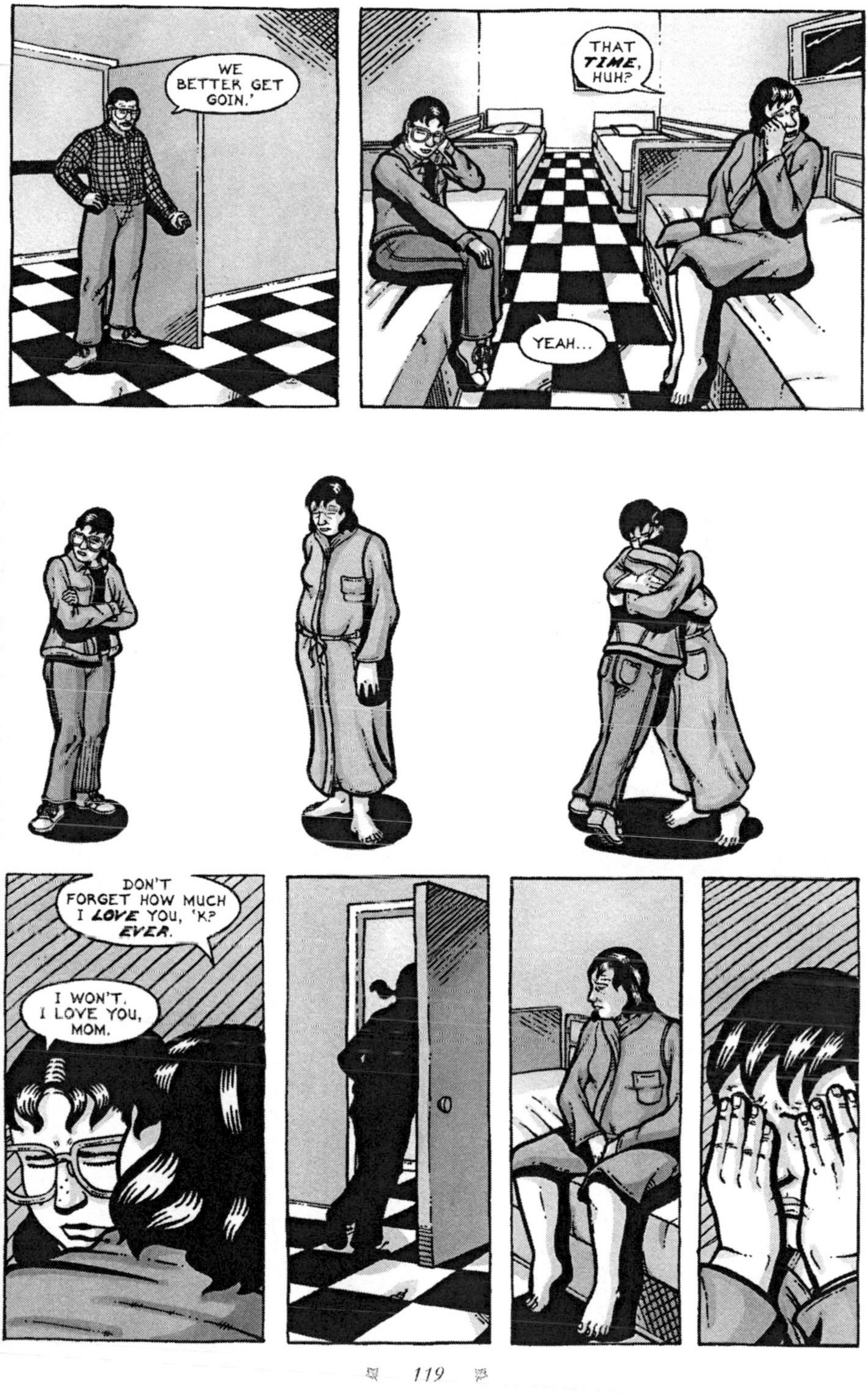
WE BETTER GET GOIN.'
THAT TIME, HUH?
YEAH...
DON'T FORGET HOW MUCH I LOVE YOU, 'K? EVER.
I WON'T. I LOVE YOU, MOM.

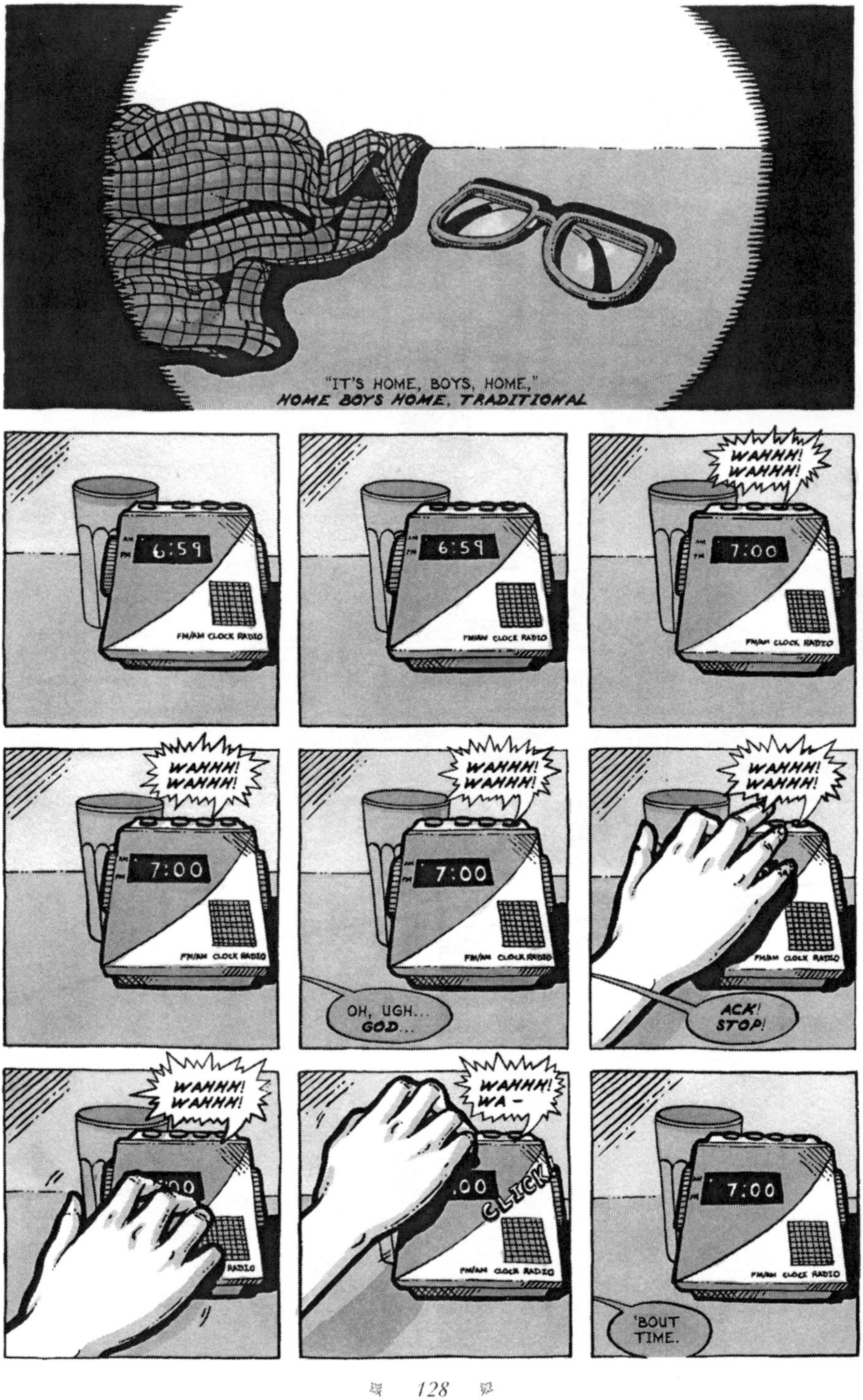
"IT'S HOME, BOYS, HOME,"
HOME BOYS HOME, TRADITIONAL
6:59
FM/AM CLOCK RADIO
6:59
FM/AM CLOCK RADIO
WAHHH! WAHHH!
7:00
FM/AM CLOCK RADIO
WAHHH! WAHHH!
7:00
FM/AM CLOCK RADIO
WAHHH! WAHHH!
7:00
FM/AM CLOCK RADIO
OH, UGH... GOD...
WAHHH! WAHHH!
FM/AM CLOCK RADIO
ACK! STOP!
WAHHH! WAHHH!
RADIO
WAHHH! WA–
CLICK!
FM/AM CLOCK RADIO
7:00
FM/AM CLOCK RADIO
'BOUT TIME.

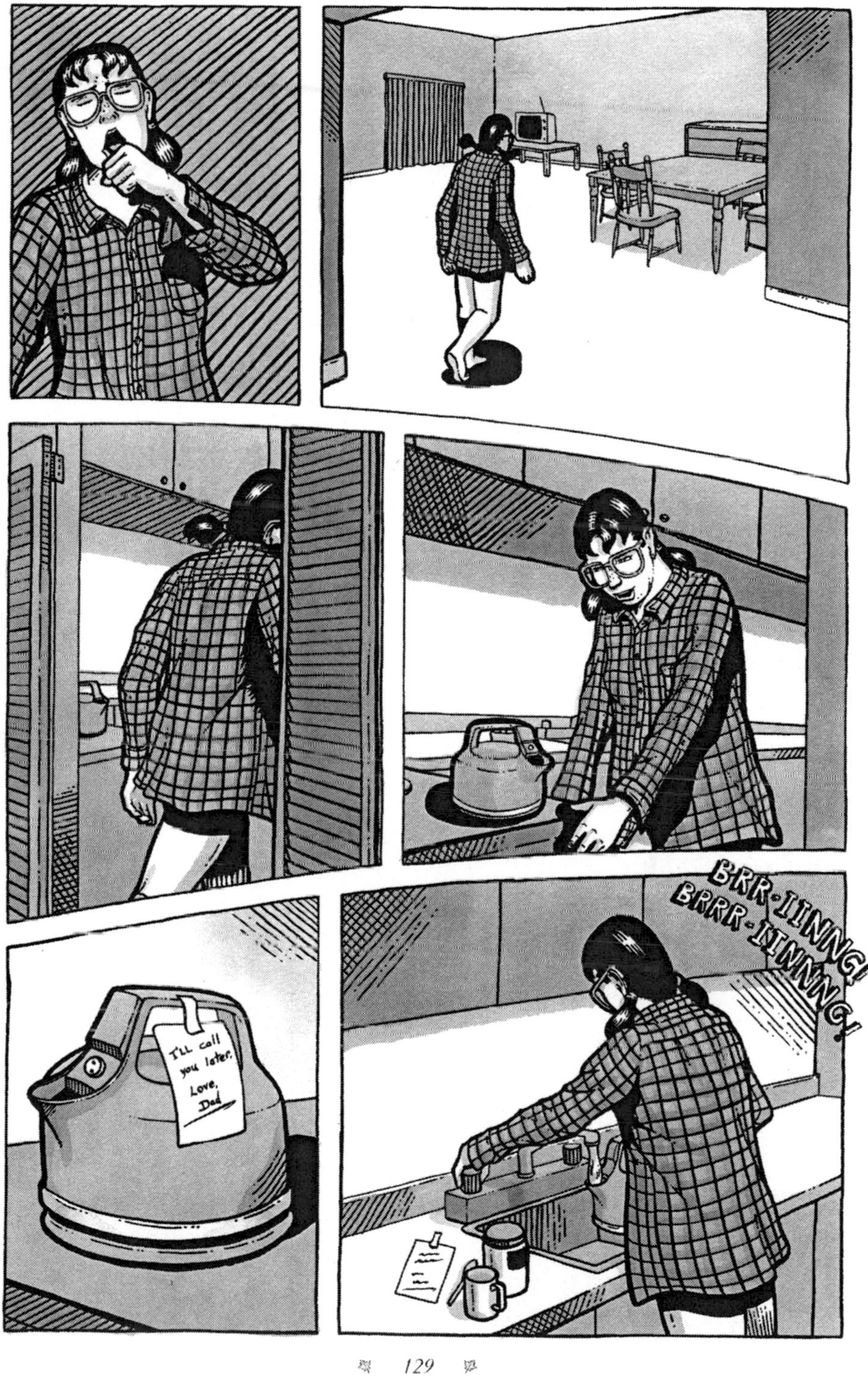
I'll call
you later,
Love,
Dad
BRR-IINNG!
BRRR-IINNNG!

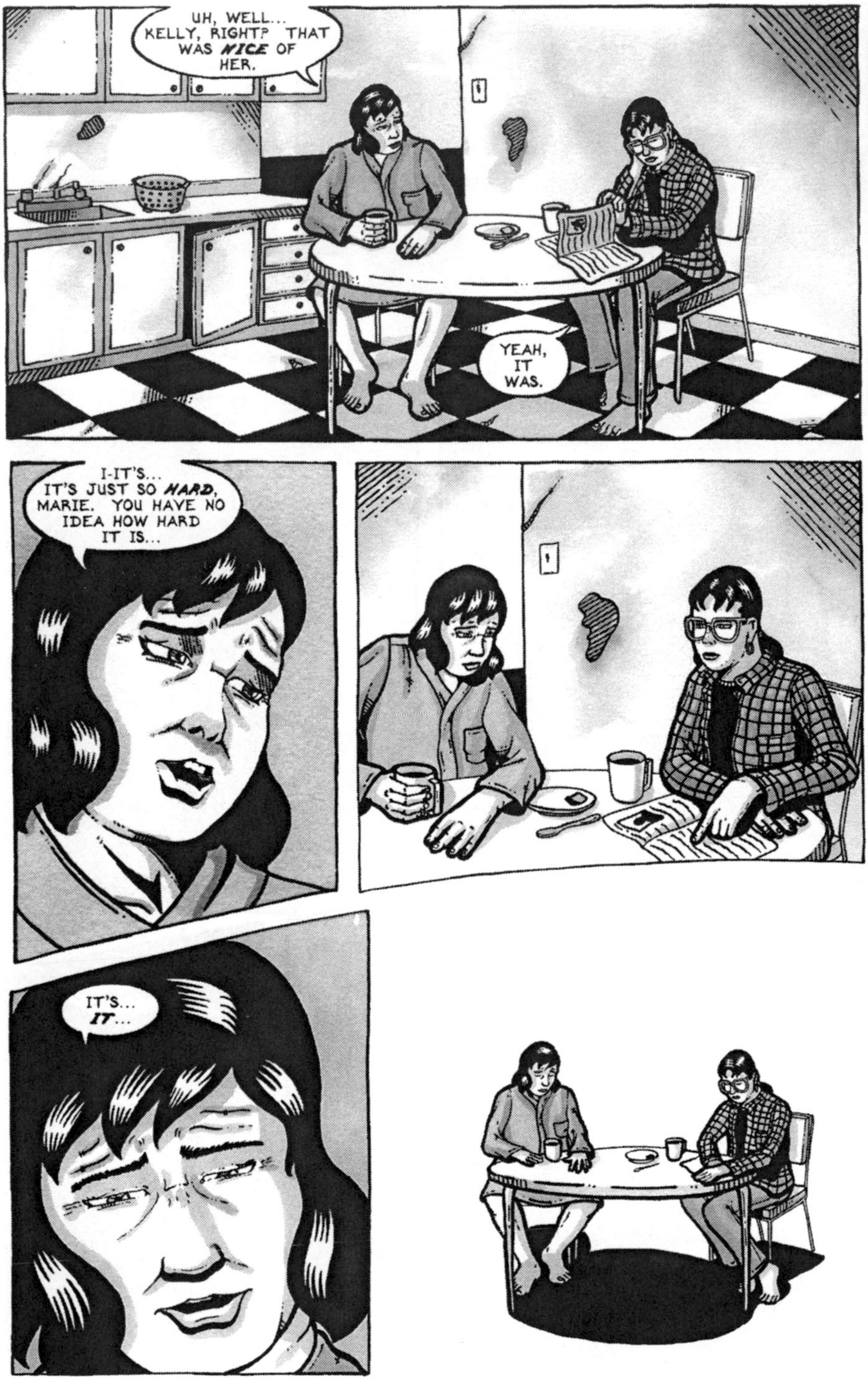
UH, WELL... KELLY, RIGHT? THAT WAS NICE OF HER.
YEAH, IT WAS.
I-IT'S... IT'S JUST SO HARD, MARIE. YOU HAVE NO IDEA HOW HARD IT IS...
IT'S... IT...

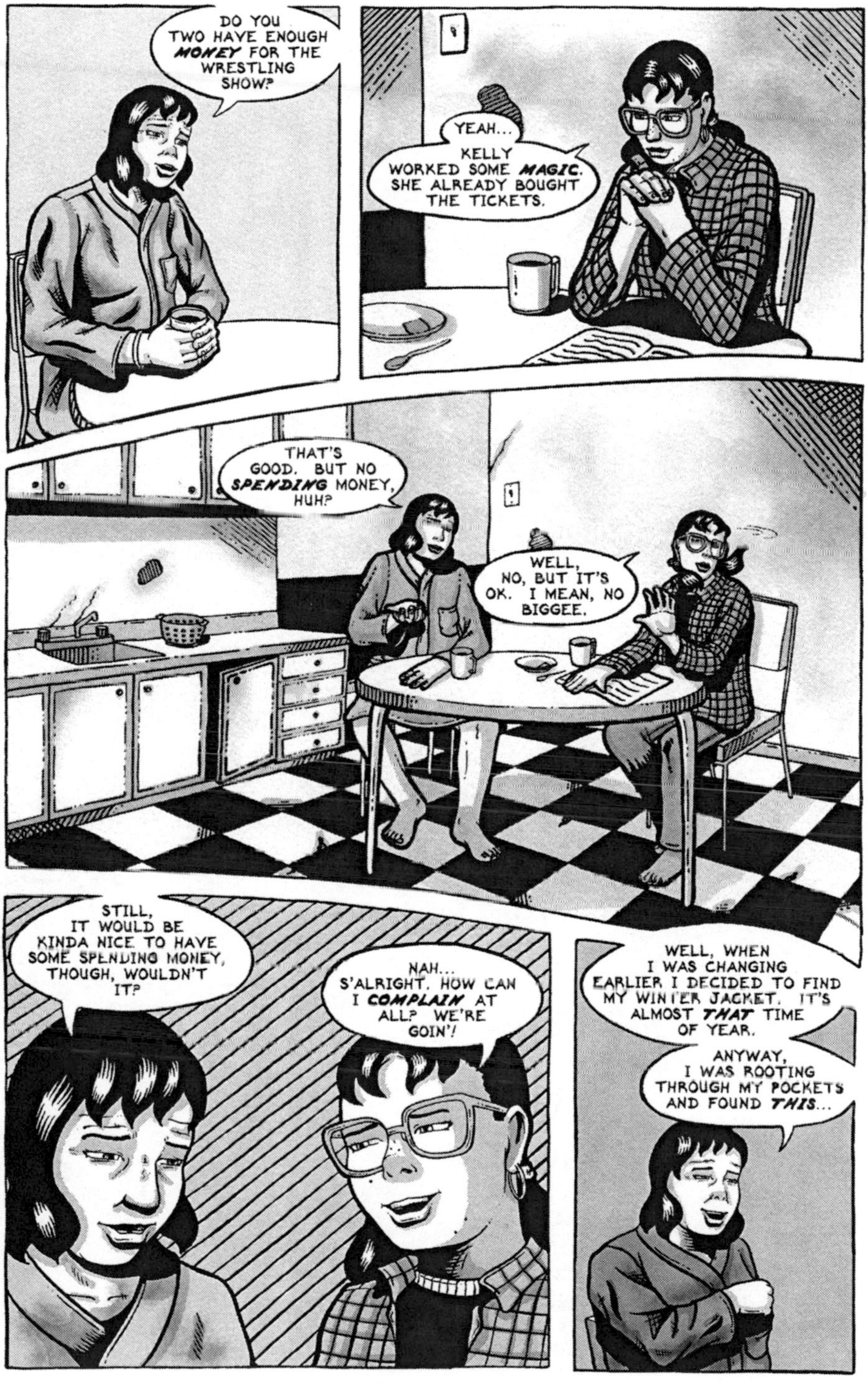
DO YOU TWO HAVE ENOUGH MONEY FOR THE WRESTLING SHOW?
YEAH... KELLY WORKED SOME MAGIC. SHE ALREADY BOUGHT THE TICKETS.
THAT'S GOOD. BUT NO SPENDING MONEY, HUH?
WELL, NO, BUT IT'S OK. I MEAN, NO BIGGEE.
STILL, IT WOULD BE KINDA NICE TO HAVE SOME SPENDING MONEY, THOUGH, WOULDN'T IT?
NAH... S'ALRIGHT. HOW CAN I COMPLAIN AT ALL? WE'RE GOIN'!
WELL, WHEN I WAS CHANGING EARLIER I DECIDED TO FIND MY WINTER JACKET. IT'S ALMOST THAT TIME OF YEAR.
ANYWAY, I WAS ROOTING THROUGH MY POCKETS AND FOUND THIS...

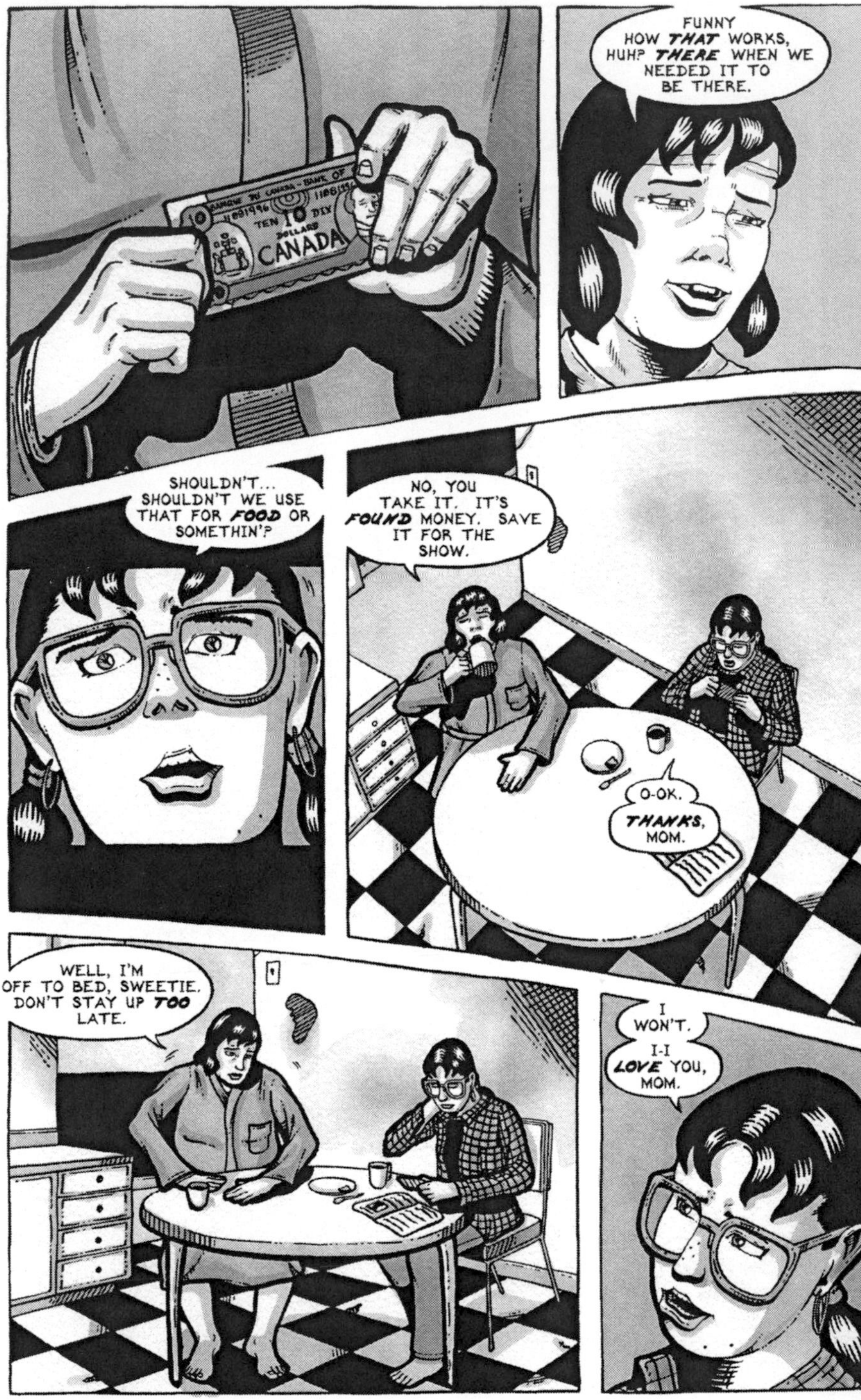
BANQUE DU CANADA · BANK OF CANADA
TEN 10 DIX
DOLLARS
CANADA
FUNNY HOW THAT WORKS, HUH? THERE WHEN WE NEEDED IT TO BE THERE.
SHOULDN'T... SHOULDN'T WE USE THAT FOR FOOD OR SOMETHIN'?
NO, YOU TAKE IT. IT'S FOUND MONEY. SAVE IT FOR THE SHOW.
O-OK. THANKS, MOM.
WELL, I'M OFF TO BED, SWEETIE. DON'T STAY UP TOO LATE.
I WON'T. I-I LOVE YOU, MOM.

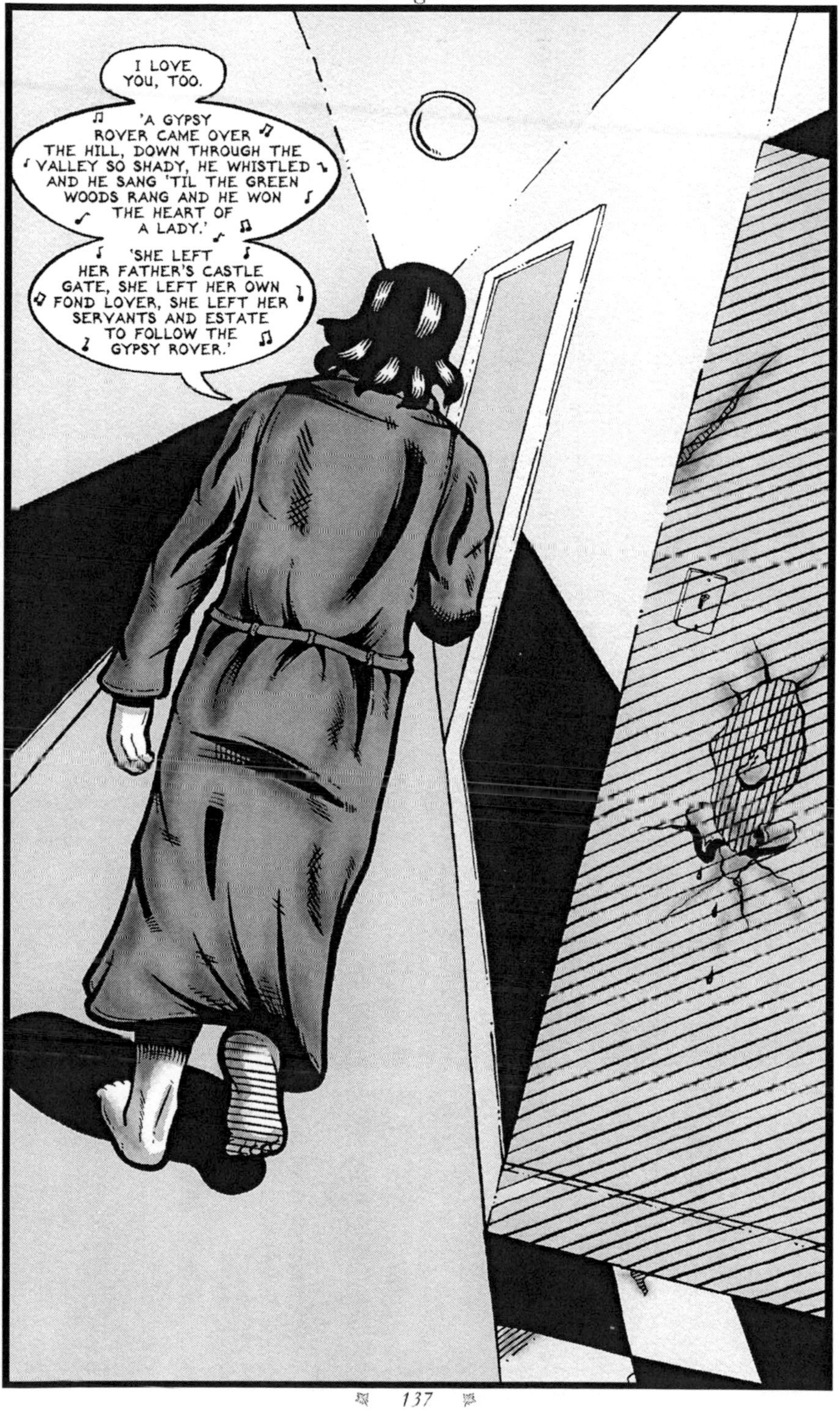
I LOVE YOU, TOO.
'A GYPSY ROVER CAME OVER THE HILL, DOWN THROUGH THE VALLEY SO SHADY, HE WHISTLED AND HE SANG 'TIL THE GREEN WOODS RANG AND HE WON THE HEART OF A LADY.'
'SHE LEFT HER FATHER'S CASTLE GATE, SHE LEFT HER OWN FOND LOVER, SHE LEFT HER SERVANTS AND ESTATE TO FOLLOW THE GYPSY ROVER.'

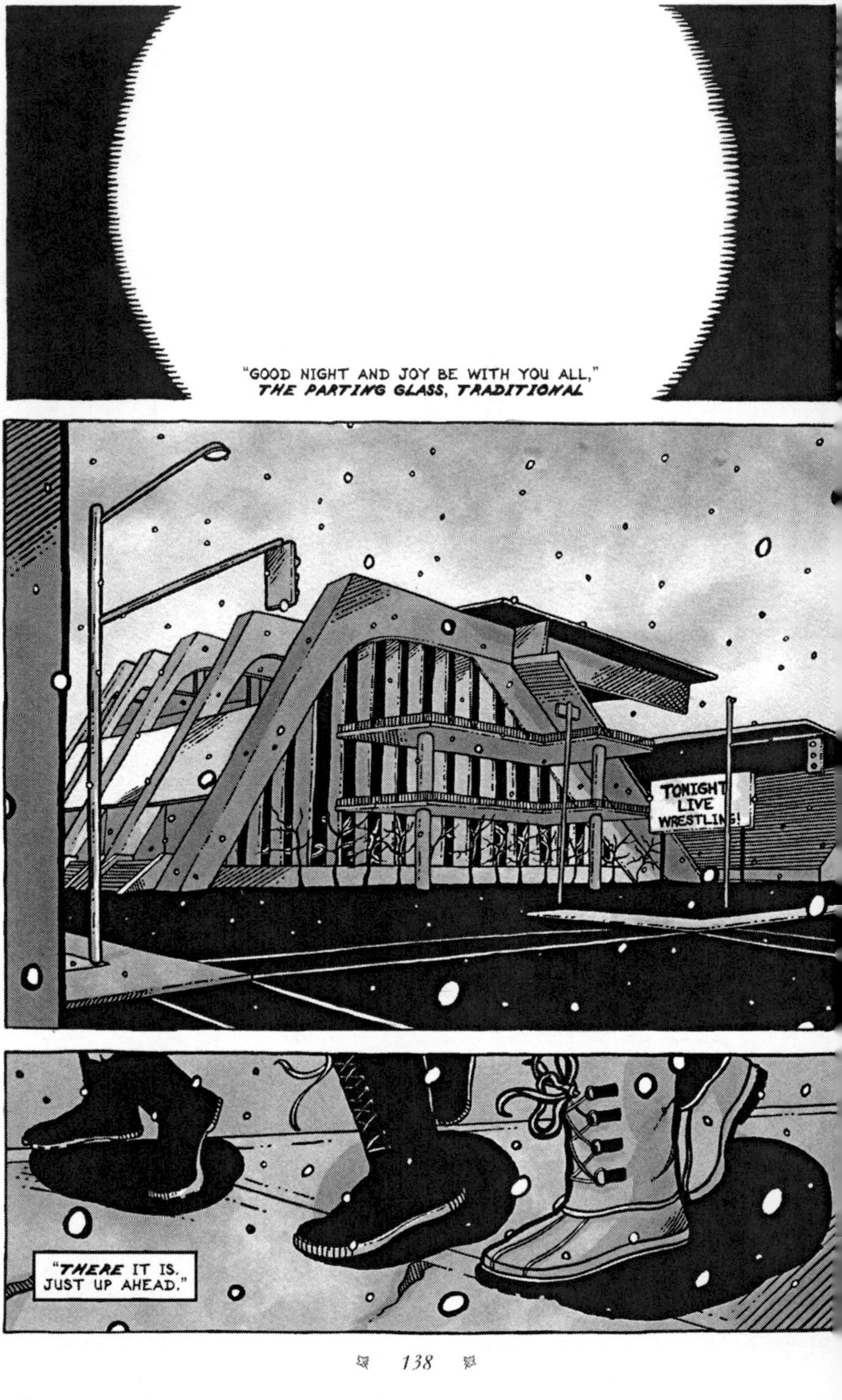
"GOOD NIGHT AND JOY BE WITH YOU ALL,"
THE PARTING GLASS, TRADITIONAL
TONIGHT LIVE WRESTLIN!
"THERE IT IS. JUST UP AHEAD."

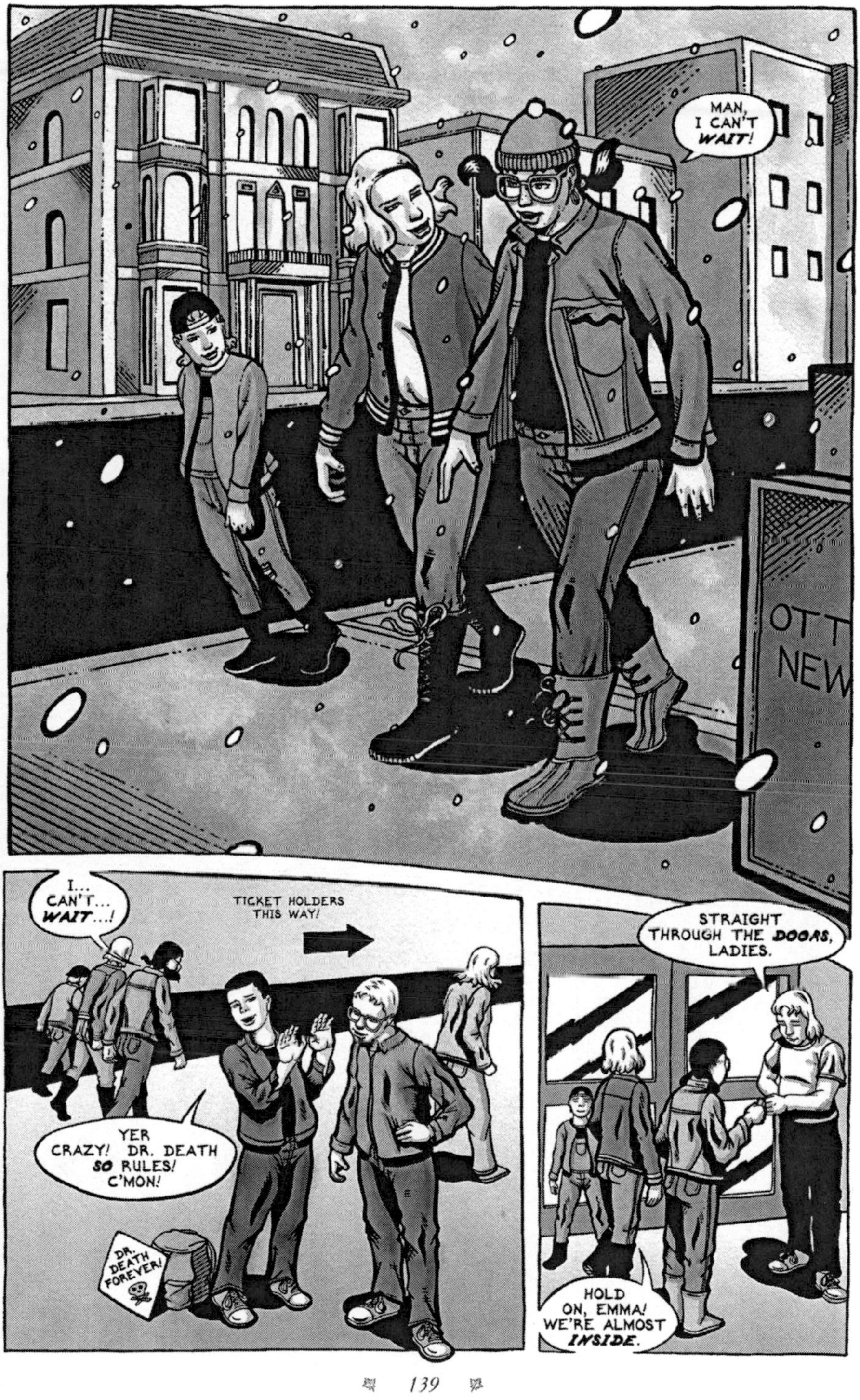
MAN, I CAN'T **WAIT**!
OTT
NEW
I... CAN'T... **WAIT**...!
TICKET HOLDERS THIS WAY!
YER CRAZY! DR. DEATH **SO** RULES! C'MON!
DR. DEATH FOREVER!
STRAIGHT THROUGH THE **DOORS**, LADIES.
HOLD ON, EMMA! WE'RE ALMOST ***INSIDE***.

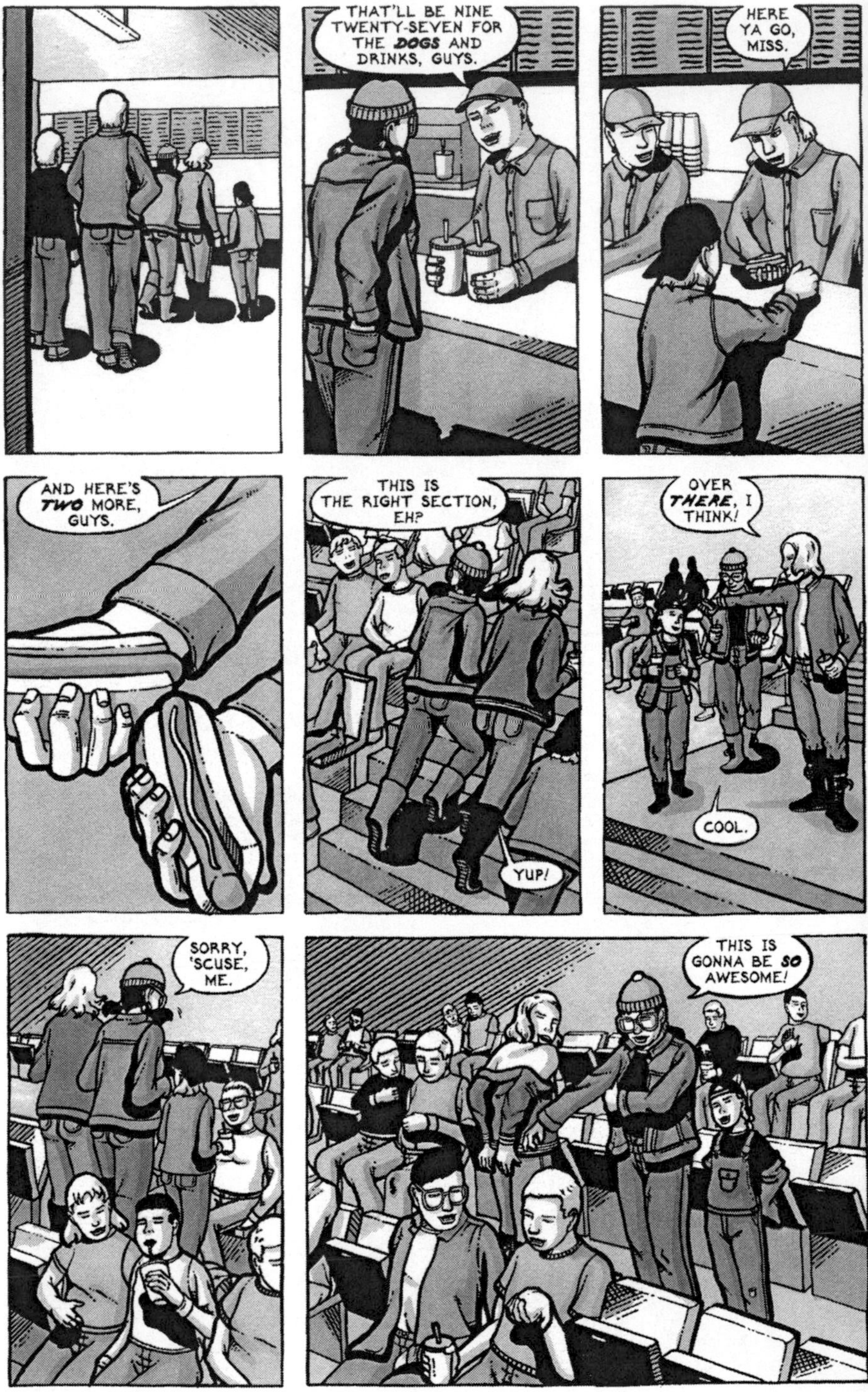
THAT'LL BE NINE TWENTY-SEVEN FOR THE DOGS AND DRINKS, GUYS.
HERE YA GO, MISS.
AND HERE'S TWO MORE, GUYS.
THIS IS THE RIGHT SECTION, EH?
YUP!
OVER THERE, I THINK!
COOL.
SORRY, 'SCUSE, ME.
THIS IS GONNA BE SO AWESOME!

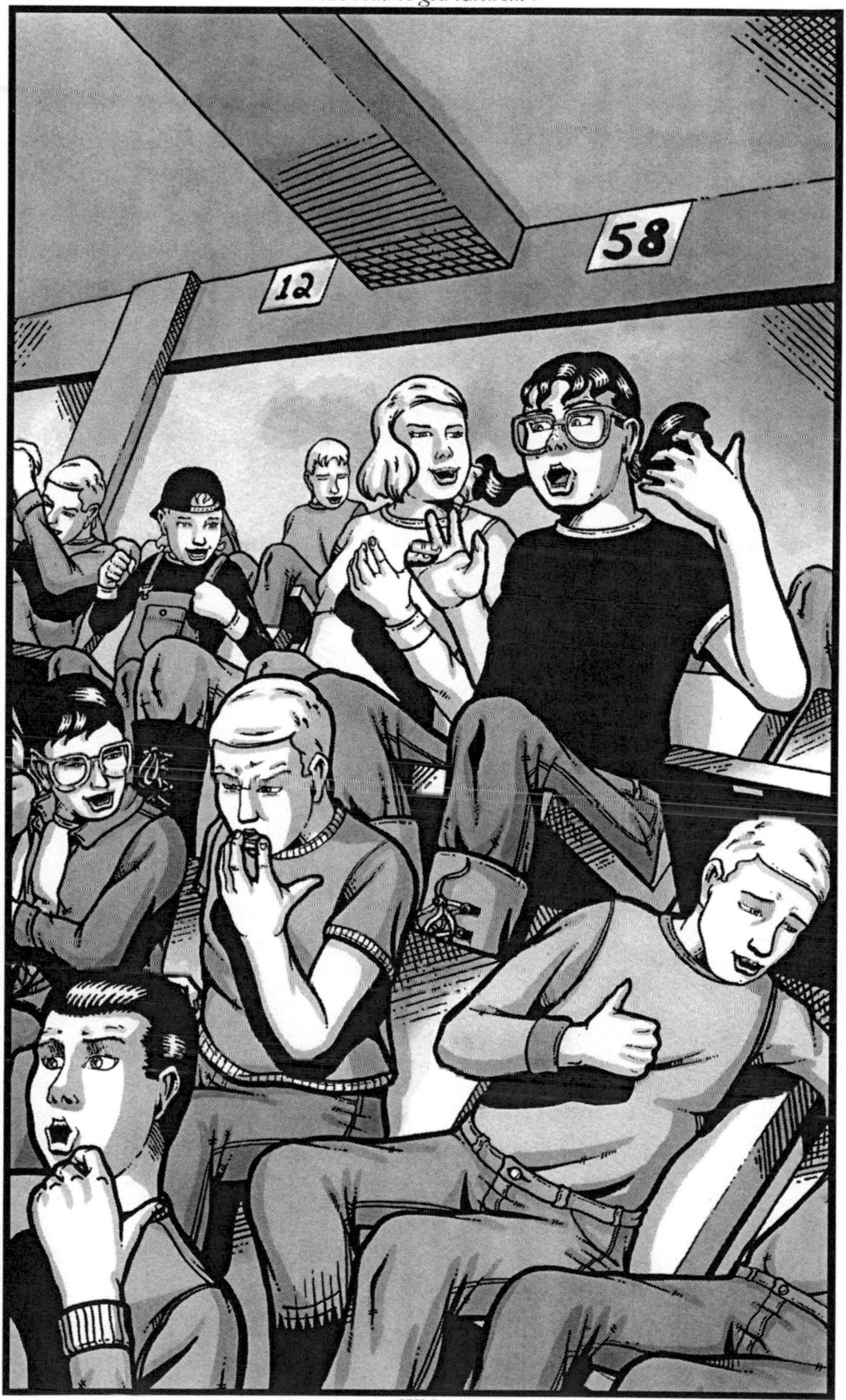
58
12

FIN

About Von

Von Allan was born red-headed and freckled in Arnprior, Ontario, just in time for Star Wars: A New Hope. The single child of two loving but troubled parents, Von split most of his childhood between their two homes and, consequently, spent a lot of time in the worlds of comics and wrestling. And, to be perfectly honest, what comics and piledrivers didn't teach him, science fiction did. He managed a small independent bookstore in Ottawa, Ontario for many years, all the while working on story ideas in his spare time-- eventually, he decided to make the leap to a creative life, and *the road to god knows...*, an original graphic novel, was the result.

Von currently lives in Ottawa, Canada, with his writer/editor geek wife, Moggy; a husky dog, Rowen; and two feisty cats, Bonny and Reilly.

Von loves to hear from people who've read and (hopefully!) enjoyed his work. Feel free to write him at von@vonallan.com. Both Moggy and Von update their blog quite regularly at http://vonandmoggy.livejournal.com. Von's website is at http://www.vonallan.com and is the best place to go for updates, art, essays and the like.

Von's next project is *Stargazer*. The story can be found at http://stargazer.vonallan.com

CPSIA information can be obtained at www.ICGtesting.com
232377LV00002B/179/P

9 780978 123703